The Kansas Journey

by Jennie Chinn

In cooperation with the Kansas State Historical Society

Gibbs Smith, Publisher
Salt Lake City

ABOUT THE AUTHOR

Jennie Chinn is executive director of the Kansas State Historical Society. Previously Jennie served as the director of education for the Society. She holds a B.A. in Humanities from the University of California, Berkeley and an M.A. in folklore and mythology from the University of California, Los Angeles. Jennie taught history, language arts, and speech at the middle school level. She served as co-chair of the Kansas history curriculum standards in both 1999 and 2004. Jennie also teaches folklore classes at Washburn University.

This book is dedicated to
Carl and George Magnuson,
who gave me the time,
and the kids of Kansas,
for giving me the inspiration.

Published by
Gibbs Smith, Publisher
P.O. Box 667
Layton, Utah 84041
800-748-5439
www.gibbssmitheducation.com

Photo Research: Diane Good
Managing Editor: Carrie Gibson
Assistant Editor: Courtney J. Thomas
Book Design: Alan Connell
Cover Design: Alan Connell

Cover Photos: Aerial of the Flint Hills ©1999 James Nedresky
Plane No. 5 built by Albin K. Longren courtesy of The Kansas State Historical Society

Printed and bound in the USA
ISBN 1-58685-286-8

22 21 20 19 18 17 16 15   16 17 18 19 20

RESEARCH ASSOCIATE

Diane L. Good started her professional career with the Kansas State Historical Society as an archeologist. Diane is currently an Education Specialist with the Society. She has a Master of Arts degree in Anthropology and a Master of Library Science degree. Diane has taught as adjunct faculty at Emporia State University and Washburn University. She is the author of numerous publications, for both adult and student audiences.

ADVISORS

Bobbie L. Athon serves as public information officer for the Kansas State Historical. She has a bachelor's degree in communication arts-radio/TV and a master's in journalism. Her experience includes television promotion, writing numerous articles, conducting advertising campaigns and audience research, and writing and producing video projects.

Virgil W. Dean holds a Ph.D. in U.S. history from the University of Kansas and is editor of *Kansas History: A Journal of the Central Plains*. He taught history in the public schools for nine years before joining the staff of the Kansas State Historical Society. He has taught Kansas history at Washburn University. Virgil has authored numerous scholarly articles, encyclopedia entries, and book reviews.

Lois J. Herr works as Outreach Coordinator for the Kansas State Historical Society where she writes curriculum, manages educational programs, participates in exhibit development, and has coordinated Kansas History Day. Lois received her B. A. degree in history and political science from the University of Wisconsin-Parkside and her Masters in historical administration from Eastern Illinois University.

Robert J. Keckeisen is the Museum Director for the Kansas State Historical Society. He began his career in the archives division of the Society. Bob holds B.A. and M.A. degrees in history from Wichita State University where he serves as an Adjunct Instructor in the Public History program teaching graduate-level classes in museum administration. The Kansas Museum of History, which Bob directs, has won many national awards.

Mary W. Madden is a graduate of the American Studies program at Bowling Green State University, Ohio. She received her Masters of Liberal Arts from the University of Kansas in American Studies. Mary serves as Interim Director of the Education and Outreach Division at the Kansas State Historical Society. Mary is the managing editor of the Society's children's magazine *Kansas Kaleidoscope*.

Patricia A. Michaelis is Director of the Library and Archives Division of the Kansas State Historical Society and serves as the State Archivist. Pat has an undergraduate degree from Kansas Wesleyan in Salina and a Ph.D. in U.S. History from the University of Kansas. Pat has served as state coordinator for History Day and as project director for Territorial Kansas Online, a digital repository of Kansas territorial era primary sources.

Kim Ramussen is currently curriculum coordinator for USD437 Auburn Washburn district. For eight years she was the social studies consultant at the Kansas State Department of Education where she facilitated the development of state standards and assessment in history, government, geography and economics. Kim has served on numerous state and national curriculum and assessment teams. She was a teacher and a coach.

Sherry Reed is a curriculum coordinator for USD437 Auburn Washburn school district. She has served on numerous standards writing committees and has written assessment items for several states. Sherry has consulted in school improvement, curriculum and assessment for more than 100 districts in Kansas as a service center consultant for Greenbush. She taught history for many years in Fort Scott, Kansas.

Virginia A. Wulfkuhle is public archeologist at the Kansas State Historical Society. She received a B.A. in anthropology from the University of Kansas and an M.A. in anthropology from the University of Texas at Austin. Previously Virginia worked at the Texas Historical Commission and the Museum of the Big Bend. Virginia coordinates the Kansas Archeology Training Program and edits *The Kansas Anthropologist* and *Kansas Preservation*.

TABLE OF CONTENTS

MAPS, CHARTS, AND GRAPHS

PORTRAITS

ACTIVITIES

WHAT DO YOU THINK?

HOW DO WE KNOW THIS?

THINK ABOUT IT!

SPECIAL FEATURES

WORDS TO UNDERSTAND
absolute location
aquifer
arid
basin
conterminous
cultivate
drought
ecosystem
erosion
folklore
organic
physical feature
physiographic region
precipitation
primary source
relative location
sediment
shelterbelt

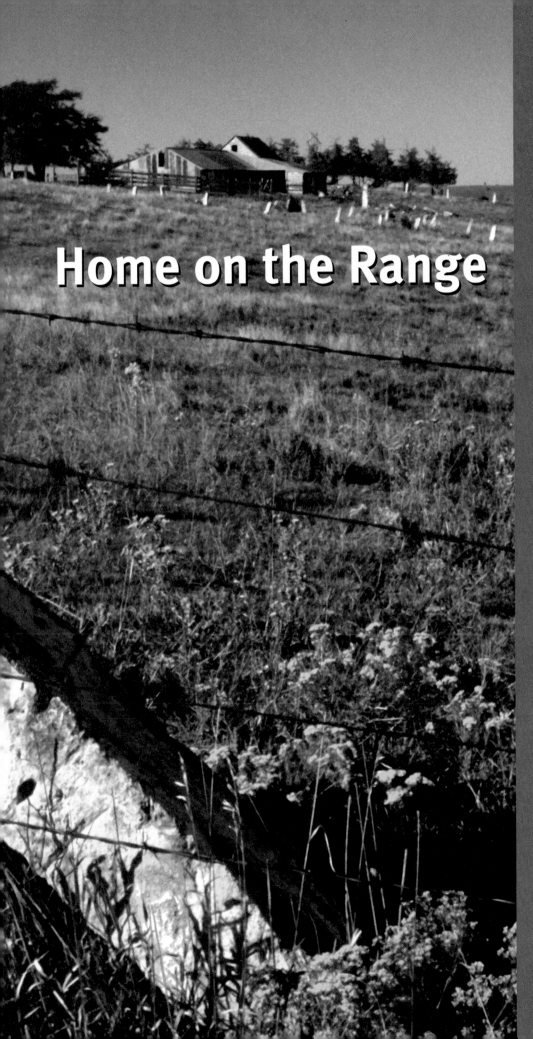

Home on the Range

Kansas is a land of diversity in landscape and people. In the past and present, Kansans have used the natural landscape to meet their needs. This photograph shows fence posts made from limestone.

Photo by Gene Berryman

History and Geography

Kansas is a land of great beauty, but it has changed in dramatic ways over time. People, land, waterways, animals, and plants all have a story to tell. In order to understand the present and make good decisions about the future, it is important that we learn about the past. History tells us about the people who came before us. Geography introduces us to the natural features of Earth. Both history and geography look at where and how people live.

In geography we study location, place, regions, movement, and the interaction between humans and the environment. People, land, water, animals, and plants depend on each other for survival. It is important to understand these relationships.

Location

Kansas is called "America's heartland." This nickname says a lot about where Kansas is located and its role in American history. Kansas truly is the center of the United States–the *conterminous* United States, that is. The 48 states that are enclosed within one common boundary form the conterminous United States. The actual center is located in Smith County, near Lebanon. North Dakota becomes the geographic center of the country when the states of Alaska and Hawaii are included.

"This is the finest country and the most beautiful land in the world; the prairies are like seas, and filled with wild animals...in such quantities as to surpass the imagination."

—French explorer Etienne Veniard de Bourgmont, 1700s

Smith County

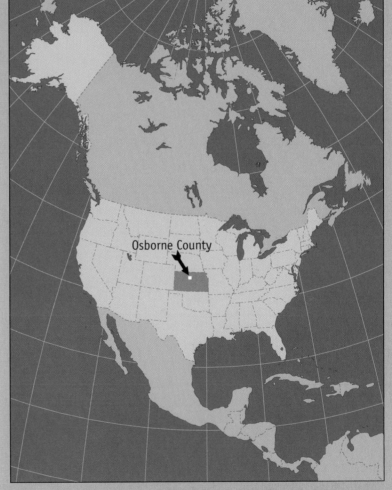

History and geography are concerned with how and where people live. This farm in Kingman County has a story to tell. What allows the wheat to grow? Why do people want to grow it? How have they changed the land by growing wheat? These are some questions answered by history and geography.

How to Find a Location

To find the *absolute location* of Kansas we use latitude and longitude. Kansas is located between the 37th and 40th parallels north latitude. It is between 94 and 102 degrees of west longitude. This tells us that Kansas is north of the equator and west of the prime meridian. What place is on the opposite side of Earth from Kansas? If you stayed in the northern hemisphere and followed the latitude and longitude lines half way around the world, you would end up in Jiuquan, which is in the Kansu Provence of China. Can you find this place on a globe?

A *relative location* explains where a place is in relation to other places. Kansas is next to Colorado and below Nebraska. Kansas is often referred to as being landlocked. We are surrounded by other states but not by any oceans.

Kansas is shaped like a rectangle with a "bite" taken out of the northeast corner. That "bite" is the result of Kansas' only natural border, the Missouri River. The Missouri River has changed its course several times, but the border remains the same.

Mapping Point of North America

Did you know that all distances in North America are calculated from a point in Kansas? To accurately map Canada, the United States, and Mexico, a consistent point of origin is needed. That point is located in the pastureland of Osborne County.

Kansas

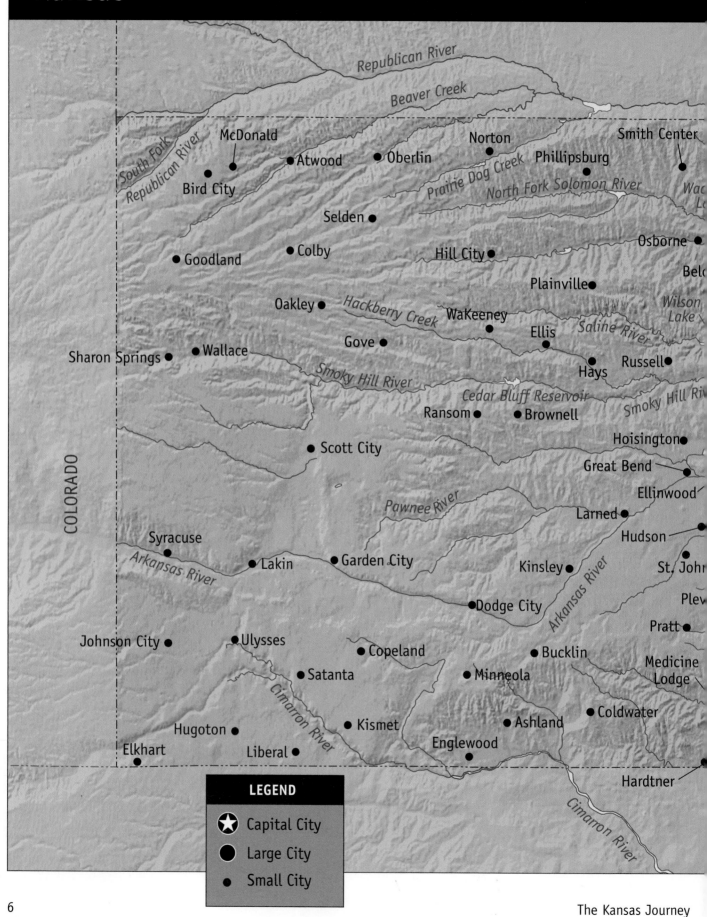

COLORADO

Republican River

Beaver Creek

South Fork Republican River

McDonald

Atwood

Oberlin

Norton

Phillipsburg

Smith Center

Bird City

Prairie Dog Creek

North Fork Solomon River

Wac
L...

Selden

Osborne

Goodland

Colby

Hill City

Belo...

Plainville

Wilson
Lake

Oakley

Hackberry Creek

WaKeeney

Saline River

Gove

Ellis

Sharon Springs

Wallace

Russell

Smoky Hill River

Hays

Cedar Bluff Reservoir

Smoky Hill Riv...

Ransom

Brownell

Hoisington

Scott City

Great Bend

Ellinwood

Pawnee River

Larned

Hudson

Syracuse

Kinsley

St. John

Lakin

Garden City

Arkansas River

Arkansas River

Plev...

Dodge City

Pratt

Johnson City

Ulysses

Copeland

Bucklin

Medicine
Lodge

Satanta

Minneola

Coldwater

Cimarron River

Kismet

Ashland

Hugoton

Englewood

Elkhart

Liberal

Hardtner

Cimarron River

LEGEND

⭐ Capital City

⬤ Large City

• Small City

6

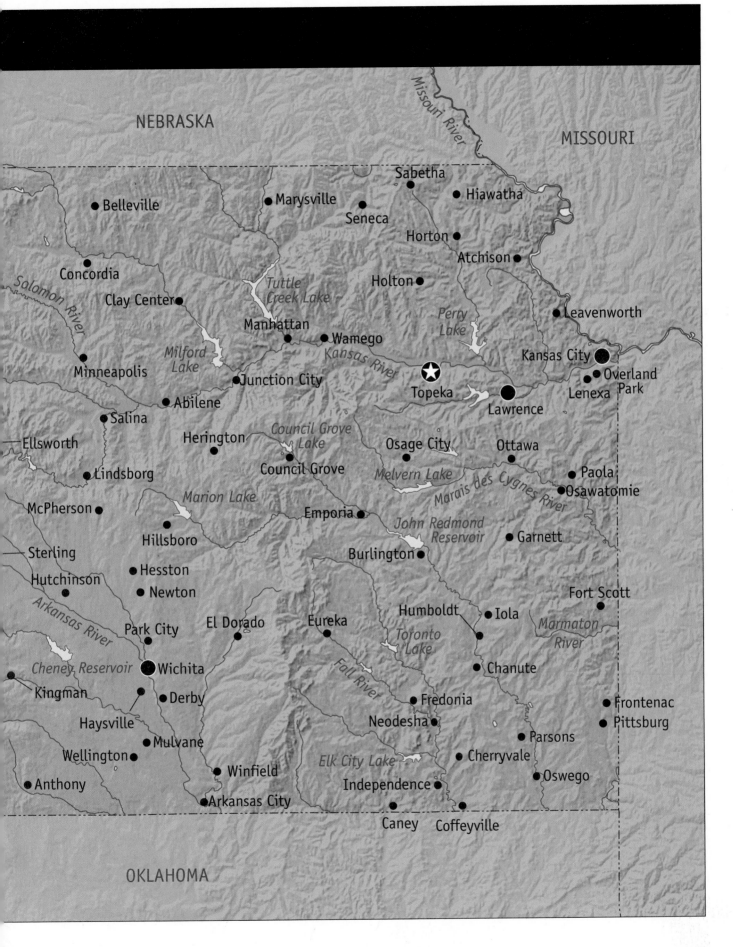

You can see a variety of landforms and plants in the Flint Hills.

The Kansas Journey

Castle Rock in Gove County contains many fossils of prehistoric organisms.

Place

All locations have *physical features* that make them different from other places. Features natural to the environment include rivers, hills, soil, and rocks. Some features are dramatic, like the ancient chalk spire known as Castle Rock. Kansas also boasts the beauty of the native prairies.

The Kansas landscape has been described as subtle. Perhaps this is because we have no mountains. Yet the state is not flat. The southeast corner is less than 700 feet above sea level. Kansas rises to more than 4,000 feet at its western border. How can that be?

The elevation rises gradually on an incline at approximately 10 feet per mile. If you were to walk across Kansas from east to west, you would climb a total of 3,325.5 feet. If this rise occurred within a space of just 100 miles, it would have the same appearance as some of the peaks in the Appalachian Mountains.

Rolling Hills, Plains, and Prairies

Kansas is environmentally diverse. Great differences exist between the eastern and western parts of the state. Eastern Kansas has wooded areas and rolling hills. Western Kansas has high plains. A plain is a flat, treeless landscape that receives low levels of rainfall. This area is the heart of the Great Plains. The Great Plains stretch through the central portion of the North America from Texas into Canada.

One of the most striking physical features in Kansas is the prairie. Today about one-third of Kansas is prairie. The development of a prairie is tied to rainfall. In an area too wet to be a desert, but too dry to be a forest, prairie grasses grow.

Did you know that 80 percent of a prairie is underground? Prairie plants have very long root systems that can survive grazing animals, floods, and fire. The long roots allow the plants to come alive again each spring. The prairie is one of the world's most complicated *ecosystems*.

Kansas is big. It is 208 miles from north to south and 411 miles from east to west. This makes Kansas larger than the combined nine smallest states– Rhode Island, Delaware, Connecticut, Hawaii, New Jersey, Massachusetts, New Hampshire, Vermont, and West Virginia. In terms of area, Kansas is the fourteenth largest state.

The highest point in Kansas is Mount Sunflower in Wallace County. Monuments created by humans mark the spot.

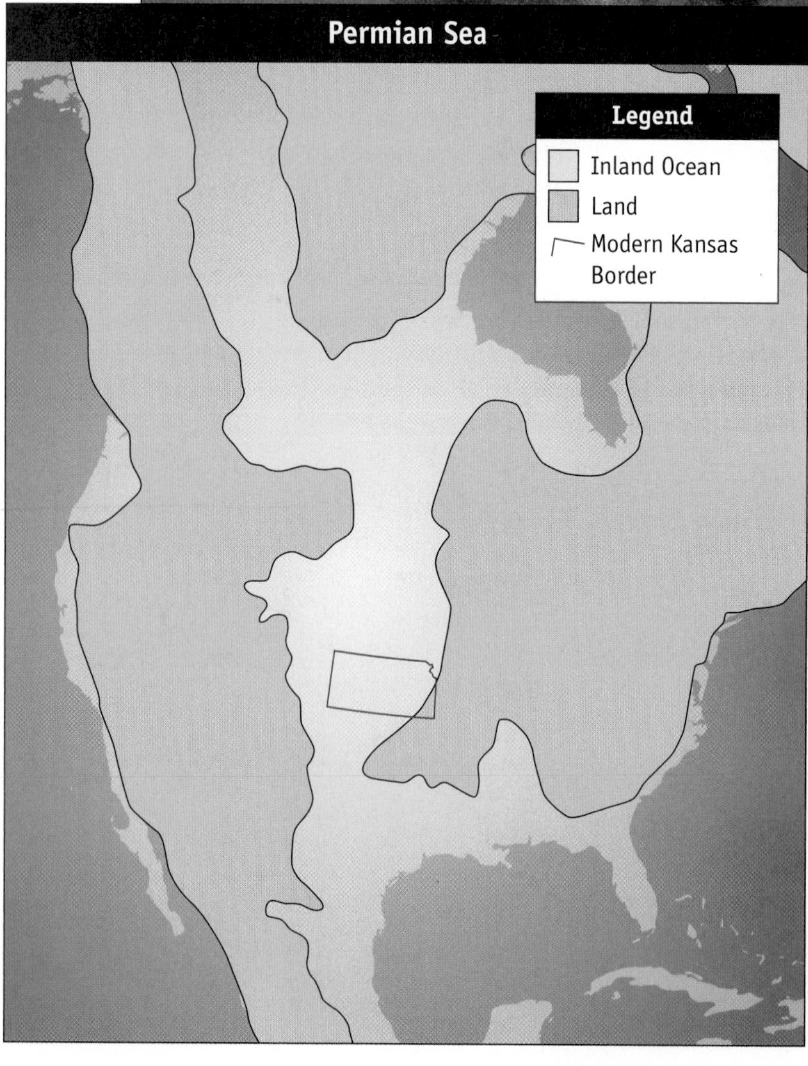

Mosasaurs were giant water reptiles that once lived in the Permian Sea. Mosasaurs could grow to 50 feet in length.

The Permian Sea

The physical features you see today are the result of a great inland sea. If people lived here at that time, they would have traveled by boat. This is because Kansas was covered by a shallow ocean of salt water called the Permian Sea. The warm ocean was home to many plants, huge fish, swimming birds, and reptiles. Some of the creatures found in the sea were as long as the width of a basketball court. Some fish had enormous mouths that opened 8 feet high.

This great sea created many of the natural resources we have today. As the plants and animals that lived in the sea died, they dropped to the bottom of the ocean floor. ***Organic*** material decayed and compressed over millions of years, and limestone was formed. Deposits of natural resources such as coal, oil, and natural gas, formed. The ocean even left behind thick layers of salt.

How Do We Know This?

The land in Kansas is very old. How do we know this? Evidence of our geologic past is buried underground. Preserved in the layers of rocks are fossils—outlines or body parts of plants or animals from ancient times.

How do we know that Kansas was once covered by an inland sea? Kansas rocks are full of marine animal fossils. Clams and oysters, fish and sharks, and even reptiles have been found in fossilized form.

George Sternberg was a famous fossil hunter who came from a family of fossil hunters. When he was only nine years old, he wandered away from his father's excavation in Gove County and discovered a plesiosaur skeleton. Sternberg eventually worked at Ft. Hays State University developing a museum. Today, the Sternberg Museum in Hays is named for his family.

The most photographed fossil in the world is a Xiphactinus. George Sternberg found it in Kansas. This fossil is a fish 14 feet long with an entire 6-foot fish inside it. How do you think one fish got inside the other fish?

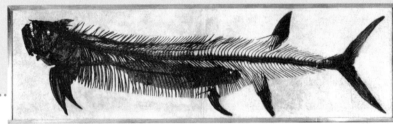

One of the most famous fossils ever found is the Xiphactinus "fish within a fish" fossil.

Tallgrass Prairie National Preserve

Land that today looks like a sea of grass was formed out of the bottom of the ancient Permian Sea. The Flint Hills are part of a rolling landscape. With flat tops and concave slopes, the hills are formed of limestone and shale deposits. Within the Tallgrass Prairie National Preserve visitors can experience the land much like American Indians, explorers, and settlers once did. Over 400 varieties of plants, almost 150 species of birds, 39 different reptiles and amphibians, and 31 species of mammals live in the preserve.

Tallgrass is just one type of prairie in Kansas. At one time tall grass prairie covered more than 140 million acres of the central United States. Most of the original prairie has been plowed under for agricultural purposes, helping the United States feed the world. Today, less than 4 percent of the original tallgrass prairie exists, making it one of the most endangered ecosystems on Earth.

Cattle still graze on the Tallgrass Prairie National Preserve.

Tallgrass Prairie ●
National Preserve

The Legend of Waconda Springs

A mysterious crater of water once drew visitors from near and far. This large saltwater spring was believed to have spiritual and healing powers.

Waconda means "spirit" for many Plains Indians. The Pawnee strived to live in harmony with the universe and looked to animals to provide spiritual guidance to reach this goal. The Pawnee traveled to the springs to make offerings and to gain wisdom to treat disease.

Later, settlers also believed Waconda Springs had healing powers. People built a hotel near the springs, and it served as a spa. For nearly 50 years people came "to take the cure." The water, it was believed, could cure a variety of medical conditions.

Today, Kansans can no longer "take the cure" at Waconda Springs. The place was covered by water after a dam was built on the Solomon River.

In western Kansas, land is irrigated. Center pivot irrigation makes circular patterns seen from the air.

Water

Water is necessary to sustain life. Our economy is also tied to water. Kansas often has too much water or too little.

American Indians and early settlers lived close to rivers and streams. Their trails followed the rivers. Water was important for drinking, and streams and rivers held fish, a source of food. Larger rivers served as transportation corridors for boats, carrying both people and supplies. Land near water is often level and, therefore, easier for overland travel. The most fertile land for agriculture is usually found near water.

The Arkansas River is the only major river in the state that originates in the mountains. Other streams and rivers begin on the flatlands east of the Rocky Mountains. All of the rivers and streams in Kansas eventually drain into the Mississippi River, which flows into the Gulf of Mexico.

The Ogallala Aquifer

Under the farms and ranches of western Kansas lies an underground reservoir called the Ogallala Aquifer. The *aquifer* runs under other states, too. This source of water was created millions of years ago. In some places the water is 500 feet deep.

The greatest use of this water has been for irrigation. There is not enough rainfall in western Kansas to grow corn—yet corn is needed for the livestock and meatpacking industries that are important to the state. Irrigation from the aquifer allows farmers to grow much-needed corn.

It is very difficult to replenish the water. When it rains in western Kansas, the dry winds evaporate the water. Rivers can only replenish the aquifer when they are flowing. When the water level is low, the rivers actually drain water from the aquifer. There is also a crusty substance that lies below the soil in some areas that prevents rainwater from draining into the aquifer.

Years of pumping water from the aquifer and repeated years of drought have reduced the amount of water available. At one time, people thought the Ogallala Aquifer would never run out of water. Now people are no longer sure. A variety of solutions are being proposed to manage this valuable water source. Some people support programs that restrict irrigation, whereas others believe we need to find a way to increase rainfall.

Cheyenne Bottoms is a natural lake that has been turned into a wetlands for migratory birds.

Lakes

Kansas is a land of few natural lakes. Almost all of the large lakes we see in Kansas today are the result of flood-control projects, where dams are built to control the flow of water. Although the primary purpose of these lakes is to prevent rivers and streams from flooding, many of the lakes are used for recreation and wildlife conservation. Some lakes are also used to provide water to towns and to irrigate agricultural land.

Cheyenne Bottoms

Cheyenne Bottoms, north of Great Bend, is one of the few natural lakes in Kansas. However, it no longer remains a completely natural environment. In order to provide wetlands for migratory birds, the water levels have been altered. The natural *basin* is partially surrounded by low sandstone bluffs. Waterfowl stop and feed in the large pools of water and the mudflats. Nearly half of the bird species in the United States can be found here on their seasonal migrations. Endangered birds, including the whooping crane, peregrine falcon, and bald eagle, can be seen here.

Protecting Our Water

Because water can be scarce in Kansas, we need to be protective of this resource. For this reason, the state of Kansas enters into agreements about water rights with surrounding states. Kansas took legal action against Colorado for the rights to the water in the Arkansas River. Kansas claimed that Colorado used more than its share of the water. This left the Arkansas River with extremely low water levels by the time it flowed into Kansas. The state estimated we lost enough water to fill a football field 70.82 miles deep. The United States Supreme Court unanimously ruled in favor of Kansas. The Court agreed that for 44 years Colorado had been depriving Kansas of its water.

The Kansas River is a source of controversy of another kind. The river is the subject of a fight over water quality. Sometimes, people have different views about how resources should be used. Some people want to keep rivers as natural habitats. Others want to use them for recreation, and still others need them for agricultural or industrial uses. Different uses can affect what goes into the water.

What do you think?

Water is a precious resource that cannot be taken for granted. A problem for state government is how much to regulate and monitor water quality and usage. What do you think the government's role should be in protecting this resource? How do we balance the needs of all living things, especially human and business desires?

Home on the Range

Kansans face weather extremes and natural disasters such as this ice storm in Chanute.

Highs and Lows

Temperatures change with the seasons. The average Kansas temperature is moderate, but weather here is rarely average. The highest recorded temperature is 121 degrees, and the recorded low is 40 degrees below zero. The temperature can drop below freezing every month of the year. At the same time, the temperature can be over 100 degrees from March to October. The weather can shift so quickly that in just one day, Harper, Kansas, reported a tornado, a serene sunset, lightning, rain, ice, sleet, and snow.

Climate

If the landscape of Kansas can be called subtle, then the climate of Kansas must be classified as dramatic. In Kansas, weather is everyone's favorite topic. It is changeable, extreme, and unpredictable. There is more *folklore* in Kansas about weather than about any other topic. Here is one folktale about a Kansas farmer:

> *A Kansas farmer was driving his cattle and realized the heat was tiring them out. He rushed to get a bucket of water for the cows to drink. When he returned with the water, he realized that one of his cows had died from heat stroke. As he was turning around to check on the rest of his cattle, the weather changed. The wind began blowing from the north. In an instant, the farmer looked down at his bucket to find it was now solid ice!*

Wind Chill

Wind is a dominant feature of the Kansas climate. The state's name comes from the Kansa who called themselves "the people of the south wind." Due to the wind and other factors, the temperature feels even more extreme. The temperature of the air does not always tell you how warm or cold

Kansans have learned to use the wind to their advantage. A family from the 1880s poses in front of their sod house and windmill. They used the windmill to get water from the ground.

you will feel. The "wind chill" is part of our weather forecasts. How the temperature feels is affected by the speed of the wind and the amount of moisture in the air.

Precipitation

When meteorologists measure annual *precipitation*, they are measuring the amount of moisture that reaches the ground each year from rain, snow, sleet, hail, and mist. The average precipitation in Kansas varies from east to west. In eastern Kansas the average is around 40 inches, but in the *arid* western part of the state we are likely to record just less than 18 inches of precipitation per year.

Tornados, Blizzards, Droughts, and Floods

L. Frank Baum's *The Wonderful Wizard of Oz* has a special place in the hearts of many Americans. When Dorothy's house "whirled around two or three times and rose slowly through the air," tornados became linked with Kansas. It is an image we cannot escape. Despite its reputation, Kansas is not the state with the most tornados. In terms of deadly tornados, Kansas is not even in the top 10 states. However, tornados do happen here, and they can be highly destructive.

Blizzards are also an extreme weather condition here. Folklore tells us "it has to warm up to snow." Blizzards usually begin with a warm winter day. Blowing snow can be extremely dangerous. In the Blizzard of 1886, nearly 80 percent of the cattle died and almost 100 people froze to death. This had a lasting effect on the state's economy. With the loss of this many cattle, many people lost their source of income.

Kansas is also subject to the extremes of both flood and *drought*. Excessive rain in a short time caused one of the most significant floods in our history. The 1951 Flood resulted in such damage that it led to building the network of reservoirs we see today.

On the other extreme, the effect of extended periods of drought is hard on plants and animals. Dust storms can develop, blowing away valuable topsoil.

An Oz-like tornado touches down to begin its 15-minute journey over an open field near Clearwater, Kansas.

Activity

Reading the Newspaper

A *primary source* is a first-hand account of an event. This includes newspapers, letters, and diaries. Documents such as census records and wills, as well as photographs, are also primary sources. Primary sources help us interpret what happened in the past. We can see different points of view and learn about how people in the past felt about their world.

The following two newspaper accounts are from different time periods. Both describe tornados. Read the accounts, and then answer these questions:

1. What descriptive words are used to portray the tornados in each article?

2. What main point did each reporter try to convey?

3. Is there a difference in how the events are reported?

4. Based on these two articles, do you think people have changed the way they report the news?

Primary Source 1

A Terrible Cyclone

Many of the people of this city watched the progress of this storm with bated breath as it threatened to turn and pass over us. As these clouds approached each other there was a constant succession of the most vivid lightning flashes ever witnessed. These were accompanied by the most alarming peals of thunder.

The whole heavens in the vicinity of the storm appeared to be in a towering rage, and the furious contortions of the angry clouds, the sharp, piercing thunder and the mad lightning formed a terribly grand and impressive picture that those who witnessed will never forget. This wild wrangling of the mad elements lasted for nearly an hour, the clouds seeming to hover over one locality.

About this time the mad flashes of lightning suddenly ceased, the thunders hushed and a dark, ugly, muddy, funnel-shaped cloud was formed about the center of the storm, and it rose and fell and began to sweep on down the river everybody turned pale and spoke in whispers. Everybody knew what it meant. Everybody knew that the ruin and death would mark its course.

They watched its progress, saw the formation of the cyclone, and saw it rushing wildly and madly over the country, tearing up trees, carrying off buildings and leaving nothing but ruin in its track.

—*Osage City Free Press*, June 13, 1881

Primary Source 2

Over 20 reported killed; injured besiege hospitals

More than 20 people were reported dead late Friday night, victims of one of the worst tornado-spawning storms to ever strike the Wichita area.

The small Butler County community of Andover, just east of Wichita, was hit hardest. At midnight, officials there said they had found eight bodies and knew of 12 more that had not been taken from the ruins of a mobile home park. The National Guard moved into Andover at 9 p.m. and sealed off the city to prevent looting and keep out unnecessary traffic.

The storm first struck about 5:30 p.m. northeast of Clearwater, then moved into Haysville, dropping down at Broadway and 55th South and 47th South and K-15 before it hit McConnell Air Force Base, said officials with the National Weather Service. After McConnell, the funnel moved on to Greenwich Road, then to Andover and toward El Dorado.

Wichita hospitals were swamped with injured people, and one estimate was that more than 200 had been treated. HCA Wesley Medical Center had seen as many as 50 victims by 8:30 pm.–including three families from the Andover area.

—*Wichita Eagle*, April 27, 1991

Native Plants

Kansas plants must grow and prosper in extreme temperatures and with uncertain precipitation. It does help that the state has some of the best soils in the world.

Grasslands

Kansas prairies are characterized by either tall grasses or short grasses. If you divide the state into three sections from east to west, you will travel first through tall grass prairie, then mixtures of tall and short grasses, and complete your journey among the short grasses of western Kansas.

Big and little bluestems are the most common of tall grasses. They are commonly called "turkey foot" because the seed heads branch into three parts, resembling a foot of a turkey. Bluestem and buffalo grasses, part of the Kansas landscape, are favorite foods for animals. This natural resource has helped to make Kansas a leading state in cattle ranching.

Native grasses are a valuable resource for many reasons. Much of the most fertile land lies beneath the grasses. The grasses protect the soil from *erosion*. They also catch the rainwater, helping to provide moisture to the soil below. It is interesting that, in addition to the native grasses, most of the crops *cultivated* today are members of the grass family. This includes wheat and hay.

Kansas is known as the "sunflower state." Twelve species of sunflowers bloom from the middle of summer through the fall.

Sunflowers provide food for small birds and animals. Farmers plant and harvest sunflowers in large fields. In addition to the sunflower, Kansas is home to over 1,600 varieties of blooming plants, including many beautiful wildflowers.

Prairie Fires

Fires are part of the life cycle of the prairie and actually contribute to its growth and stability. One of the reasons we do not find more forests in Kansas is that the burning of dead grasses destroys much of the early tree growth. These fires that were once ignited naturally by lightning strikes are now set on purpose. Old growth is burned off so that new growth can begin its cycle.

Woodlands

Less than 4 percent of Kansas is covered in forests. Most woodland is in the east or confined to the banks of streams and rivers. The most common trees found in Kansas are hardwoods that lose their leaves in the fall. Cottonwood, elm, oak, and walnut trees grow here.

The cottonwood, the official state tree, is a fast-growing tree that can reach 100 feet tall. When settlers first arrived, they cut down trees for fuel and construction of homes and buildings.

Prairie fires contribute to the health of the prairie.

Have you seen a pronghorn antelope?

Animals

The lyrics to the state song "Home on the Range" plead, "Give me a home where the buffalo roam, where the deer and the antelope play." The image is of an ideal life, surrounded by nature on the peaceful prairie. In reality, once humans arrived there were tough times ahead for many animals.

The native buffalo almost stopped roaming when too many were hunted for their hides and meat. The pronghorn antelope nearly stopped playing. Larger predators, such as mountain lions, grizzly bears, black bears, and gray wolves disappeared. Smaller animals, such as river otters, swift foxes, and black-footed ferrets, became endangered. Once the human population of Kansas grew, the landscape was altered and the different types of animals found here decreased.

The animals that live in Kansas today have adapted to the prairie and can survive the extremes of climate. There are almost 700 species of fish, amphibians, reptiles, birds, and mammals. Since large lakes are not natural to Kansas, most of the native fish inhabit the rivers and streams of eastern Kansas. Waterways in western Kansas often run dry, so few fish are found there. During early spring evenings we hear the sounds of frogs and toads. The state also is home to salamanders, snakes, and turtles. Deer are plentiful today, and on occasion an opossum, raccoon, jackrabbit, or prairie dog can be seen.

Buffalo once again roam in Kansas.

Insects

Amazingly there are over 3,500 different types of insects in Kansas. This makes insects the most numerous type of animal in the state. Insects play an important role in the environment. Despite popular opinion, only 1 percent of insects are harmful to plants. Many insects help pollinate flowers and serve as food to bigger animals. Whether we see them or not, insects are part of our daily life. In late summers, it is hard to ignore the ever-present sound of the cicadas. We rarely see them, but we hear their buzzing all around us.

How would you describe the sound of cicadas?

Invasion of the Grasshoppers!

One type of insect that can be destructive to plants is the grasshopper. They feed on an area of vegetation until they completely devour it. With almost 150 species of grasshoppers in Kansas, they are one of our more common insects.

In the 1870s, Kansas had a terrible grasshopper invasion. Grasshoppers became so numerous that they blocked out the sun, and the loud buzzing of their wings sounded like rain. It was reported that the ground was covered with up to six inches of the insects. The grasshoppers ate everything in sight as the citizens of Kansas looked on in fear. Gardens and fields of grain disappeared almost instantly. Some people reported that grasshoppers ate the clothes off their backs and the hair on their heads.

GRANGERS VERSUS HOPPERS — KANSAS 1874 '75.

Henry Worrall drew this cartoon to show the grasshopper invasions of 1874 and 1875. What does it say about how people felt about the insects?

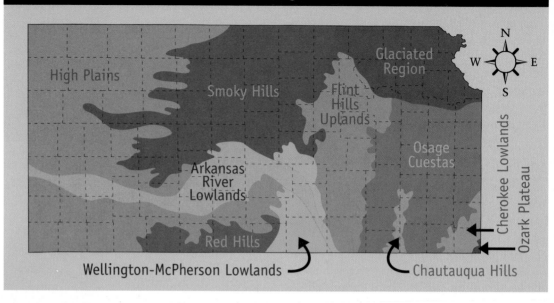

High Plains

Smoky Hills

Glaciated Region

Flint Hills Uplands

Osage Cuestas

Arkansas River Lowlands

Cherokee Lowlands

Ozark Plateau

Red Hills

Wellington-McPherson Lowlands

Chautauqua Hills

Regions of Kansas

A region is a subdivision of a larger area. As large as a continent or as small as a neighborhood, a region is an area with one or more characteristics or features that make it different from surrounding areas. States are often divided into land regions based on common physical or human characteristics. Geologists look at geologic processes that shape the landscape. Using this approach Kansas can be divided into 11 *physiographic regions*.

High Plains

The High Plains are flatlands, originally formed by *sediments* from the Rocky Mountains. Parts of the mountains eroded into sand and rock that were carried east by streams and rivers. Over many years, this

The Gypsum Hills of Clark County are known for their beauty. They are part of the Red Hills Region.

debris was deposited onto the High Plains. Outcroppings of sandstone can be found among the desert vegetation.

Red Hills

The Red Hills region is different in appearance from most of Kansas. The area contains hills red with iron oxide. Plains Indians believed in the healing powers of the hills and streams. The magnesium sulfates found in the water are better known as Epsom Salt and are used to heal some wounds.

Glaciated Region

The Glaciated Region gets its name from the glaciers that once covered the northern part of the United States. In some places the ice was 500 feet thick. As the ice moved from the north, it broke off boulders in South Dakota, Iowa, and Minnesota and deposited them in Kansas. These red quartzite boulders can be seen today.

Ozark Plateau

The Ozark Plateau extends into Missouri, Oklahoma, and Arkansas. This region has the oldest surface rock in the state. The limestone here formed millions of years ago when this region alternated between being below the sea and above it. The land is hilly and covered with hardwood trees. Caves can be found here.

The Kansas landscape is often referred to as a sea of grass.

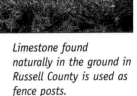

Limestone found naturally in the ground in Russell County is used as fence posts.

Arkansas River Lowlands

The Arkansas River Lowlands is formed of rocks from the Rocky Mountains that were carried east by the Arkansas River. For many years, the river has been carrying debris. When the river loses much of its water on the High Plains, the river dumps sediment in the Arkansas River Lowlands.

Wellington-McPherson Lowlands

The Wellington-McPherson Lowlands contains sand dunes covered with grasses. Underground are two important resources: water and salt. The water is part of an aquifer that now supplies water to Wichita, McPherson, and Newton. The Hutchinson salt bed is one of the largest in the world.

Cherokee Lowlands

The Cherokee Lowlands is a gentle rolling landscape of very fertile soil. This makes the region good for agriculture. It is also a coal-mining region. Many years ago, this area was swampland. Dead plant matter fell into water, eventually turning to coal.

Chautauqua Hills

The Chautauqua Hills region consists of low hills topped with sandstone. Hardwood trees, such as oaks, and medium-tall grasses cover the hills. For this reason, the land is not cultivated but is used as grazing land.

Smoky Hills

The Smoky Hills region gets its name from the haze visible in the valleys early in the morning. About 100 million years ago, this region was under an ocean that created the sandstone, limestone, and chalk found in the region today. Settlers to Kansas used the limestone as fence posts since there were few trees to use.

Flint Hills Uplands

The Flint Hills Uplands region is a well-known ranching area. The erosion of limestone and shale formed the rolling hills. The limestone contains flint that creates a rocky soil. This region is one of the last tallgrass prairies in the country. There are few trees, except on the stream bottoms.

Osage Cuestas

Cuesta is the Spanish name for hill or cliff. The Osage Cuesta region contains east-facing cliffs with gentle slopes to the west. The ridges are 50 to 200 feet high. The slopes contain layers of shale.

This aerial photograph of snowy Topeka shows the dramatic impact of humans on the environment.

Humans have tried to learn to work with the environment. Harnessing wind power has had an effect on the way we live. Planting trees as *shelterbelts* and changing agricultural practices have prevented precious topsoil from blowing away. The survival of both human beings and the environment are forever linked.

Interaction of Humans and the Environment

Just as there are physical features that define a place, there are also human characteristics. What we build and how we change the environment over time make a place distinct. Throughout history, people have adapted to and changed the environment. But nature has also had a huge impact on humans. People and the environment have a very complex relationship.

From the beginning, people used the natural resources available to them. Trees were cut down, stone was removed from the ground, and water was consumed from the rivers. The Pawnee built earthlodges and the Wichita constructed grass houses on the prairie. Settlers came to Kansas and built homes out of sod and wood. Town sites were laid out, and railroad companies laid tracks across the state.

Today, as we plow and irrigate the prairies, we change the environment to meet our needs. Over time, technology has given us the ability to remove oil, gas, coal, zinc, and other resources from below the ground. These activities show human impact on the environment.

Nature alters our lives as well. In the early 1900s, agricultural practices overworked the land. Then nature gave Kansans drought and windstorms, and the three factors together created the Dust Bowl. Kansans built towns and developments near major rivers. In the 1950s, nature provided excessive rainfall. This created great floods.

Movement of People, Products, and Ideas

People travel from place to place, sharing knowledge and ideas. Kansas has always been a crossroads. People have traveled to, from, and through the state. Plains Indians seasonally left their homes to hunt buffalo. Settlers passed through Kansas before it was open for settlement. American Indians from the East were moved first in and then out of the region. Later, immigrants from foreign lands brought with them their customs and beliefs. As people move, so do ideas and information.

New forms of communication linked Kansas to a wider and wider network. The Pony Express once traveled through Kansas carrying mail on horseback from Missouri to California. The transcontinental telegraph line later connected Kansas to the rest of the country. Today, Kansans are linked to the world through the Internet, cable television, and satellite telephone services. Goods and services are moved in and out of our state. The wheat grown in western Kansas and the airplanes built in Wichita are exported all over the world. In turn, many types of goods are brought into the state.

As we extract natural resources from the ground, we change the environment. In Cherokee County we see the results of strip mining.

Chapter 1 Review

What Do You Remember?

1. How are history and geography alike, and how are they different?
2. How can Kansas appear relatively flat but climb over 4,000 feet in elevation from east to west?
3. What are the Great Plains?
4. Why is the prairie partly underground?
5. How did Kansas get its deposits of coal, oil, natural gas, and salt?
6. What do fossils tell us about our state's geologic past?
7. Name at least two reasons why American Indians and settlers lived close to rivers and streams.
8. Why can't the water in the Ogallala Aquifer be easily replenished when it rains?
9. How were most of the larger lakes in Kansas formed?
10. In what ways can the Kansas weather affect our economy?
11. Why are native grasses valuable to the state?
12. Why are native fish more plentiful in the eastern side of the state?
13. What is the most numerous kind of animal in the state?
14. Give at least two examples of how humans and the environment interact with each other.
15. Give the definition of a region, and describe one of Kansas's physiographic regions.
16. In what ways do you see Kansas linked to other parts of the world?

Activities

1. On a map of Kansas, indicate the three different types of prairie: short grass, tall and short grass, and tall grass. Research the rainfall in Kansas, and indicate the average annual rainfall in each prairie region. Do you see a connection between precipitation and the type of plants that have adapted to the environment?
2. Kansas has had several different lawsuits against surrounding states over water rights. Look in old newspapers or on the Internet for information about these lawsuits. Debate the merits of one of the lawsuits with your class.
3. Interview someone in your community who has witnessed a tornado. Present your interview in a display, a paper, or a verbal report.
4. Research the cultivation of sunflowers in Kansas today, and write about or draw the products that come from sunflowers.

Think About It!

1. Many of today's industries are made possible because of prehistoric developments. For example, coal or salt formation took place during prehistoric times and now these resources support industries around which communities are built. What is the relationship of prehistoric developments and the industries in your community?

PEOPLE TO KNOW
Arapaho
Cheyenne
Comanche
Francisco de Coronado
Kansa
Kiowa
Kiowa Apache
Jacques Marquette
Osage
Pawnee
Plains Apache
Satanta
Wichita

PLACES TO LOCATE
Gulf of Mexico
Medicine Lodge
Platte River

Early People: Migration and Adaptation

Timeline of Events

7000 B.C.
Big Game Hunters
living on the plains use
spears to kill
mammoths, mastodons,
and giant bison.

6500–3500 B.C.
Major climate changes
create a hotter and drier
climate and more seasonal
changes.

7000 B.C. 6000 B.C. 5000 B.C. 4000 B.C. 3000 B.C.

7000 B.C.–A.D. 1
People hunt deer and other small
animals using an atlatl and darts.
They also gather wild plants for foods.

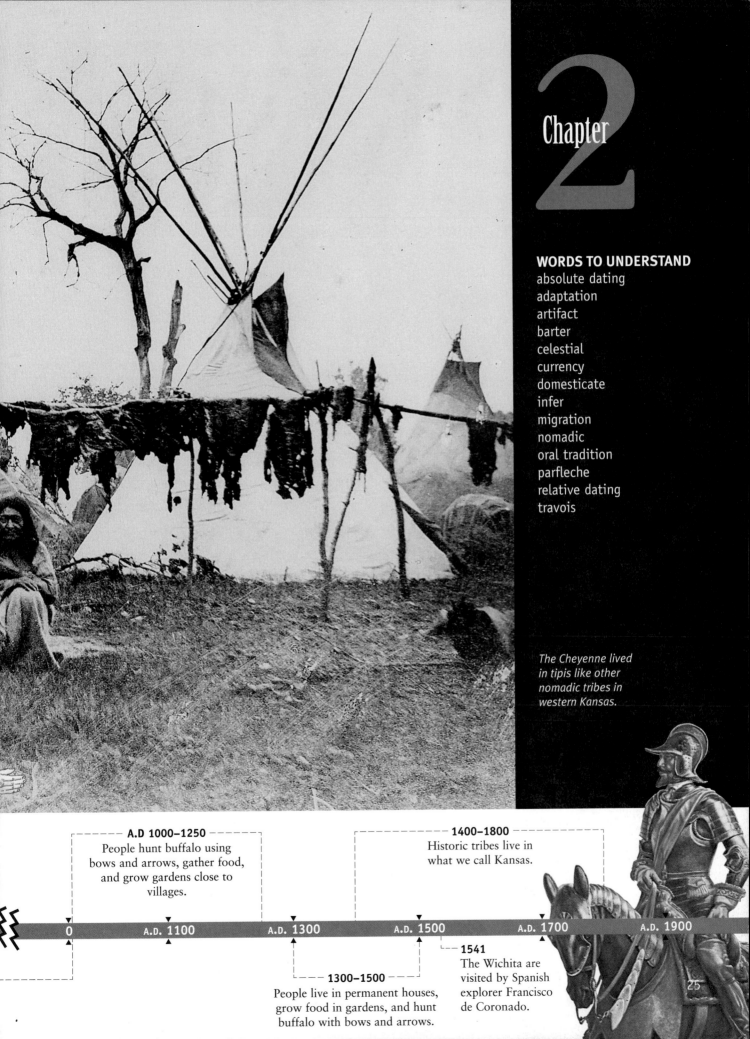

Chapter 2

absolute dating
adaptation
artifact
barter
celestial
currency
domesticate
infer
migration
nomadic
oral tradition
parfleche
relative dating
travois

The Cheyenne lived in tipis like other nomadic tribes in western Kansas.

A.D 1000–1250
People hunt buffalo using bows and arrows, gather food, and grow gardens close to villages.

1400–1800
Historic tribes live in what we call Kansas.

| 0 | A.D. 1100 | A.D. 1300 | A.D. 1500 | A.D. 1700 | A.D. 1900 |

1541
The Wichita are visited by Spanish explorer Francisco de Coronado.

1300–1500
People live in permanent houses, grow food in gardens, and hunt buffalo with bows and arrows.

25

Mastodons were an important source of food for the Big Game Hunters.

The Earliest People

There are many ideas about how people first came to live on this land. Each culture has its own beliefs about how the world began.

The Kansa, for whom our state is named, tell a story of creation that begins with the Great Spirit creating man and woman. The two lived on a small island surrounded by a lot of water. As more and more children were born to the couple, the island became so crowded it was necessary to push the extra people into the sea. The woman felt compassion for her children and prayed to the Great Spirit to save them by providing more land. The Great Spirit responded by sending down animals such as beavers and turtles for the purpose of expanding the island. The animals worked for many years gathering materials from the bottom of the great sea to create more and more land. Eventually, Earth was the size it is today. From the falling leaves of the trees that grew along the rivers, the Great Spirit created birds, deer, buffalo, and other animals.

This story has been passed on for generations among the Kansa. It is part of their *oral tradition*. Traditional stories are one way we learn about how people view their past.

There is more we don't know about the earliest inhabitants of Kansas than we do know. We have physical evidence that people have lived here for thousands of years. We learn about earlier people from *artifacts* and records they left behind. The story of the early people is one of *migration*, *adaptation*, and technological change.

This unique ceramic head shows how people in Kansas viewed themselves 5,000 years ago. Why is it important? Today we document our lives through pictures. This ceramic head might have been one way early peoples documented themselves.

Migration

The earliest people we know about are called Big Game Hunters. They migrated from the north when the glaciers pushed south. Their world was very different from what you know today. Mammoths, mastodons, and giant bison roamed the area. The land was covered with different and more diverse plant and animal life. The environment was ideal for hunting and gathering food. The climate was less dramatic than it is today, with warmer winters and cooler summers.

There are many mysteries surrounding the Big Game Hunters. We do not know what they called themselves or what language they spoke. They were named Big Game Hunters by archaeologists because of the hunting tools found with mammoths and bison remains. There is no evidence to speculate on what type of houses they built or how they actually lived. It is thought that people socialized and worked in small family units, but we do not know for sure. One interesting thing that is known is that these early people had *domesticated* dogs. Dogs were important work animals for the early people.

Adaptation

Eventually, the climate began to change. They were not small changes like we see from season to season, but big, life-altering, changes. These changes did not happen overnight. It took many, many years for the climate to become hotter and drier. The seasons became more like what we experience today, with hot summers and cold winters. This change was very hard on plants and animals. Some were unable to adapt and became extinct.

This chain of events must have also been stressful for humans. They depended on plants and animals for food just like we do today. What would it be like if some of your food sources became extinct? Just like you adapt your clothing to the season, so did the people living at the time of the climate change. How they lived and built their houses probably changed too.

There is so much we do not know. We can assume people adapted because they stayed. The climate change was slow enough that people had time to alter their

patterns of living. They used their old skills at hunting and gathering, but adapted them to new plants and animals. People hunted animals that were similar to those we know today, including buffalo, elk, and deer. People ate grains and seeds.

The photo above is a scene in western Kansas. Early people crossed landscapes like this in search of food.

What do you think?

Some people today think that the climate may be changing again. Some think this is a natural process. Others think that human beings are disregarding the environment and causing global warming. What do you think? If the climate changed dramatically, do you think humans could adapt?

Early People: Migration and Adaptation

Boiling Stones

American Indians created methods for heating food using fire. How did they boil the soup without burning the pot? They used a buffalo stomach for a cooking pot. Suspended from a tripod of sticks, the stomach held water. It could expand as the water got hotter, and it could be easily taken down and carried from one place to another.

But, putting a buffalo stomach cooking pot over an open fire is a recipe for disaster. Flames would quickly burn a hole through the pot. Plains Indians figured out a way to heat their soup without burning a hole in the pot. They heated stones in the coals and used forked sticks to transfer them to the buffalo stomach cooking pot. Hot rocks heated the stew enough to cook it. Only certain stones would work, however. Sandstone and limestone would shatter when the hot rock hit the liquid of the stew. Stones carried south by glaciers were the best to use for cooking with the "boiling stone" method.

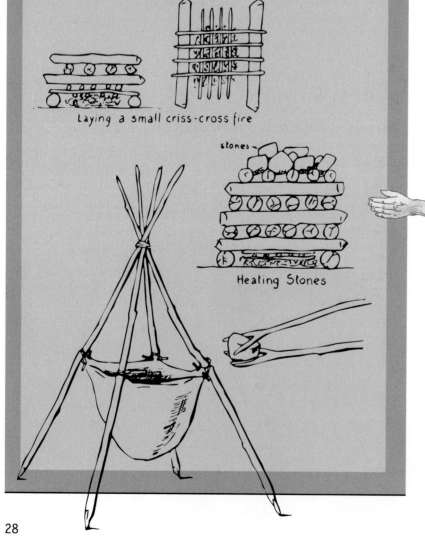

Laying a small criss-cross fire

stones

Heating Stones

Technology

Just as new technology changes our lives today, it also changed life for the early people. How do people get new technology? Sometimes we invent new ways of doing things, either by accident or on purpose. Sometimes new ideas come from other places in the world, and technology improves that way.

As time went on, people living in Kansas received new ideas from people living to the east. Some of the new things were pottery vessels, the bow and arrow, and the process of cultivation.

Pottery vessels improved food storage and possibly changed cooking methods. The bow and arrow became a common hunting weapon. Old methods of hunting used an atlatl. This was a throwing stick used to propel darts. The bow and arrow improved performance. Smaller arrows traveled farther and the bow provided more force.

As people began cultivating plants, their lifestyle saw major changes. In addition to gathering wild foods, the people grew gardens. They got more food this way.

With these new technologies, the population in Kansas began to grow. The people could get more food by having better hunting tools and growing gardens. They could also store food in their pots for longer periods of time.

People used an atlatl for hunting. Later they developed the bow and arrow.

28

How Do We Know This?

No written records exist to tell us about the people who lived in Kansas before the 1500s, yet we know a great deal about these people. How do we know this? Archeology helps us to understand human groups through things discarded or left behind. People changed the land where they lived by digging holes to build houses and fire pits. They discarded broken tools and household items that were no longer needed. Archeologists use these artifacts to piece together the stories of the past.

Archeologists establish dates and develop sequences for the artifacts they study. In order to tell the story of the early people, we need to understand which artifacts are from the same time period and how they relate to each other.

There are two ways to place artifacts in chronological order. *Relative dating* can order things in relation to other things. When archeologists investigate a site, they carefully record the location of what they find. This helps to establish the chronology. If a site is undisturbed, the artifacts found closer to the surface are the youngest. The deeper an archeologist digs, the older the artifacts are.

Absolute dating is done through scientific study of the actual artifact. Archeologists often use a method called radiocarbon dating to learn the approximate calendar year for an item that is made of organic materials.

Taken together, all this information gives us a picture of what life might have been like. Archeologists must assume the relationship between the artifacts and *infer* their meaning to construct what may have taken place many years ago.

Archeologists experiment with how the Wichita might have lived hundreds of years ago. This student is demonstrating how a scapula hoe might have been used.

Activity

Interpreting Archeological Evidence

Near the town of Minneapolis, in Ottawa County, archeologists have found the remains of a village where people lived more than 500 years ago. The village is located near sources of wood, water, and good soil. Patterns and relationships among artifacts that were found there

What Was Found	Background Information
Projectile (arrow) points Small triangular points, unnotched or with side notches, chipped from locally available gray stone.	Types of stone can be identified and sometimes related to a specific geologic source. The size of the point suggests the weapon on which it was used. The shape of a point tells the general time period when it was made.
Grinding slabs Grinding slabs of sandstone and handstones of quartzite, both locally available stones.	Grinding slabs are heavy and not easily carried from place to place. Grinding seeds makes them easier to use as food. Gathering wild seeds is unpredictable and does not always produce large quantities, so grains obtained from the wild are usually eaten raw or cooked in an unaltered form.
Bone fragments and tools Bones from small game (including fish, reptiles, amphibians, birds, and small mammals) and from larger mammals, such as bison and deer. Some bones have been cut, smashed, or burned, and others have been made into tools, including fishhooks.	We know from other sources what animals lived in the region. Scientists conduct experiments that show how bones look when humans have used them in specific ways.
Plant remains Charred but identifiable parts of corn, squash, sunflower, hackberry, and prairie turnip.	Corn and squash are cultivated crops. Sunflowers grow wild and as a domesticated plant. Hackberry and prairie turnips are wild plants.
Broken pottery Medium to large jars with rounded bodies and smaller mouths and sometimes strap handles; outer surface rarely decorated.	Breakable pottery vessels are not practical for people who move around. The construction and style of pottery vessels can identify the group of people who made it.
Posthole pattern A rectangular pattern of postholes showing large central support posts and fragments of daub (fired clay with grass and stick impressions).	Postholes are the remains of posts set into the ground to support a substantial house. Daub results from the burning of mud or clay that was used as plastering material.
Digging tool Made from the shoulder blade of a bison.	The size and shape of the scapula tell us that it came from a bison. Such digging tools were used to loosen and move soil in the garden.

30

The Kansas Journey

tell a story. The chart below gives you the pieces of that story. To interpret the evidence and tell the story, several clues must be put together. To do this, we must infer what the story might be. After studying the chart, fill in the missing pieces. How would you tell the story?

Questions	What It Means (Interpretation)
• How big is the point? • What type of stone is the point made of? • What is the style of the point?	Small points were attached to arrow shafts that were shot with a bow for hunting and warfare. The stone is found in the local area, indicating that it was available without needing to obtain it through trade. From this information we can infer that the people had an effective technology for making tools and for hunting and that their diet included meat.
• Why would you need a grinding stone? • What quantity of grain would need to be available to make such a stone practical?	Because grinding slabs are not easily moved, we can speculate that this village is fairly permanent. We also can infer that these people cultivated some crops and that their diet included cultivated grains.
• Can we figure out what type of meat people ate from these pieces of bone? • Can we tell how they prepared it?	We can conclude that these people had a diversified protein diet, eating both red meat and fish. We know from the arrow points and fish hooks that they had hunting and fishing technologies.
• Why were the plant remains preserved? • Can we tell what the people ate? • Can we tell if they were gardeners? • Can we tell how they prepared their food?	We can conclude that some corn, squash, and probably sunflowers were grown in gardens. The presence of grinding slabs contributes to our deduction that this was a permanent village. Wild plants also were part of the diet.
• Do the pottery pieces represent a single style?	Because many pieces of similar pottery were found, we can conclude that this was a permanent village with a fair number of inhabitants. The style of the pottery identifies it with the group of people at this and other sites.
• Are these remains of a permanent structure? • What shape was it? • Is there any indication of what the walls were made of?	*How would you interpret this?*
• What is the digging tool made from? • Where did it come from? • How was the tool used?	*How would you interpret this?*

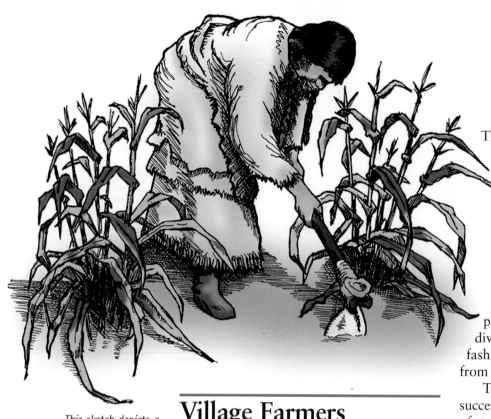

This sketch depicts a woman gardening using a hoe made from the shoulder blade of a bison. How is this farming tool different from the ones we have today?

Village Farmers

Around 800 years ago, many different cultures existed in Kansas. Some people began to live in permanent villages. Located on bluffs, the villages overlooked rivers and streams. These villages included two to 20 structures. Evidence suggests that houses were built with poles buried in the ground.

The homes appear to have been covered with thatched grasses and plastered over with clay. Because these homes would have been difficult to move, people think the structures were permanent rather than mobile.

Another indication that the villages were permanent is the cultivation of corn, beans, squash, pumpkins, and sunflowers. These cultivated crops, along with wild plants, buffalo, and fish, made for a diverse diet. In order to live in this fashion, people made a variety of tools from stone, bone, shell, and wood.

The people appear to have been highly successful. Why do we think that? Evidence of storage pits indicates an abundance of food. Stored or saved food is a sign of success. There is also evidence of trash or items being discarded. People only throw things out if they can replace them. We also find indications of trade among people. That is one explanation of why shells from the Gulf of Mexico are found in Kansas.

Where Is the Money?

When you purchase something today, you use money to pay for it. Both the buyer and the seller know the value of the *currency* you use and the value of the item. Our culture depends on a system of money to keep our economy stable from day to day. The value of items stays constant from one purchase to the next.

When archaeologists study sites where American Indians lived many years ago, one thing they do not find is money. They find items that came from far away, such as pieces of stone from the volcanic mountains of the Northwest. We can infer that Kansas Indians traded with other groups of people to get these items. For such a trade to work, both groups must agree on the value of the items being traded. They might discuss this value until both sides agree, and then the items are exchanged. This type of trade is called *barter*. No money is exchanged, and the value of items might change from one encounter to the next.

The economy of early tribes relied on barter. Tribes traded with other tribes. When French traders came to Kansas, they knew the Indians were experienced in barter. Indians traded furs for French items of metal and glass. In successful barter, the two groups meet the wants and needs of each other.

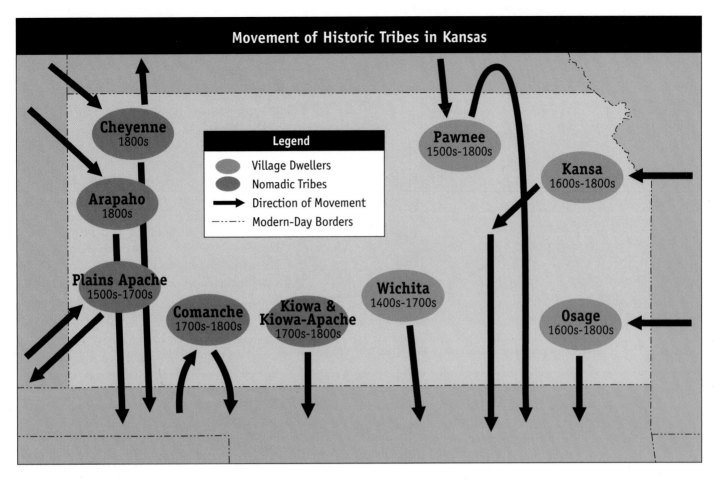

Movement of Historic Tribes in Kansas

Cheyenne
1800s

Legend
- Village Dwellers
- Nomadic Tribes
- → Direction of Movement
- — — — Modern-Day Borders

Pawnee
1500s-1800s

Kansa
1600s-1800s

Arapaho
1800s

Plains Apache
1500s-1700s

Comanche
1700s-1800s

Kiowa & Kiowa-Apache
1700s-1800s

Wichita
1400s-1700s

Osage
1600s-1800s

Historic Tribes

The Indians who are called "historic tribes" by historians are really part of the same cultures that were in Kansas for a very long time before Europeans entered the region. The term "historic" in this case only means that the evidence we have of their lives includes written documents.

The historic period in Kansas begins when written records begin. The first written records we have about American Indians on the plains are from a Spanish explorer's expedition. His name was Francisco de Coronado.

Tribes on the Plains

American Indians have moved in and out of this region for thousands of years. The historic period begins just a few hundred years ago. The people of this period lived in large family units, sometimes referred to as tribes. The Wichita, Kansa, Osage, Pawnee, and Plains Apache descended from the American Indians who lived in Kansas before them. These tribes

did not speak the same language or share the same customs. They wore varying styles of clothing, ate different foods, and created art specific to their culture. Some time later the Comanche, Kiowa, and Kiowa-Apache came to the region. Eventually, Arapaho and Cheyenne also came.

These early tribes, although different, shared things in common. They all lived in what came to be called the Great Plains, giving them the distinction of being Plains Indian tribes. Each tribe controlled a certain area of land, but the boundaries were fluid and changed over time. Unlike Americans today, they did not think of themselves as landowners. They did not exchange money for the use of land. But the people did have land they considered their own. They depended on it for hunting and living.

Over time, tribes moved in and out of Kansas from all directions.

Francisco de Coronado's exploration of the plains yielded the first written records of the Wichita.

Hide paintings depicted important events such as a raid by the Kansa on a Pawnee village to obtain horses.

Horses and Buffalo

It is impossible to determine exactly when horses came to the plains, but we know the animals were acquired from the Spanish in the Southwest. Using horses was an easy adaptation from using dogs as pack animals. Horses could carry bigger and heavier loads. Some tribes called horses "big dogs."

Horses also helped the people hunt buffalo. The buffalo was an extremely valuable resource for all of the people living on the plains. Although many of the tribes lived in permanent homes, they left those homes seasonally to hunt buffalo. The tipi, whether used as a primary dwelling or a home away from home, is another thing the Plains Indians had in common.

Is It a Buffalo or a Bison?

Bison is the scientific name for buffalo. The true buffalo is found in Africa and Asia. English settlers, using a variation of the French word "les boeufs," named the American "buffalo." The buffalo is the largest land mammal in North America, weighing about as much as a small car.

An estimated 40 million buffalo once roamed North America. The buffalo was very important to the Plains Indians. They considered the animal to be the giver of life and to have great spiritual power. The buffalo was the mainstay of the Plains Indians. It provided food, shelter, and clothing. The people made use of all parts of the buffalo.

- Meat and marrow were eaten.
- Skins were made into blankets, tipi covers, *parfleches*, drums, shields, saddles, clothing, and game balls.
- Hair was used to weave ropes and to provide stuffing for game balls, saddle pads, and pillows.
- Horns were used for spoons, bowls, and cups.
- Bones were made into tools, knives, flutes, and needles.
- Tails became fly swatters.
- Stomachs were used to cook stew and were later eaten.
- Bladders served as containers.
- Tendons and sinew were used as thread.
- Fat was made into soap.
- Tongues made hairbrushes.
- Hooves could be processed into glue.
- Buffalo dung could be burned as fuel.

Not all American Indians are Plains Indians

When early explorers came to North America, there were hundreds of Indian nations living here. Each nation had different cultures with different languages, customs, and beliefs that changed over time. Each culture adapted to its specific environment. Historically, many Plains Indians used tipis for shelter and decorated buckskins for clothing with porcupine quills and later, glass beads. American Indians in other parts of the United States lived in different ways that were unique to their culture and environment.

American Indians living on the Northwest Coast carved totem poles from tall tree trunks and used animals and birds as symbols.

American Indians living on the Great Plains used parts of the buffalo to make clothing and shelter. Quill and bead designs were mostly geometric.

American Indians living in the Great Lakes used birch bark from the numerous trees to make canoes, boxes, baskets, and even to cover house frames. Porcupine quill designs were of flowers and leaves.

American Indians living in the Southeast wove baskets of cypress and cane that grew in the swamplands. Zigzag patterns, popular in baskets, were also constructed in cloth as designs for clothing.

American Indians living in the Great Basin and California made tightly woven baskets out of grasses that grew in the region. Shells and bird feathers were often attached to the baskets.

American Indians living in the Southwest built houses of stone and adobe, known as pueblos. Painted pottery was made from local clays.

Homes

The Wichita built beehive-shaped grass lodges as permanent homes. Willows and cottonwood trees grew in central Kansas, and grasses were in abundance. The whole family worked together gathering needed materials, but the women and children actually constructed the lodge. The Wichita entered their homes through very low doorways on the east and west sides. Light entered the lodge through these doors, as well as through an opening in the roof.

The Pawnee made their home in a different environment than the Wichita. They built round homes covered with earth. The Pawnee placed grasses on top of a wooden structure. Then they covered the exterior with packed soil. Before the earth was applied, a Pawnee earth lodge looked similar to a Wichita grass lodge. Building an earth lodge was a communal effort, with neighbors helping neighbors. The Pawnee entered their earth lodges through tunnel-like openings that were wide enough to stable horses in the winter.

Both the Wichita and the Pawnee used the tipi as temporary housing when they hunted buffalo. The men of both tribes hunted year round, but they went on extended buffalo hunts with their families twice a year. Buffalo migrated, making it necessary to follow the herds.

Wichita grass lodges were constructed using frames of wood covered with bundles of grass.

Wichita and Pawnee

Wichita oral tradition tells us that the Wichita and the Pawnee are related. They migrated from Arkansas and Louisiana to the Platte River in Nebraska where they split into two groups. The Pawnee stayed in Nebraska and northern Kansas, and the Wichita moved south to central Kansas.

The door of a Pawnee earth lodge faced east towards the rising Morning Star.

Shar-I-Tar-Ish was a Pawnee chief. He is wearing a traditional warrior's roach. A roach is a headpiece made from deer hair and turkey beard.

Crops, Clothing, and Traditions

Corn was an important crop cultivated by both the Wichita and the Pawnee. Squash and pumpkins were also grown in gardens. To preserve them, vegetables were cut in strips and dried. The strips were pounded flat and woven into mats for storage. Pieces of the mats were torn off later to use in stews and soups. The Wichita traded pumpkin and squash mats to the Kiowa and Comanche who did not grow crops. The Wichita received additional buffalo meat in exchange.

Wichita and Pawnee women made clothing from tanned animal skins. Their style of dress was similar. Women wore moccasins, leggings, and skirts to protect their skin from the tall grasses.

Wichita men adorned themselves by piercing their ears. Both women and men tattooed their bodies. Young Wichita boys received their first tattoo on their hand when they had successfully learned to hunt.

Pawnee men wore their hair in a distinctive style, removing all but a narrow strip on top. The Pawnee were considered to be good warriors. War drums were decorated with symbols of *celestial* powers, such as the moon and the stars.

What's in a Name?

From the historic period forward, we refer to American Indians by their tribal names. Where did these names come from? Most American Indian cultures referred to themselves in their own language as "The People." When Europeans and Americans came to Kansas, they often struggled with the languages of the American Indians. When recording the names of the Indians, they wrote down what they thought they heard. This accounts for why some American Indians have been referred to by a variety of names.

In the early 1700s, French explorer Jacques Marquette visited the people living near the river that emptied into the Missouri River. He asked them what they called the river. He wrote down what he thought he heard, and from that time on the Kansa people were referred to by that name. Over time, the pronunciation and spelling has changed. There are more than 125 recorded variations of the name. Today, the people refer to themselves as the Kaw.

This illustration was published in London in 1857. It depicts a conference between the Kansa and the U.S. Commissioner if Indian Affairs. Why do you think people in London would be interested in this conference?

This picture of Osage men was taken in a formal studio.

Kansa and Osage

The Kansa and the Osage shared similarities in language. Their relationship is similar to that of cousins. Oral tradition tells us they may have lived as one tribe with the Quapaw, Omaha, and Ponca.

Homes

The Kansa and the Osage came to Kansas from the forested Southeast, bringing with them their knowledge of bark construction. Even in Kansas, the Kansa lived in permanent longhouses covered with bark. The Osage lived in long wood-framed lodges covered by cattail stems, bark, hides, or woven grass mats. Two related families lived in a lodge, one at each end of the structure.

Crops, Clothing, and Traditions

Both the Kansa and the Osage cultivated corn, beans, and squash. They also relied on the buffalo, and they traveled to hunt the large animals. The Osage, however, did not take tipis on the hunt.

They followed the Black Dog Trail, named after the chief who established it. Along the trail there was a series of framed structures built one day's travel apart from each other. As the people moved, they carried hide coverings from structure to structure.

Kansa men plucked hair from their eyebrows, chins, arms, and heads. Osage men shaved their heads except for a narrow band of hair running from the forehead to the back of the neck. Like the Kansa men, they wore ornaments in their pierced ears. Kansa warriors wore bear claws around their necks. Osage men adorned themselves with bracelets and tattooed their bodies for certain ceremonies. The women wore less elaborate clothing, but they did tattoo their bodies with colorful patterns.

When the Kansa feared their traditions were in jeopardy of being lost, they taught the Osage one special dance so that it would be preserved. For over 100 years, the Osage have danced the "I lon shka" with a drum given to them by the Kansa. Interestingly, in recent times, the Osage returned the drum to the Kansa.

The Kansa brought their skills of working with bark from the Southeast and then used these skills to construct their homes in Kansas.

Early People: Migration and Adaptation

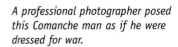
Nomadic Tribes: Cheyenne, Arapaho, Kiowa, Kiowa-Apache, and Comanche

Historic tribes of western Kansas are often referred to as *nomadic*. The scarcity of some resources in arid western Kansas forced the tribes to move often. Horses greatly increased the people's mobility.

Homes

The Cheyenne, Arapaho, Kiowa, Kiowa-Apache, and Comanche relied on the tipi for their homes. Tall poles tied together at the top and covered with hides created a structure that could be put up or taken down quickly. American Indians did not have wheels. The nomadic tribes transported their tipis on a frame called a *travois*.

A tipi was lightweight, but at the same time could withstand the winds of western Kansas. The outside of the tipi was often highly decorated. Arapaho tipis were decorated with porcupine quills in symbols that protected the well being of the occupants. Kiowa men painted their tipis to tell the story of a hunt or a battle.

Clothing

Like other Plains tribes, the American Indians of western Kansas used hides to make clothing. The Kiowa decorated their clothing with elk teeth, bones, shells, and porcupine quills. The nomadic peoples also adorned their bodies in a variety of ways. Comanche women painted the insides of their ears red. They also enhanced their beauty by painting orange and red circles on their cheeks and red and yellow lines around their eyes. Arapaho women painted their hair, scenting it with seeds and herbs. Fringed and embroidered bags were made to carry face paint and porcupine-tail brushes.

Satanta

1830–1878

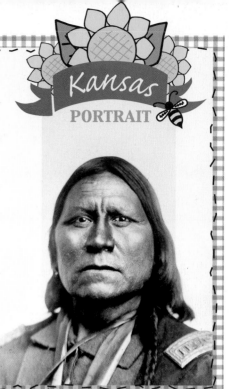

Satanta was a Kiowa chief, born before Kansas was open for settlement. In his lifetime, he saw his people at the height of their power, but he also witnessed the Kiowa restricted in their movement by the U.S. government.

Satanta gained his stature from being a strong warrior. He fought in wars against the Cheyenne and the Ute. He negotiated with the U.S. government to maintain the *sovereignty* of the Kiowa. Satanta represented his tribe at the Medicine Lodge Treaty Council. He spoke so well in defense of his people that he became known as the "Orator of the Plains."

I love the land, the buffalo, and will not part with it....I have heard that you intend to settle us on a reservation near the mountains. I don't want to settle. I love to roam over the prairies. There I feel free and happy, but when we settle down we grow pale and die....A long time ago this land belonged to our fathers; but when I go up to the river I see camps of soldiers....These soldiers cut down my timber, they kill my buffalo; when I see that, my heart feels like bursting; I feel sorry.

Moving Around for Food

The nomadic nature of their existence, and the limited access to water, meant that these tribes did not cultivate gardens. Instead, they hunted and gathered wild plants for food. The buffalo was probably more important to the nomadic tribes than it was to other Plains Indians because the nomadic tribes used buffalo as a trade item as well. When they needed cultivated crops like corn to eat, they would trade buffalo meat to get it.

Telling Stories and Keeping Record

The Cheyenne used animal skins as canvases to paint stories. Bold colors depicted horses during the heat of battle or during a hunt. Some hides were decorated with abstract designs. The Kiowa kept a pictorial account of the history of their tribe. Called winter and summer counts, they depicted important events. Painted on buffalo hide, they served as historical calendars for the tribe.

Nomadic tribes traveled long distances to hunt buffalo. This photograph shows how they used a travois to carry supplies.

Interaction and Trade

The horse made travel over long distances much easier. A great deal of trading took place among the tribes. The tribes in the West offered dried meat, hides, deerskin clothing, and decorative objects for trade. The tribes in the East grew gardens and offered nuts, corn, squash, and pumpkins.

In the very earliest of times, there is no real evidence of serious hostilities among the tribes. Conflict arose as the populations grew in Kansas. The Pawnee traded less with their neighbors because they considered many of them enemies. The Pawnee engaged in long-standing conflicts with the Osage and the Kansa. The Cheyenne and the Arapaho forced the Kiowa and the Kiowa-Apache south. The Kiowa and the Comanche banded together for raids into Mexico.

When Europeans and Americans eventually entered Kansas, relationships became more complicated between tribes. Life for the Plains Indians changed dramatically.

The horse allowed Plains Indians great mobility to both trade and hunt. This photograph shows Eagle Shirt (on horseback) and Black Horse of the Cheyenne.

Chapter 2 Review

What Do You Remember?

1. Why do we not know more about the earliest people of Kansas?
2. How did people adapt to the major climate change?
3. Name at least two technological changes that led to an increased population.
4. Explain the difference between relative dating and absolute dating.
5. What evidence do we have that the village farmers lived in permanent villages?
6. How did the American Indians use a system of barter?
7. What do archeologists mean when they say they "infer meaning"?
8. What advantages did the horse bring to the Plains Indians?
9. Explain the similarities and differences in Wichita and Pawnee housing.
10. What did the Osage use instead of tipis during the buffalo hunt?
11. Name at least five ways the Plains Indians used the buffalo.
12. Give a definition of "nomadic" and explain how the term describes some of the Plains Indians.
13. Why were there no serious hostilities among the earliest people of Kansas? Why did hostilities increase among tribes?

Activities

1. The Plains Indians of western Kansas are not the only nomadic people in the history of the world. Research a nomadic people from another part of the world. What was the climate like where they lived? Describe their clothing, food sources, and culture. How is their lifestyle similar to the nomadic Plains Indians? How is it different?

2. You have read that the Cheyenne, Arapaho, Kiowa, Kiowa-Apache, and Comanche are referred to as nomadic tribes. The Wichita, Pawnee, Kansa, and Osage are sometimes referred to as sedentary tribes. It means that, while they did move around to find food and hunt, they had permanent villages. Choose one nomadic tribe and one sedentary tribe to learn more about. Describe and compare their housing, art, customs, food, and culture.

Think About It!

1. Compare ways the American Indians lived off the land with our use of natural resources today. How are they alike? How are they different? Which lifestyle appeals most to you?

2. Archeological techniques help us lean more about prehistoric people. Can you think of other uses for archeology? For example, some archeologists also work with law enforcement to solve crimes. Law enforcement agencies use archeologists to uncover evidence and record the key findings for use in court.

Kansas As a Crossroads:
Invasions and Encounters

Timeline of Events

44

1540

1670

1720

1740

1541
Explorer Francisco
Vasquez de Coronado
makes contact with the
Wichita.

1719
Claude Charles Du
Tisne travels to the
lower Arkansas
River valley.

1744
The French b[...]
Fort Cavagnia[...]
near present-d[...]
Leavenworth.

1673
Louis Jolliet and Jacques
Marquette find the Missouri
River and later place the name
"Kansas" on a map.

1723
Etienne Veniard de
Bourgmont establishes
Fort Orleans on the
Missouri River.

WORDS TO UNDERSTAND
assimilate
boarding
botanical
chain mail
commerce
confluence
eminent domain
entrepreneur
manifest destiny
monarchy
New World
ration
reservation
sanitation
sovereign right
synonymous
transcribe
vocation

This mural depicts Coronado coming to Kansas. It was painted by Kansas artist David H. Overmyer and is displayed in the State Capitol. Coronado was part of the first group of Europeans to visit Kansas.

1803
The United States purchases Louisiana Territory from France.

1806
Zebulon Pike explores the southern portion of the Louisiana Purchase.

1822
Explorer Stephen Long publishes a map that describes Kansas and surrounding areas as "The Great Desert."

1825
Indian tribes from the East begin relocation to Kansas.

1843
About 900 emigrants travel the Oregon-California Trail.

1800 1810 1820 1830 1840

1804
The Lewis and Clark expedition reaches Kansas as it travels along the Missouri River.

1821
Mexico wins independence from Spain. William Becknell becomes the first to travel the Santa Fe Trail to trade legally with Mexico.

1830
U.S. Congress passes the Indian Removal Act that trades Indian lands in the East for reservation lands in the West.

45

Europeans Invade Kansas

For thousands of years, countries invaded and explored other lands. Encounters between native peoples and foreign explorers always resulted in changes to both cultures. What motivated these early explorers? Some were driven by a desire to spread religious beliefs. Others were motivated to conquer new lands. Exploration was also fueled by a need to establish trade routes and obtain precious resources such as gold or spices. A thirst for new knowledge was also a motivating factor.

European explorers came to the land that was to become Kansas. The Spanish were the first to arrive, followed by the French.

Francisco Vasquez de Coronado

By the 16th century, the Wichita were actively trading with the Indians of the Southwest. This gave them experience with people of other cultures. But we can only imagine what the Wichita thought when the first Europeans arrived at their villages. The Spanish came on horseback, wearing shiny metal helmets and protective vests of *chain mail*. Although few in numbers, the Europeans must have been a sight unlike any other. We have no records to tell us how the Wichita felt. Were they curious, afraid, or indifferent?

We know much more about the Spanish point of view. Francisco Vasquez de Coronado was born into a wealthy family in Spain. He came to the *New World* at the age of 25 to serve in the government of New Spain. He heard stories about seven cities of gold. Although already wealthy, he wanted more. His search for treasure led him to present-day New Mexico and beyond, but he found no gold.

Quivira

Among the men in Coronado's expedition was an Indian slave called "Turk." He told the Spaniards about the land of Quivira. A wide river with fish the size of horses could be found there. Large

Chain mail armor was worn by Spanish explorers for protection. Chain mail was also used to protect their horses. This small piece of horse chain mail was found in a large Indian village site in central Kansas. This and other artifacts have led some people to speculate that Coronado made it as far north as Lindsborg before returning to Mexico. How does a piece of chain mail tell us the Spanish were here? What else might it mean?

The Kansas Journey

boats with golden eagle statues on their bows sailed up and down the river. The king of this great land slept each night beneath a tree of golden bells. The blowing wind made soft music. Even the common people of Quivira were surrounded by great wealth. They ate from plates of silver and were served from bowls of gold.

Although Coronado and his men began to doubt the stories about Quivira, the allure of this mythical place was strong. Eventually, Coronado and about 40 men made their way to present-day Kansas in search of Quivira. They found no gold or silver, no river with fish as big as horses. They did, however, encounter Wichita villages. The Wichita lived in grass lodges, raised gardens, and hunted buffalo. They worked with stone tools. The only metal Coronado found was a necklace of copper worn by a Wichita chief.

Disappointed, Coronado eventually returned to Mexico, where his expedition was considered a failure. Within a short time, Coronado lost his job with the Spanish government, was put on trial, and was found guilty of mistreating native peoples.

The Wichita lived in grass lodges for most of the year. After harvest, the people went on an extended winter hunt as they followed the buffalo herds.

Coronado was told about great shaggy cows that roamed the plains. His report to the king of Spain mentions that the Wichita followed the "cows" and used them as a source of food, clothing, and shelter. This is an early picture of a buffalo. Does it look like a shaggy cow?

Coronado's Report to the King of Spain

As was customary with Europeans at the time, Coronado asked the Wichita to give their "obedience" to the king of Spain and to place themselves under his "royal overlordship." On October 20, 1541, Coronado wrote to the king of Spain about his visit to the Wichita villages that he called Quivira. He described the people he encountered and his opinion of the land:

> *I arrived at the province they call Quivira, to which the guides were conducting me, and where they had described to me houses of stone, with many stories; and not only are they not of stone, but of straw. . . .The diversity of languages which exists in this country and my not having anyone who understood them, because they speak their own language in each village, has hindered me.*
>
> *The province of Quivira is 950 leagues from Mexico. . . The country itself is the best I have ever seen for producing all the products of Spain, for besides the land itself being very fat and black and being very well watered by the rivulets and springs and rivers, I found prunes like those of Spain & nuts and very good sweet grapes and mulberries. . . . I remained twenty-five days in this province of Quivira. . . . And what I am sure of is that there is not any gold nor any other metal in all that country, and the other things of which they had told me are nothing but little villages, and in many of these they do not plant anything and do not have any houses except of skins and sticks, and they wander around with the cows; so that the account they gave me was false.*

What do you think?

When Coronado writes to the King of Spain, he seems to contradict himself. Coronado writes first about the Wichita living in "straw houses," but later refers to houses of "skins and sticks." Considering what we know about the Wichita and other tribes, what do you think is going on here? Is Coronado confused? Is there a logical explanation?

The state of Kansas is named for the Kansa. This illustration by George Catlin was painted at a Kansa village in 1830. The village was about 70 miles west of the place where the Missouri and Kansas Rivers meet. Catlin traveled to the homelands of American Indians to paint and sketch them. His work gives us an early record of native peoples.

French Exploration of Kansas

More than 100 years after Coronado visited the Wichita, French explorers from Canada followed the Mississippi River to the Missouri River. One of the explorers, Louis Jolliet, placed the names "Kansas" and "Missouri" on a map for the first time. Jolliet never actually explored Kansas but was responsible for gathering information on the lands beyond the Missouri River.

Fort Cavagnial

The French had already developed trade relationships with American Indians north and east of Kansas. Trading guns, alcohol, and metal for furs was profitable, and the French wanted to make even more profit. They also heard that the Spanish might be moving into territory already claimed by France. The French sent expeditions into Kansas to persuade the Indians who lived here to form trade relationships with the French, not the Spanish.

Claude Charles Du Tisne

France sent Claude Charles Du Tisne to contact the Comanche. The Comanche were a powerful nation that had obtained horses from the Spanish. This helped them control

parts of the plains. They took horses and mules from others and traded them to the Spanish. They even captured Indians of other tribes and traded them as slaves. The French saw the Comanche as a possible barrier to relations with other tribes, so they wanted to form a relationship with them.

Du Tisne failed to reach the Comanche, but he did manage to make contact with the Osage and the Pawnee, and he traded guns and ammunition for information. This alarmed the Spanish. Neither the Spanish nor the French wanted the other to take control of Kansas.

Etienne Veniard de Bourgmont

Four years after Du Tisne's trip, France sent another explorer to try to gain control of present-day Kansas. Etienne Veniard de Bourgmont was sent to establish a relationship with the Kansa and the Plains Apache and set up a fort on the Missouri River. A year after Fort Orleans was established, de Bourgmont made a 10-day trip west to meet the Plains Apache. The Frenchman convinced the Plains Apache to enter into a peace agreement with other tribes.

Although the French continued to trade in Kansas, they began to lose influence. When the traders could not supply trade items the Indians wanted, the agreements dissolved. The British also became increasingly interested in trade. The goods offered by the British were often superior to those of the French, so tensions increased between the French and the Indians. To help regulate the fur trade, the French built Fort Cavagnial.

Trading Kansas

When the Europeans first arrived, many Indian tribes had already made Kansas their home. It was usual for European explorers and traders to claim the land and its resources in the name of their king or queen. Indians were asked to give their allegiance to the *monarchy*, or royal family. Over time, Spain and France traded Kansas back and forth without consulting, or even informing, the American Indians who lived here. The *sovereign rights* of the native peoples were ignored.

The interest of the Europeans in Kansas had both immediate and long-term effects on the native populations. The Spanish chose to rule the area from afar, but the French lived among the native peoples, often marrying Indian women. The Spanish were not allowed to provide guns and ammunition to the Indians, but the French freely traded firearms.

Contacts between Indians and Europeans were sometimes friendly and sometimes hostile. Trade brought the native peoples new products, such as metal tools and cloth, but it also created economic needs. Although trade and conflict existed among Indian tribes before the Europeans arrived, the presence of the Europeans increased tensions. Some Indians stole from each other and even sold members of other tribes into slavery.

Encounters with Europeans also brought new diseases to the plains. Smallpox, measles, whooping cough, and influenza had a devastating effect on the Indians of Kansas. Sometimes the population of an entire village died from these diseases.

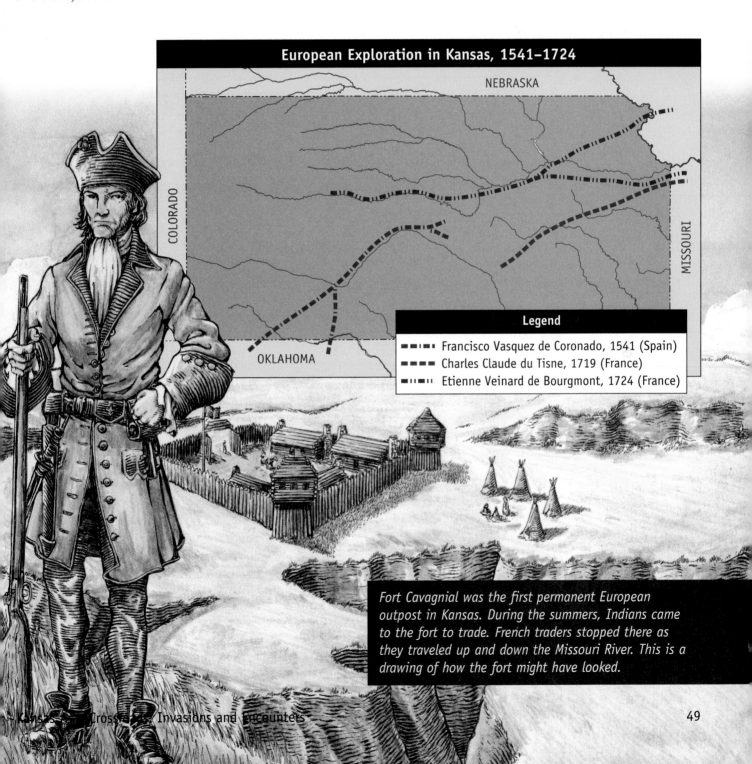

European Exploration in Kansas, 1541–1724

NEBRASKA

COLORADO

OKLAHOMA

MISSOURI

Legend
- ■-■-■- Francisco Vasquez de Coronado, 1541 (Spain)
- ■-■-■- Charles Claude du Tisne, 1719 (France)
- ■-■■-■■ Etienne Veinard de Bourgmont, 1724 (France)

Fort Cavagnial was the first permanent European outpost in Kansas. During the summers, Indians came to the fort to trade. French traders stopped there as they traveled up and down the Missouri River. This is a drawing of how the fort might have looked.

American Explorers in Kansas

When France claimed most of the place that became Kansas, it was part of a huge area of land called Louisiana. Napoleon Bonaparte, emperor of France, saw England as his enemy. By selling the entire Louisiana Territory to the United States, Napoleon was able to prevent it from becoming part of England. Plus, the money he received would help pay for any military action against his rival. The United States, on the other hand, gained enough land to double its size and open up possibilities for westward expansion.

Meriwether Lewis and William Clark

Once again the land that was home to the Wichita, Kansa, and other tribes was delivered into the hands of another nation. This happened peacefully–but without a vote by the people who lived here.

Once the United States owned the land called Louisiana, they needed to know what was out there. President Thomas Jefferson selected his personal secretary, Meriwether Lewis, to lead the exploration. Lewis chose William Clark as his partner. Both men had military experience that would serve them well. President Jefferson gave Lewis and Clark very specific directions: "The object of your mission is to explore the Missouri River. . .and other river [s which] may offer the most direct. . .water communication across the continent." This meant the men were to search for a water route that went all the way to the Pacific Ocean. The American explorers were also to establish relationships with the American Indians and to record information about the natural environment.

Lewis and Clark traveled up the Missouri River, struggling against the current. One hundred twenty-three miles of their entire route was in Kansas. Clark recorded in his journal what he had heard about the Kansa. Although the information Clark collected was invaluable, he was a notoriously bad speller:

This great river of the Kansas . . . recves its names from a nation which dwells at this time on its banks & 2 villages . . . those Indians are not verry noumerous at this time, reduced by war with their neighbours, . . . above this river in an open & butifull plain and were verry noumerous at the time the French first Settled the Illinois, I am told they are a fierce & warlike people, beinmg badly Supplied with fire arms, become easily conquered by the Aiauway & Saukees who are better furnished with those materials of war, This nation is now out in the plains hunting the Buffalow.

Lewis and Clark seemed to like Kansas. They mentioned that there was a variety of game and that the prairie held great beauty. Deer seemed to be plentiful, and wild raspberries were abundant. Clark did remark, however, that the water in the Kansas River tasted "disagreeable" to him. All of this information would be valuable to future settlers on the prairie.

Lewis and Clark celebrated Independence Day near Atchison on July 4, 1804. The members of the expedition wore dress uniforms and fired the keelboat's gun.

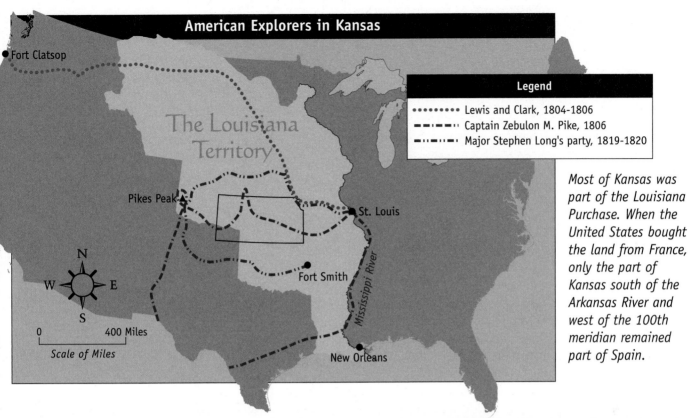

American Explorers in Kansas

Legend
- ••••••••• Lewis and Clark, 1804-1806
- –•–•–•–•• Captain Zebulon M. Pike, 1806
- –••–••–••• Major Stephen Long's party, 1819-1820

The Louisiana Territory

Fort Clatsop

Pikes Peak

St. Louis

Fort Smith

Mississippi River

New Orleans

N
W E
S

0   400 Miles
Scale of Miles

Most of Kansas was part of the Louisiana Purchase. When the United States bought the land from France, only the part of Kansas south of the Arkansas River and west of the 100th meridian remained part of Spain.

Kansas As a Crossroads: Invasions and Encounters

Zebulon Pike came in contact with the Pawnee shortly after Spanish soldiers asked the Pawnee to pledge their allegiance to the king of Spain. Pike asked the Pawnee to take down the Spanish flag and to "acknowledge their American father."

How Do We Know This?

We know a great deal about Lewis and Clark, Pike, and other expeditions. How do we know this? Explorers wrote journals. They kept notes on what they saw and what they thought. Their accounts were published so others might learn from their observations.

Pike published An Account of Expeditions *in 1810. Pike was not a trained astronomer, surveyor, or guide, and therefore he made errors on his expedition. His work was still valuable, as he gathered a great deal of scientific information.* An Account of Expeditions *was widely read. Pike was the first to recommend that trade with Spain could be accomplished with an overland trail.*

AN ACCOUNT OF EXPEDITIONS
TO THE
Sources of the Mississippi,
AND THROUGH THE
WESTERN PARTS OF LOUISIANA,
TO THE SOURCES OF THE
ARKANSAW, KANS, LA PLATTE, AND PIERRE
JAUN, RIVERS;
PERFORMED BY ORDER OF THE
GOVERNMENT OF THE UNITED STATES
DURING THE YEARS 1805, 1806, AND 1807.
AND A TOUR THROUGH
THE
INTERIOR PARTS OF NEW SPAIN,
WHEN CONDUCTED THROUGH THESE PROVINCES,
BY ORDER OF
THE CAPTAIN-GENERAL,
IN THE YEAR 1807.

By MAJOR Z. M. PIKE.

ILLUSTRATED BY MAPS AND CHARTS.

PHILADELPHIA:
PUBLISHED BY C. & A. CONRAD, & Co. No. 30, CHESNUT STREET. SOMER
WELL & CONRAD, PETERSBURGH. BONSAL, CONRAD, & Co. NORFOLK.
FIELDING LUCAS, JR. BALTIMORE.

John Binns, Printer.—1810.

Zebulon Pike

Before Lewis and Clark returned from their expedition, Zebulon Pike began his exploration of the plains. Unlike Lewis and Clark, who traveled by boat, Pike became the first American to travel over land.

General James Wilkinson, governor of Louisiana Territory, sent Pike on a mission to return around 50 Osage who were held by the Potawatomi. Pike was to make peace between the Osage and the Kansa. He was also to establish a friendly relationship with the Comanche, but to do so he needed the help of the Pawnee. In many ways, Pike's assignment mirrored President Jefferson's instructions to Lewis and Clark. He was to observe the animals and plants around him and return with mineral and ***botanical***, or plant, specimens.

Spain was not pleased with the United States' purchase of Louisiana. The Spanish became nervous as American explorers pushed into the interior of the plains. This put precious trade relationships with American Indians at stake. In response to Pike's expedition, the Spanish sent their own force onto the plains. By the time Pike reached the Pawnee, the Spanish were already there.

A Desert

While exploring the lands at the foot of the Rocky Mountains, Pike and his men found themselves unprepared for winter. Pike crossed into land claimed by Spain and was captured. He was held for several months, and some of his papers were taken by the Spanish officials. He managed to hide his journal. After he was released, Pike wrote down details of his journey in an attempt to replace the lost papers.

In his accounts, Pike wrote his opinion of what is now Kansas. He described the land as a desert:

> *In the vast country of which we speak, we find the soil generally dry and sandy, with gravel, and discover that the moment we approach a stream, the land becomes more humid with small timber; I therefore conclude, that this country never was timbered, as from the earliest age, the aridity of the soil having so few water courses running through it, and they being*

Stephen H. Long published this map in his popular atlas. Across Kansas it reads, "The Great Desert is frequented by traveling bands of Indians who have no place of residence but roam from place to place in quest of game."

principally dry in summer, has never afforded moisture sufficient to support growth of timber. . . .These vast plains of the western hemisphere, may become in time equally celebrated as the sandy desarts of Africa; for I saw in my route, in various places, tracts of many leagues, where the wind had thrown up the sand, in all the fanciful forms of the ocean's rolling wave, and on which not a speck of vegetable matter existed.

Pikes description helped begin a national debate over whether this land could be cultivated. It was an important issue, because in the 19th century the ability to grow crops was a primary requirement for American settlement.

Stephen H. Long

Stephen Long had much in common with other 19th century American explorers who mapped the West. He was a college-educated member of the Army Corps of Engineers. Long was familiar with the technology of his age.

Long's mission was to map the southwestern portion of the plains. One thing that made Stephen Long's expedition unique was that he traveled by steamboat. The boat, called the *Western Engineer*, traveled from Pittsburgh, Pennsylvania, down the Ohio River to the Mississippi River and then into the Missouri River. When Long reached the **confluence** of the Missouri and the Kansas Rivers, he attempted to navigate onto the Kansas River. The river was filled with mud from a

recent flood, and the expedition was forced to return to the safer waters of the Missouri. Although some of Long's men were dispatched into Kansas, Long himself continued north into Nebraska.

The impact of Stephen Long on the history of Kansas is a story told on a map. Long was the first to publish a U.S. atlas with state and territory maps. The book was very popular. Long labeled the area that was to become Kansas as "The Great Desert." In Long's opinion, "It is almost wholly unfit for cultivation, and of course uninhabitable by a people depending on agriculture for their subsistence." This view of Kansas as a desert stuck, and it influenced U.S. government's settlement policies for years to come.

Members of Long's expedition met with the Kansa. This sketch was made by one of the members of the expedition. It is a drawing of a traditional Kansa dance.

This map from the 1830s shows what the United States looked like at the time of the Indian Removal Act.

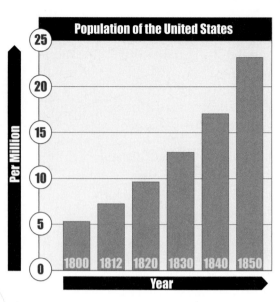

Thirst for Land

As the population of the United States grew, so did American's desire for land. New immigrants were coming to the country's shores and the birth rate was rising. The American economy was based on agriculture, so the country needed large amounts of land. The United States feared that European countries might invade. Settlement in the West would create a barrier to possible European invasions.

At the time of the Louisiana Purchase, President Jefferson wanted to move American Indians from the East to lands in the West. This would free up land for agriculture and white settlement. The plan was tested on a voluntary basis and failed.

Indian tribes were placed under a great deal of pressure. Some chose to protect what was left of their land. To do so, some tribes chose to *assimilate* to the American way of life. Other tribes sold parts of their land to the U.S. government in an attempt to maintain control over what land was left. Others simply refused to move, even if it meant going to war.

Indian Removal Act

About 20 years after the Louisiana Purchase, President Andrew Jackson pushed for the Indian Removal Act. The act allowed the president to move Indian tribes in the East to lands west of the Mississippi.

President Jackson felt American Indians stood in the way of progress.

What good man would prefer a country covered with forests and ranged by a thousand savages to our extensive Republic, studded with cities, towns, and prosperous farms embellished with all the improvements which art can devise or industry execute, occupied by more than 12,000,000 happy people, and filled with all the blessings of liberty, civilization and religion?

The Indians saw it from a different point of view. Chief John Ross of the Cherokee nation protested the treatment of his people:

We are stripped of every attribute of freedom and eligibility for legal self-defense. Our property may be plundered before our eyes; violence may be committed on our persons; even our lives may be taken away, and there is none to regard our complaints. We are denationalized . . . We are deprived of membership in the human family!

Indian Relocation to Kansas

Even before the Indian Removal Act was passed, present-day Kansas was considered a potential home for Indian tribes from the East. Some white people also wanted to protect the Indians.

Isaac McCoy was a Baptist minister who worried that American influence would bring about the end of the Indian's way of life. McCoy wanted to create an Indian state where native peoples could live in peace and gradually be assimilated and converted to Christianity. Many thought this plan was humane, even though it required the Indians to change their traditional ways.

Indian removal in Kansas really began when Superintendent of Indian Affairs William Clark, of Lewis and Clark fame, arranged to give part of the lands of the Kansa and the Osage to Indian tribes from the East. Within a 25-year period, more than 25 tribes were given land in Kansas. These tribes became known as emigrant Indians.

The Emigrant Indian Experience

Indian tribes forced to emigrate to Kansas were assigned to *reservations*. Some Indian tribes split apart with the stress of relocation. A large number of Potawatomi living in Indiana refused to move until they were forced by the military to flee to Canada. Only a portion of the Potawatomi came to Kansas.

The government's policy of relocation was difficult to implement because lifestyles varied greatly among tribes. Hunting was an important part of Ottawa and Shawnee life. The Iowa and Kickapoo were farmers. The Miami were known as traders. Some tribes had already adopted white ways before relocation. The Wyandot wore the clothing and practiced the customs of the Americans. Other tribes, such as the Sac and Fox, held on to their traditions.

Upon arrival in Kansas, many tribes found the living conditions to be unfamiliar and difficult. The Potawatomi, who had depended on a diet of fish, found themselves in a place with very few fish. For tribes such as the Ottawa, the changes were disastrous. During their first two years in Kansas, more than 300 of the 600 Ottawas died due to extreme weather, disease, and lack of food.

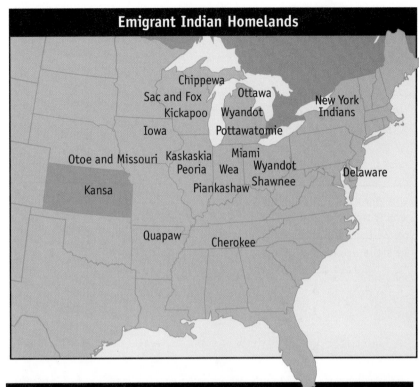

Emigrant Indian Homelands

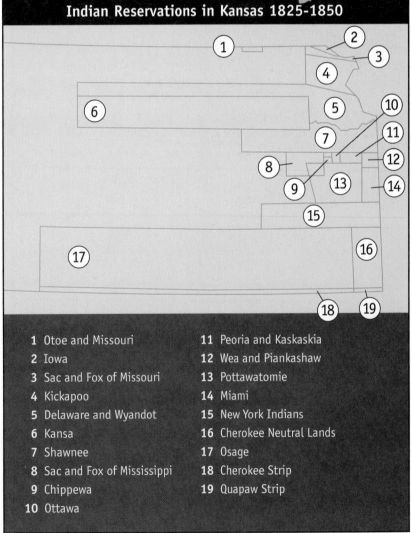

Indian Reservations in Kansas 1825-1850

1 Otoe and Missouri	11 Peoria and Kaskaskia
2 Iowa	12 Wea and Piankashaw
3 Sac and Fox of Missouri	13 Pottawatomie
4 Kickapoo	14 Miami
5 Delaware and Wyandot	15 New York Indians
6 Kansa	16 Cherokee Neutral Lands
7 Shawnee	17 Osage
8 Sac and Fox of Mississippi	18 Cherokee Strip
9 Chippewa	19 Quapaw Strip
10 Ottawa	

The Sac and Fox was one of the tribes that relocated to Kansas. Traditionally, they lived in bark-covered lodges. They moved from a land that was heavily forested. Based on what you know about the Kansas environment, can you speculate why it might have been difficult to build this type of lodge in Kansas?

What do you think?

During the period of Indian removal, American Indians were not given the rights of citizens. The U.S. government did make attempts to compensate tribes for losses. In some cases this was more successful than others. The tragedy of Indian removal is that native peoples did not have a choice. Could this happen to you today?

Within our country we believe in the power of ***eminent domain***. This means that the government can take the property of an individual for the sake of the common good. Federal, state, and local units of government have this right. The Fifth Amendment to the U.S. Constitution says that no property may be taken without just compensation. Much discussion has taken place about what constitutes "just compensation." What do you think? What justifies the taking of personal property for the common good? Who should decide what is fair compensation?

Letter to William Clark, Superintendent of Indian Affairs, from Richard W. Cummins, Indian Agent

Richard Cummins was a government agent who worked in Kansas with emigrant Indians. In this letter, Cummins expresses concern for the Delaware and Wea under his supervision. Indians had been forced to move across the country without proper time to prepare for the long journey. At times, Indians were forced to move during very bad weather.

Shawanee and Delaware Agency
2d April 1831

Genl. William Clark
Sup't of Indian Aff's

Sir,

I have furnished the Delawares with as much provisions only as was actually needful to keep them from suffering . . .when they came last fall their horses were poor, oweing to the very extreme Hardness of the winter, the Indians generally as weel as the Delawares lost most all their horses. They have none fit for service, a great many of the Indians, are in a suffering condition . . . I believe it to be my duty to have some provisions Waggoned to them, particularly, to the Delawares Chief Anderson & his counsel men says that it was understood last fall on White river that the supplementary article to their treaty was ratified, That immediately the white people moved in among Them and took possession of their farms. Commenced seeding their fields and selling whiskey to his people so that he was compelled to move. I have also furnished that half of the, Weas, that have been in the Mississippi swamps, for some time past with Two wagon loads of Corn and pork. They came and joined their, Nation on their Land this spring, in a starving condition, their Friends were unable to help them many of whom I was informed by the trader divided their corn with their horses as long as they had a ear, they are now trying to work but their diet is so weak, they are not able to do much. I think the past winter, will learn the Indians in future to be more provident. They stand much in need of provisions, I would like to receive some instructions from You on the subject of furnishing them.

Respectly Your Most
Obedt. Servt.
(Signed) Richd. W. Cummins
Indn. Agent

*This is the actual letter written by Cummins. When historians **transcribe** primary source documents, they write down exactly what is written, including misspelled words.*

What do you think?

If you were in Cummins' position, and your job was to take care of the Indians, what would your response be to this situation? What would you say to the Superintendent of Indian Affairs who was in charge of relocating Indians to the West? How would you try to solve the problem?

Missionaries

During the period of Indian relocation, the only non-Indians allowed to legally live in present-day Kansas worked for the U.S. government or traveled with the emigrant tribes. Missionaries, traders, and Indian agents became an integral part of the displaced Indians' lives.

Missionaries set up schools to convert the Indian children to Christianity and to teach them *vocational* skills. The missionaries' motives varied. Some sincerely believed that their work would help the Indians.

The Indian reaction to the mission schools was mixed. Some Indians felt no need to change their way of life and preferred their own spiritual beliefs. Others welcomed what the missionaries could give, including food and clothing.

Missionary schools were built on reservation lands and were usually supported by government funds as part of treaty negotiations. Children often lived apart from their families by *boarding* at the school. The quality of the experience varied from mission to mission. At some, the children were required to speak English only. A few missions allowed students to speak their native language. Nevertheless, the main goal at all missions was to change the culture of the child—to Americanize the Indian.

The service to a new pupil was to trim his hair closely; then with soap and water, to give him or her the first lesson in godliness, which was a good scrubbing, and a little red precipitate on the scalp, to supplement the use of a fine-toothed comb; then he was furnished with a new set of clothes, and taught how to put them on and off. They all emerged from the ordeal as shy as peacocks just plucked. A new English name finished the preparation for the alphabet and the English language.

–Dr. Wilson Hobbs, superintendent,
Friend's Mission, Kansas

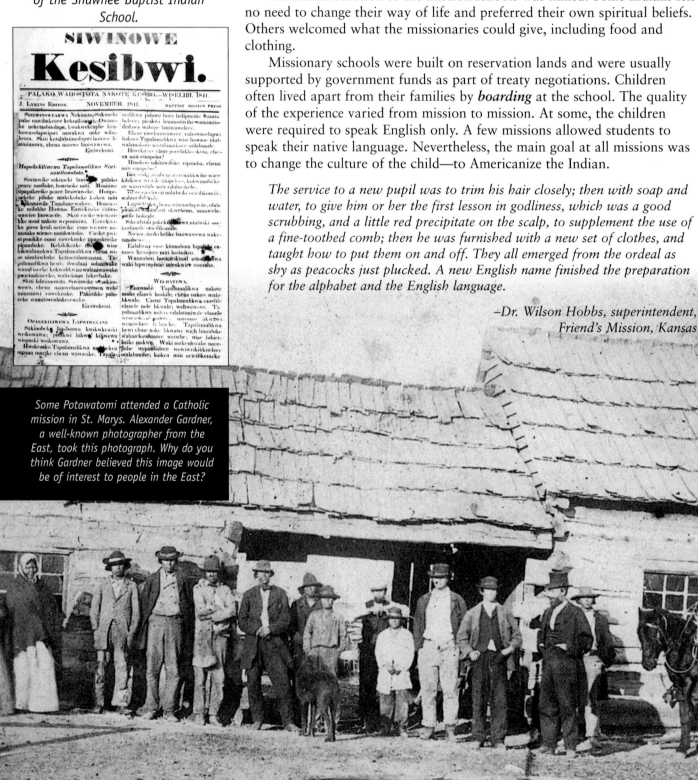

The first newspaper in Kansas, Siwinowe Kesibwi (Shawnee Sun), was printed in the Shawnee language. Missionary Jotham Meeker brought the first printing press to Kansas and operated the paper out of the Shawnee Baptist Indian School.

Some Potawatomi attended a Catholic mission in St. Marys. Alexander Gardner, a well-known photographer from the East, took this photograph. Why do you think Gardner believed this image would be of interest to people in the East?

The Kansas Journey

Activity

A Day at the Mission

Mission life was very structured. Missionaries wanted Indian children to assimilate quickly. Indian parents were encouraged not to visit their children. How do these school experiences compare to your school day? Study the chart below, and find similarities and differences to your school experience.

Time	Indian Mission School Activities (1840s)
5:00 am	Religious worship
6:00 am	Breakfast
7:00 am	Girls learn to knit and sew; boys learn to farm
9:00 am	Girls and boys study spelling, reading, arithmetic, geography, and writing
10:30 am	Continue academic instruction
12:00 noon	Dinner meal, followed by recreation period
1:00 pm	Continue studying spelling, reading, arithmetic, geography, and writing
2:45 pm	Continue academic instruction
4:00 pm	Boys work the farm, raising corn, vegetables, and livestock; girls are instructed in sewing, knitting, housekeeping, and food preparation
5:30 pm	Supper, religious worship, and a short exercise period
7:00 pm	Religious instruction, including singing hymns and reading the Bible

Students learned from books like McGuffy's Reader.

Kansas PORTRAIT

Annie Marshall Grinter
1820–1905

Annie Marshall's mother was a member of the Delaware tribe. Her father was a fur trader who became an Indian agent. As an Indian agent, her father assisted the Potawatomi in relocating to the reservation in Kansas. Growing up, she was educated at the Osage Mission.

At age 16, Annie Marshall married Moses Grinter, and they moved onto the Delaware reservation in what is today Wyandotte County. It was because of her Indian heritage that they were able to have a home and run a business in Kansas during this time period.

Grinter and her husband operated a ferry boat on the Kansas River. For five years in the mid-1850s, they also operated a trading post. They exchanged clothing, ammunition, perfume, sugar, scissors, and other goods for furs and cash from the Delaware. The Grinters were also farmers. They raised chickens and grew apples.

Annie Grinter was proud of her Delaware roots. Throughout her life, she spoke both English and the language of the Delaware.

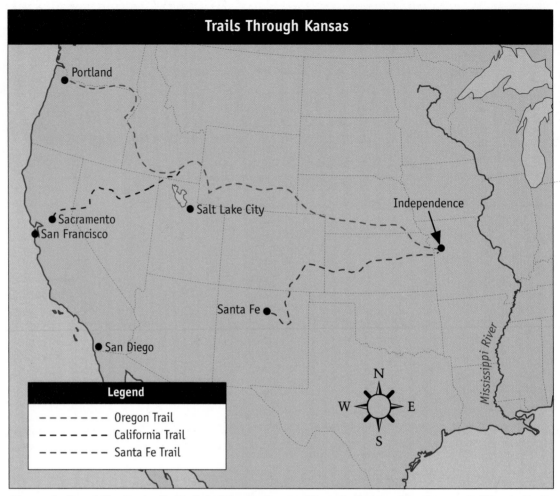

Trails Through Kansas

Portland

Salt Lake City

Independence

Sacramento
San Francisco

Santa Fe

San Diego

Mississippi River

Legend
- - - - - - Oregon Trail
- - - - - - California Trail
- - - - - - Santa Fe Trail

N
W · E
S

The majority of the Santa Fe Trail (489 miles) goes through Kansas. The Oregon-California Trail passes through northeast Kansas for 165 miles.

Crossing Kansas

In the early 1800s, people traveled through Kansas to trade or settle in the West. Long before air travel and interstate highways, people traveled west on trails. Two great trails of the 19th century went through Kansas. The Santa Fe Trail was primarily a *commerce* route, connecting the United States to Mexico. The Oregon-California Trail was an emigrant trail, carrying families west to find prosperity and new lives.

The Santa Fe Trail

William Becknell is often called the father of the Santa Fe Trail. A trader from Missouri, Becknell was out of money and risking jail time for debts. To earn money, he decided to haul

trade goods from Kansas City to Santa Fe. At first, Becknell and other traders used pack mules, limiting the amount they could carry. Becknell eventually found a route that would accommodate wagons, which increased the amount of freight he could transport. This, of course, increased his profit.

The Santa Fe Trail became an important international trade route, attracting *entrepreneurs* from all over the world. Wyandotte Chief William Walker rented warehouses in Independence, Missouri, to store trade goods. Hiram Young, a former slave who bought his own freedom, became a wealthy man making wagons to carry goods on the trail. One Missouri woman invested $60 in one of William Becknell's early trips and received $900 on her investment. The Santa Fe Trail made money for people.

What Was Life Like on the Santa Fe Trail?

An average wagon train had about 26 wagons. It took about 35 men eight weeks to make the trip from Independence, Missouri, through Kansas and on to Santa Fe. They rode or walked through dust or mud. Gnats, mosquitoes, and glaring heat were constant problems. Food was scarce, so it had to be *rationed*. Flour, sugar, bacon, and coffee were staples. It was a treat once a week to have beans. Dried apples were an even greater treat, as they were available about twice a month. When buffalo could be hunted, everyone was glad for the fresh meat it added to the menu.

Weather on the plains was unpredictable and could be harsh. James Ross Larken, who traveled on the Santa Fe Trail, wrote about camping near the Arkansas River:

Oct. 9th

After traveling a good distance camped near the Arkansas—there being a storm coming up—Had hardly got settled down before on it came, raining & blowing a gale—during the night the thunder & lightning was tremendous—I was quite uneasy in my wagon with so much iron—my guns, pistols, powder &c, but not struck—altho' much exposed on a hill.

Pawnee Rock was a landmark on the Santa Fe Trail. Once a wagon passed by Pawnee Rock, the travelers knew they were halfway to their destination. Pawnee Rock State Historic Site looks a little different today. Railroad companies and settlers who were in need of building stone destroyed much of it.

What Was It Like on the Oregon-California Trail?

Travel on the trail was not easy. Many travelers had little or no experience with oxen or mule teams. They often had difficulty getting their animals to go in the right direction. They bumped their wagons into trees and sometimes tipped them over. One out of every 10 travelers died. Poor **sanitation**, disease, and even accidental gunshot wounds were common. Many of the emigrants, including children, had to walk the 2,000 miles. Most emigrants had only one or two changes of clothing for the entire trip. By the end of the trip, their shoes had worn out.

Not all emigrants finished the trip; some returned home. John H. Clark kept a diary of his 1852 trip. He commented about the tragedies on the Oregon-California Trail:

> *May 10 - Saw the first dead ox on the road today, and passed two or three graves, the occupants of which, it is said, died of small pox. Met a young man with two small children returning to the states; he said he had buried his wife and one child just beyond. We felt for the poor fellow as he every now and then turned his look toward the wilderness where lay his beloved ones.*

Oregon-California Trail

The Oregon-California Trail was different than the Santa Fe Trail. Its purpose was to move people, rather than freight. The trail was the only practical way to get through the western mountain ranges. It took emigrants four to six months to make the trip from western Missouri to the West Coast. The only other way west was by sea, around South America, and the journey took an entire year.

The Oregon-California Trail served families wanting to make a better life in the West. It was a 2,000-mile journey and most of it had to be walked. Emigrants used small farm wagons to transport their supplies. The wagon box only measured four by ten feet. All their supplies for the journey had to fit in the wagon, leaving very little room for personal belongings. A family of four needed over 1,000 pounds of food to make the journey. Food supplies included flour, sugar, salt, coffee, and bacon. Just a few miles on the trail and most families

Over a 25-year period, nearly 400,000 people traveled on the Oregon-California Trail. Those who went to Oregon were seeking good farmland and a better life. People also traveled to California for a chance to strike it rich in the gold fields. This mural by Charles Goslin can be seen at the Hollenberg Station State Historic Site.

realized they had over-packed their wagons. The trail was littered with discarded family treasures.

Travel on the Oregon-California Trail was seasonal. Travelers started in late April or early May so they would arrive before winter. In the spring, there was sometimes congestion on the trail.

American Indians and Emigrants on the Trails

One of the great cultural myths about the trails is that travelers were frequently attacked by Indians. Actually, there were more cases of cooperation between Indians and travelers than conflicts between them.

In Kansas, the Santa Fe Trail passed through the homelands and hunting grounds of the Osage, Kansa, Comanche, Kiowa, Cheyenne, Arapaho, and Plains Apache. Most encounters were peaceful, particularly in the early years of the trail. Trading took place among the Indians, Americans, and Mexicans. Later, misunderstanding occurred when trail traffic

The Law of Supply and Demand

Prices for goods and services varied from place to place. Prices could also change from month to month. What determined prices? If supplies were plentiful, then prices were set lower than if an item was in short supply. Demand was another factor. If a lot of people wanted an item, then it could be priced higher than if there was little or no demand.

There were trading posts on the Oregon-California Trail. Prices for goods often rose dramatically the farther travelers got on the trail. Flour could be purchased in Independence, Missouri, for four dollars a barrel. Farther down the trail the price rose to one dollar a pint. This was because there were few places to buy flour, so the supply was scarce but the demand was high. On the other hand, bacon was often very cheap. After a while some travelers considered bacon too much trouble to transport, so they abandoned it by the side of the road. A pound of bacon at Ft. Laramie, located one third of the way to Oregon, could be purchased for one cent, rather than the customary five cents.

disrupted the lives of the Indians. Then both Mexican and American military troops were sent to escort the wagons safely through Indian lands.

Most of the encounters between Indians and emigrants on the Oregon-California Trail in Kansas were peaceful. Emigrants traded with Indians for supplies and services. Shoes wore out quickly, but travelers could purchase moccasins from the Indians. There are accounts of Indians assisting travelers by pulling out stuck wagons and rounding up loose cattle.

This painting by John Gast captures the symbolism of manifest destiny. In front of the woman floating over the plains lies the West in darkness. What message do you think the painting conveys?

Guide Books

Today, when your family goes on a trip to a new place, do you use a guidebook to tell you where to stay and what to do? Travelers on the Oregon-California Trail had the same types of guidebooks. The books gave advice about everything from what to take on the journey to how to fix a broken axle.

The *Hand-book to Kansas Territory and the Rocky Mountains' Gold Region*, published in New York in 1859, gave advice on luggage:

> *Let your trunk, if you have to buy one, be of moderate size, and of the strongest make. Test it by throwing it from the top of a three-storied house; if you pick it up uninjured, it will do to go to Kansas. Not otherwise.*

Manifest Destiny

In the 1800s, the United States had a vision of westward expansion. Politicians wanted to see the United States span from the Atlantic to the Pacific. This was called *manifest destiny*.

For many Americans, land represented opportunities and potential wealth. There was a great deal of land to be acquired in the West. Americans also took pride in their form of government and saw it as *synonymous* with freedom. The desire to take this freedom west was also part of manifest destiny.

Manifest destiny was not only a political concept. Millions of ordinary Americans believed that their best opportunities lay in the West, where land was cheap. In the first half of the 1800s, more than four million people followed this dream and moved west.

Chapter 3 Review

What Do You Remember?

1. What motivated early European explorers?
2. Compare what Coronado hoped to find in Quivira with what he actually found.
3. How did Kansas get its name? Who named it?
4. What helped the Comanche dominate the plains?
5. Why did the French and the Spanish want to maintain control of Kansas?
6. How were the sovereign rights of the American Indians ignored during the period of exploration?
7. How did Lewis and Clark describe the resources in Kansas? How do you think their description might have changed if they had visited in a year that had too much or too little rainfall?
8. What did Pike say about the resources in Kansas? Compare the route taken by Pike and the route of Lewis and Clark. Based on what you know about Kansas geography, how do the descriptions of these explorers reflect the area of Kansas they visited?
9. How did Long's description of Kansas as "The Great Desert" affect U.S. government policy in regard to Indians?
10. Why did the U.S. government want to move Indian tribes away from the East?
11. During the period of Indian relocation, who was legally allowed to live in Kansas?
12. What were the purposes of Indian missions? What feelings did the Indians have toward the missions?
13. What was the primary purpose of the Santa Fe Trail? What was the purpose of the Oregon-California Trail?
14. What hardships did travelers encounter on the Santa Fe and Oregon-California Trails?
15. What was the relationship between Indian tribes and travelers on the trails?
16. Explain the concept of manifest destiny.

Activities

1. Investigate what type of records modern explorers (astronauts and undersea explorers) keep. Compare their records to those of early explorers. What do they have in common, and how are they different?
2. Research the traditional culture of one of the emigrant Indian tribes. What natural resources were available to people in their homeland? How did resources influence their food, customs, and traditional arts? Were these resources available in Kansas? Develop a tabletop exhibit to share your research.
3. Write and produce a guidebook for travelers on the Oregon-California Trail. Base your guidebook on research, and include sketches of important points on the trail.

Think About It!

1. It was customary for European and American explorers to ask the American Indians they encountered to give their allegiance to a foreign nation. What do you think this meant to the Indians? How might it have made them feel?
2. During the period of Indian relocation in Kansas, the U.S. government made it illegal for non-Indians to live here. The only exceptions to this rule were missionaries, traders, Indian agents, and military personnel. Can you think of reasons why the U.S. government restricted settlement during this period?
3. There were many reasons that families chose to move west on the Oregon-California Trail. Can you think of some of the reasons? Can you speculate on what the families gave up to move west?

PEOPLE TO KNOW
David Rice Atchison
John Brown
Ann Clark
Stephen A. Douglas
Samuel Jones
James Lane
Abraham Lincoln
Clarina Nichols
Andrew H. Reeder
Charles Robinson
Charles Sumner
John Greenleaf Whittier

PLACES TO LOCATE
Atchison
Doniphan
Douglas County
Elwood
Illinois
Lawrence
Lecompton
Manhattan
Massachusetts
Missouri
Oklahoma
Osawatomie
Pike's Peak
Sacramento, California
St. Joseph, Missouri
Topeka
Troy

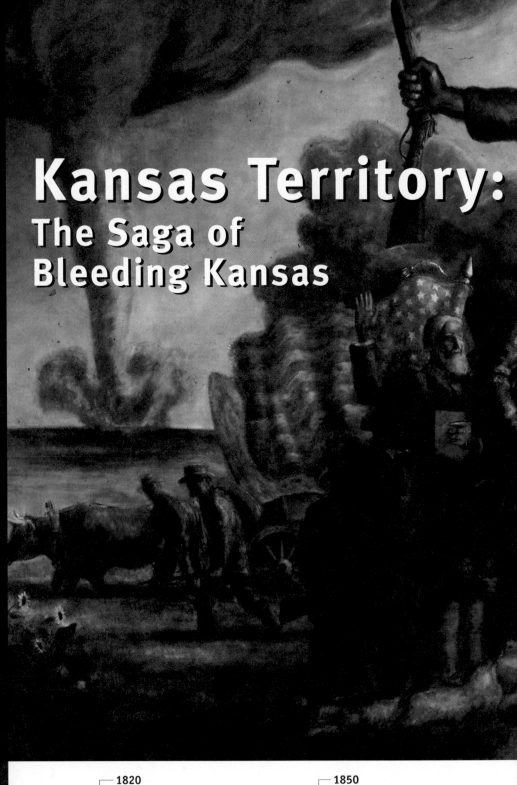

Kansas Territory:
The Saga of Bleeding Kansas

Timeline of Events

1820
The Missouri Compromise prohibits slavery in the place that became Kansas Territory.

1850
The Compromise of 1850 allows California to enter the Union as a free state. The Fugitive Slave Act is passed.

1820   1850   1852

1854
The Kansas-Nebraska Act creates two new U.S. territories and allows settlers to choose whether slavery will be allowed there.

WORDS TO UNDERSTAND
abolitionist
antislavery
border ruffian
bushwhacker
demographic
expansionist
free-stater
indentured servant
jayhawker
martyr
popular sovereignty
proslavery
repeal
siege
servitude
speculator
transcontinental
treason
unconstitutional

John Steuart Curry painted this well-known mural in the State Capitol. Curry used symbols of the territorial period to portray the emotional fight over slavery. What symbols do you see?

1855
The Bogus Legislature meets.
The Wakarusa War erupts.
The Topeka Constitutional
Convention is held.

1856
A year of violence
includes an attack
on Lawrence and
the Pottawatomie
Massacre.

1859
The Wyandotte Constitutional Convention
produces an anti-slavery constitution that
becomes the basis of our state government
today. John Brown is hanged for treason.

January 29, 1861
Kansas becomes
the 34th state.

1854   1856   1858   1860   1862

1857
The Supreme Court rules in the *Dred Scott Decision*
that slaves are not citizens of the United States.
The Lecompton Constitutional Convention is held.

1858
The Marais des Cygnes Massacre creates
tension in the nation. Gold is discovered in
western Kansas Territory. The Leavenworth
Constitutional Convention is held.

1860
The Pony Express
begins providing
fast mail service.

67

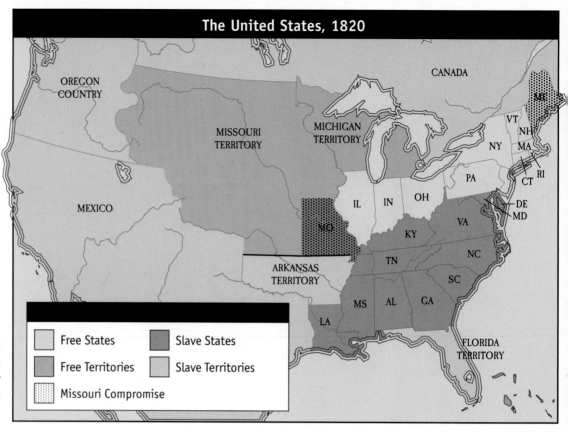

The United States, 1820

OREGON COUNTRY

MISSOURI TERRITORY

MICHIGAN TERRITORY

CANADA

MEXICO

ARKANSAS TERRITORY

FLORIDA TERRITORY

IL IN OH
MO
KY VA
TN NC
SC
MS AL GA
LA

PA
NY
VT
NH
MA
ME
RI
CT
DE
MD

Free States
Free Territories
Missouri Compromise
Slave States
Slave Territories

The United States in 1820 preserved a balance of power between free and slave states.

A Time of Turmoil

All eyes were on Kansas during the territorial period. The issue of slavery threatened to tear the nation apart. In Kansas Territory, the settlers were given the right to decide whether or not to allow slavery. At times, violence erupted over the slavery issues, and the territory became known as "Bleeding Kansas." Some people believe that the struggles in Kansas led directly to the Civil War.

The Missouri Compromise

The United States had struggled for some time with the question of whether to expand slavery into the territories. By 1820, the country had grown from the original 13 states to include 22 states. The country was split on the issue of slavery. There were 11 states that prohibited slavery and 11 that allowed it.

The Missouri Compromise allowed two additional states to enter the Union. Maine became a free state and Missouri a slave state. This maintained the balance of voting power in the U.S. Congress. But the Missouri Compromise did something else. It banned slavery in the lands of the Louisiana Purchase, north of 36, 30' north latitude. This included the land that would become Kansas.

The Compromise of 1850

The southern states were not thrilled with the Missouri Compromise. They did not like the idea that slavery was banned in such a large area. Four attempts to open the land for settlement had failed due to southern opposition. The issue of slavery was threatening to split the nation apart.

Before Kansas could become a territory, Congress once again had to reach a compromise concerning slavery. California petitioned Congress to enter the Union as a free state, but the addition of another state would tip the balance of free and slave states. The Compromise of 1850 was the answer. The compromise was that California would be admitted as a free state, but the Fugitive Slave Act would be adopted. The Fugitive Slave Act gave the southern states something they wanted. It said all citizens were required to assist in the recovery of runaway slaves, and fugitive slaves were denied the right of a jury trial.

The Shame of Slavery

To understand Kansas Territory, it is important to realize the intense emotions that surrounded the fight over slavery. The enslavement of Africans started before the United States was a country. With the early colonists came *indentured servants.* Africans and poor whites worked as laborers and were given food and housing in return. After a period of five to seven years, indentured servants earned their freedom. This meant that laborers needed to be replaced. Freed servants also competed for resources with wealthy landowners. The idea of keeping workers in life-long *servitude* became more appealing to many of the colonists.

Massachusetts became the first colony to legalize slavery. For a while, all 13 colonies permitted slavery. Virginia law stated, "All servants imported and brought to this Country…who were not Christians in their Native Country… shall be slaves." Slaves under this definition were primarily African. They were considered the property of their masters.

Most Africans had been free in their homelands. To place and keep them in servitude took great force. The white population feared rebellions. In response, the slave owners and the laws that applied to slaves became more and more brutal.

By the beginning of the 1800s, many of the northern states had outlawed slavery. It was primarily located in the southern portions of the United States. Records tell us there were more than two million slaves. Southern agriculture relied heavily on slave labor, yet only 25 percent of white southerners owned slaves. Still, the industrial economy of the North was dependent on crops grown by slaves in the South. They needed the cotton from the South to use in their textile mills in the North. The issue of slavery was creating a moral, political, and economic storm. By the 1850s, slavery had become the number-one issue in America.

The economy of the South was completely dependent on slave labor.
The economy of the North was also supported by products, like cotton, that slave labor produced.

Stephen A. Douglas was known as the "Little Giant" because he was a small man with great determination and ambition. Douglas played an important role in creating Kansas Territory. The idea of popular sovereignty in the new territories made him unpopular among those who were against slavery.

The Kansas-Nebraska Act

A senator from Illinois, Stephen A. Douglas, helped get the Compromise of 1850 through Congress. He also played a major role in the development of the Kansas-Nebraska Act. Douglas was an *expansionist*. That meant he believed that the United States should expand its boundaries to include much of the continent. As the powerful chair of the Committee on Territories, he was anxious to organize the lands of the Louisiana Purchase.

Douglas needed to offer something to the southern states in order to organize the lands west of Missouri. He thought he might gain cooperation from the South if he proposed letting the people of a new territory decide the fate of slavery in that territory. This was called *popular sovereignty*. It meant that the people who lived in the territories were given the right to decide on the issue of slavery.

With the Kansas-Nebraska Act, Congress *repealed* the Missouri Compromise. It opened two new territories for settlement: Kansas and Nebraska. Those who opposed slavery also opposed the Kansas-Nebraska Act. They did not want to see slavery permitted in the new territories.

The Kansas-Nebraska Act is considered to be one of the most important documents in U.S. history. Many people believe that the consequences of this act led to the Civil War. Today, the Kansas-Nebraska Act is preserved by the National Archives in Washington, D.C.

70

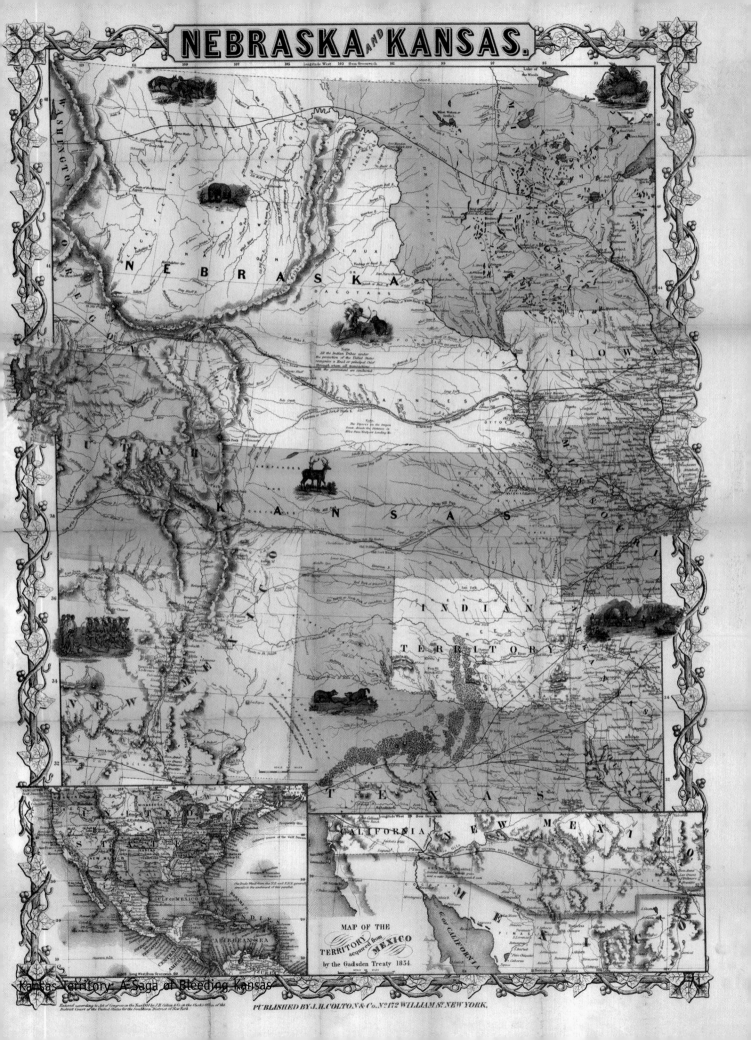

NEBRASKA and KANSAS.

Kansas Territory: A Saga of Bleeding Kansas

PUBLISHED BY J. H. COLTON & Co. No 172 WILLIAM St NEW YORK.

Activity

Lincoln's Speech on the Kansas-Nebraska Act

The Kansas-Nebraska Act stirred up politics in the country. Those who were against the act came together to create the Republican Party. Lincoln made a name for himself speaking against the Kansas-Nebraska Act and against the expansion of slavery. In Kansas, he spoke in Elwood, Troy, Doniphan, Atchison, and Leavenworth.

Eventually, Lincoln ran for the Senate against Stephen Douglas. The debates between them pushed Lincoln into the national spotlight. Although he lost the Senate seat to Douglas, Lincoln gained enough attention to eventually win the presidency.

In a speech delivered in Peoria, Illinois in 1854, Lincoln attacked the idea of popular sovereignty. He said it was not that the people shouldn't get to make the determination, but that there were some crucial issues, like freedom, which were not up to the majority to decide. Lincoln was angered by the repeal of the Missouri Compromise and felt it was a mistake for Congress to give up control over the expansion of slavery. Lincoln also questioned the morality of slavery. The following is an excerpt from Lincoln's speech. After reading it, answer the questions below:

1. What arguments does Lincoln use against the idea of popular sovereignty?
2. In his opinion, why does a doctrine of self-government not apply here?
3. To what document does Lincoln attribute the authority of his argument?

The doctrine of self-government is right–absolutely and eternally right–but it has no just application, as here attempted. Or perhaps I should rather say that whether it has such just application depends upon whether a Negro is not or is a man. If he is not a man, why in that case, he who is a man may, as a matter of self-government, do just as he pleases with him. But if the Negro is a man, is it not to that extent, a total destruction of self-government, to say that he too shall not govern himself? When the white man governs himself, and also governs another man, that is more than self-government–that is despotism. If the Negro is a man, why then my ancient faith teaches me that "all men are created equal;" and that there can be no moral right in connection with one man's making a slave of another....What I do say is, that no man is good enough to govern another man, without the other's consent. I say this is the leading principle–the sheer anchor of American republicanism. Our Declaration of Independence says:

'We hold these truths to be self evident: that all men are created equal; that they are endowed by their Creator with certain inalienable rights; that among these are life, liberty and the pursuit of happiness. That to secure these rights, governments are instituted among men, DERIVING THEIR JUST POWERS FROM THE CONSENT OF THE GOVERNED.'

I have quoted so much at this time merely to show that according to our ancient faith, the just powers of governments are derived from the consent of the governed. Now that relation of master and slaves is...a total violation of this principle. The master not only governs the slave without his consent; but he governs him by a set of rules altogether different from those which he prescribes for himself. Allow ALL the governed an equal voice in the government, and that, and that only is self-government.

The Kansas Journey

Indian Removal From Kansas

Before the Kansas-Nebraska Act, only American Indians and people representing the U.S. government could live here. The opening of the Kansas and Nebraska Territories attracted individuals and families seeking a better life. During the 1850s, people were searching for more land to settle. There was also talk of a national railroad that would connect the East and West Coasts. The most direct route for a railroad was through Indian lands. Suddenly the land in Kansas looked desirable to American settlers.

In the 1800s, most Americans had little understanding of American Indian cultures. Many people assumed it was the duty of native peoples to adjust to the American way of life. If tribes were slow to assimilate to the ways of whites, they were removed from the path of settlement.

When eastern tribes were moved to Kansas, they were told this land would belong to them forever. The idea of a "permanent Indian frontier" motivated the U.S. government to set aside land for the use of native peoples. President Andrew Jackson promised, "There your white brothers will not trouble you, they will have no claims to the land, and you can live upon it, you and all your children, as long as the grass grows or the water runs, in peace and plenty." This did not happen.

In the same month as the Kansas-Nebraska Act passed, the Delaware Indians signed a treaty, giving up much of their land in Kansas. One by one the Indian tribes left their reservations in Kansas for new lands in Oklahoma. Chief Ketchim of the Delaware expressed his frustrations:

Our Great Father told us when he gave us this land. . . . I shall never again request you to remove somewhere else. . . . Therefore I did not think . . . that he would in a few years . . . make me some other new offer for this place he had given to his Delaware children and to their succeeding generations.

George Catlin drew this political cartoon called "Pigeon's Egg Head going to and returning from Washington (1831-32)." Catlin was a defender of the native peoples. What do you think Catlin is saying about the Indians' assimilation into the American way of life?

The earliest settlers in Lawrence lived in small tent-like structures. The settlement was first called Wakarusa, Yankee-town, and then New Boston. It was eventually named Lawrence in honor of a wealthy investor who supported the free-state cause.

Settling the Territory

The Kansas-Nebraska Act opened the land for settlement. Some settlers came to Kansas Territory to make their voices heard. The concept of popular sovereignty drew people from both sides of the slavery issue. With the passage of the Kansas-Nebraska Act, some assumed that Nebraska would end up a free state and Kansas a slave state. This assumption was based on geography. Kansas sat directly west of Missouri, a slave state.

This was the first house built in Leavenworth.

For or Against?

Lots of names are used to describe people during the territorial period. If you had an opinion on slavery, you were either *proslavery* or *antislavery*. Those who believed that slavery was immoral and should be abolished without delay were *abolitionists*. But not all people against slavery were abolitionists. Some people simply did not want to see slavery expand into the territories. In Kansas, these people were called *free-staters*.

Most of the settlers who came to Kansas Territory emigrated from states nearby. Many of the earliest settlers came from the neighboring state of Missouri. Proslavery leaders from Missouri urged their people to settle Kansas to discourage the presence of a free state on the Missouri border.

Proslavery settlers founded the town of Atchison and gained an early advantage in the new town of Leavenworth. But antislavery settlers quickly moved into Leavenworth and took control. Groups formed to support free-state settlement. The first organized group of free-staters to come to the territory founded Lawrence. Free-state settlers also established the city of Topeka.

Counting the People of the Territory

Andrew H. Reeder, the first territorial governor, ordered the first census of Kansas Territory. Census takers were instructed not to count any military personnel, unless they intended to permanently stay in the territory. They were also told to ignore American Indians.

The first federal census conducted in Kansas Territory took place in 1860, five years after the one ordered by Governor Reeder. It recorded 107,209 people. Twelve percent of the population was foreign-born. Most of these immigrants came from the British Isles or Germany. Only two slaves were recorded. The number of free African Americans living in Kansas Territory had increased to 625. One hundred eighty-nine American Indians were counted. Approximately 51 percent of the population had emigrated from northern states and 37 percent from the South. The U.S. government only classified two communities as cities: Leavenworth and Atchison. All other communities were considered too small.

Governor Reeder determined the boundaries of each census district in 1855. District 17 was in present-day Johnson County. The boundaries were described as "beginning at the mouth of the Kansas river; thence up said river to the mouth of Cedar creek; thence up said creek to the Santa Fe Road; thence by said road and the Missouri State Line to the place of beginning."

How Do We Know This?

Did you know the U.S. government has gathered census data since 1790? Every decade, the United States government counts people and collects basic information about them. The information collected gives us important *demographic* characteristics of the population.

Knowing the number of people and where they live is a crucial part of our government. The number of representatives a state has in the U.S. House of Representatives is based on the state's share of the U.S. population. The U.S. Constitution requires that this be determined by a census conducted every 10 years. Today, the census numbers also affect how resources are distributed to the states. For example, the amount of federal funding for education given to each state is determined by census data.

Historians use census records from the past to study families and communities. Census records can tell us where someone came from, what type of work they did, when they were born, and even if a child attended school. Census records can give us a snapshot of a community at a specific time. They can also help us to discover how communities change over time.

Samuel Reader moved to Kansas Territory from Illinois to obtain cheap farmland. Reader painted himself staking a claim near Topeka.

Why Did They Come?

Most of the people who came to Kansas Territory came for cheap land and economic opportunities. Land could be obtained under the Preemption Act. An individual could claim up to 160 acres. The owner was obligated to pay $1.25 per acre once a public land survey was complete.

As towns developed, shares were sold to investors. Some of these investors were actual settlers, and others were absentee *speculators*. All who invested in a town hoped to make a profit. Although shares were sold for many towns in Kansas Territory, some of these towns never grew.

In an 1856 letter to her sister, Ellen Goodnow wrote, "I can say truly that I enjoy life as well here as I ever did anywhere." Ellen and her husband Isaac Goodnow had organized a company of 200 people to come to Kansas Territory. They built their new home at present-day Manhattan. Although the Goodnows were motivated to come to Kansas Territory to fight against slavery, not all settlers came for a cause.

Isaac and Ellen Goodnow built this house in Kansas Territory. Isaac founded the college that was to become Kansas State University. Today, the house is a State Historic Site.

Missourians crossed over the Kansas border to vote in elections. They hoped to make Kansas a slave state.

Proslavery Voices

Many southerners felt passionately that slavery should be extended into Kansas Territory. They felt it offered needed economic opportunities and would continue a way of life. The proslavery voices envisioned a new territory where southern farmers could prosper.

Proslavery advocates were nervous that antislavery settlers were moving into Kansas Territory. They felt that if slavery were banned in Kansas Territory this would threaten slavery in other parts of the country. Many Southerners thought their very way of life was in jeopardy. At the very least, they were worried about what would happen to the slaves being held along the border in Missouri. Because of the location of quality farmland, nearly 20 percent of all slaves in Missouri lived along the Kansas border.

Antislavery Voices

Many people came to Kansas to fight against slavery. Some came because they thought slavery was morally wrong. Others were against slavery because they believed it gave slaveholders an unfair economic advantage.

The antislavery forces wanted to take a stand in Kansas Territory. Many felt the

David Rice Atchison

David Rice Atchison, a U.S. senator from Missouri, lived very close to the Kansas border. He said, "the prosperity or the ruin of the whole South depends on the Kansas struggle." Atchison argued that Missourians had a special stake in the outcome of Kansas Territory. His belief was so strong that he encouraged Missourians to cross the border and illegally vote in Kansas elections to help sway the outcomes. He and other proslavery supporters appealed to people in the South. They asked for money, moral support, and proslavery settlers to come to Kansas Territory.

proslavery South was moving the U.S. government towards legalizing slavery on a national level.

Dred Scott

By 1857, those fighting against slavery in America could point to the *Dred Scott* decision to support this assumption.

Dred Scott was a slave who sued the government for his freedom. The U.S. Supreme Court ruled that Dred Scott and all African Americans, whether free or slave, were not citizens of the United States. It made no difference if they lived in a free or slave state. The Supreme Court went further and said it was **unconstitutional** for the U.S. government to prohibit slavery in the territories. This included Kansas Territory.

Women played a major role in the antislavery movement. In the 1830s, this image was used in needlework, publications, and on writing paper to promote the antislavery cause in America.

The first group to travel to Kansas Territory with the New England Emigrant Aid Company included these four men.

Emigrant Aid Societies

Early on, antislavery advocates flocked to Kansas Territory. Some came as individuals while others came in organized groups. One of the most influential groups was the New England Emigrant Aid Company. This organization received both financial and moral support from prominent New England abolitionists.

The company placed ads in newspapers hoping to attract potential settlers to Kansas Territory. Settlers traveled in groups at a reduced rate.

The regular price for a steamboat ride from St. Louis to Kansas City was $12. The New England Emigrant Aid Company offered the ticket for only $10. Groups as small as eight and as large as 389 came to Kansas Territory with the assistance of the Emigrant Aid Company.

Once in Kansas, the settlers were directed to available land. Rumors flew that the Emigrant Aid Company would find work for settlers or provide them with money, but this was not true. The company did help settlers in other ways. The company also raised money to construct much-needed public buildings, such as hotels and businesses. They even invested in newspapers to spread the word about the free-state cause.

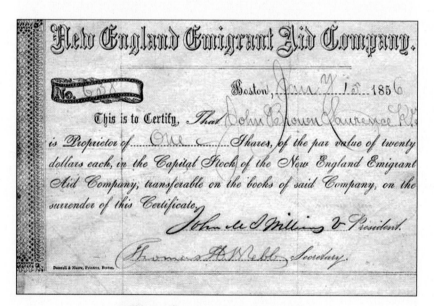

This certificate grants one share in the New England Emigrant Aid Company to John Brown.

James Lane worked for the free-state movement in Kansas Territory. Lane used the spyglass below to observe Missourians and proslavery advocates.

The Kansas Journey

Lane's Army of the North

James Lane was a U.S. representative from Indiana when he voted for the Kansas-Nebraska Act. Lane surprised many when, after moving to Kansas Territory, he took up the fight against slavery. He called slave owners in Missouri "wolves, snakes, devils." He organized 400 settlers from northern states to come to Kansas Territory. The group was called Lane's Army of the North.

James Lane became one of the first U.S. Senators from Kansas.

Activity

The Kansas Emigrant Song

John Greenleaf Whittier was born into a Quaker family in Massachusetts. He became a very well-known poet. He used his poetry to campaign against slavery. In "The Kansas Emigrant Song," Whittier encourages those against slavery to settle Kansas Territory.

1. Whittier used imagery and symbols to depict the struggle between the North and the South over the issue of slavery. For example, in the first verse, "East" refers to the northeastern states that were free of slavery. Kansas Territory is the "West" to which Whittier wants to bring "the homestead of the free." What references to the North and the South can you find?
2. This poem is written to persuade people. What opinions do you have on current events? Write a verse that uses symbolism to persuade people to your point of view.

> We cross the prairie as of old,
> > The Pilgrims crossed the sea,
> To make the West, as they the East,
> > The homestead of the free.
>
> We go to the rear a wall of men
> > On Freedom's Southern line,
> And plant beside the cotton tree,
> > The rugged Northern pine!
>
> Unbearing, like the ark of old,
> > The Bible in our van,
> We go to test the truth of God
> > Against the fraud of man.
>
> No pause, nor rest, save where the streams
> > That feed the Kansas run,
> Save where our Pilgrim [banner]
> > Shall flout the setting sun!

Slavery in Kansas Territory

One settler observed, "The roads are lined with teams from the border states, and in about every fifth or eighth wagon you will see a sprinkling of negro slaves. Don't make yourself believe the slave holders have given up Kansas!"

$200 Reward!

Ranaway from the sub-scriber, living in Saline county, on the 4th inst., two Negro men, named Jim and Jack---each aged about 25 years.

Jim

is dish-faced; has sore eyes and bad teeth; is of a light black or brown color; speaks quick, is about 5 feet 7 inches high; had on when last seen, blue cotton pants, white shirt, white fulled coat and new custom-made boots.

Jack

had on the same kind of clothing with shoes, has a very small foot, wears perhaps a No. 6 shoe, and has heavy tacks in the heels; is about the same height and color of Jim. They are doubtless aiming for K. T. **A reward of $100 each will be** given if taken outside of the State, or $50 each if taken in the State, outside of Saline county. **G. D. WILLIAMS,** Spring Garden, P. O., Pettis county, Missouri. Harrisonville, Mo., June 7th, 1860.

Many Missouri slaves escaped through the Underground Railroad in Kansas Territory. When slaves escaped, slave owners often put out wanted posters. Notice the small print on the poster. Do you see the phrase, "They are doubtless aiming for K.T." What does that mean?

Some slaves were placed in shackles by their owner. The shackles were attached to a chain with an iron ball on the end. The ball weighed over 20 pounds. Shackles made deep wounds in the slave's ankles.

Slavery existed in Kansas Territory, but on a much smaller scale than in the South. Most slaveholders owned only one or two slaves. Many slaves were women and children who performed domestic work rather than farm labor.

Marcus Lindsay Freeman was brought to Kansas Territory as a slave. When he was 59 years old, he gave the following reminiscence. Attached to his reminiscence is a note from Freeman saying that he had always liked his master and that he did not want to say anything bad about him. Even though Freeman felt this way, can you find evidence in his words that show he was not treated as a free man?

I was born in the year 1836 on the farm of George Bayne in Shelby, Kentucky. . . . He was my owner and gave me to his grandson Thomas when we were both babies. Thomas was three months older than I. His mother, having died at his birth, he was given to my mother to raise. We grew up together just as if we had been two little puppies. When he was big enough to eat at the table, he used to leave a lot of victuals on his plate and some coffee in his cup and bring it out to me to eat; for we slaves did not get such good things as were served at the white table.

Thomas Bayne brought us to his farm near Williamstown, Jefferson County, where he located in the autumn of 1854. He took up a claim there of 160 acres and bought other land. . . . I stayed for a few months, and then with his permission went back to Kansas City and married and rented my time for $200.00 a year for seven years until I was emancipated. Mr. Bayne gave me a pass which allowed me to go between Missouri and his farm in Kansas.

The Kansas Journey

Ann Clark and the Underground Railroad

The Underground Railroad was part of Kansas Territory. It was not a railroad, nor was it underground. It was a network of safe houses that helped slaves escape. There is no way to know how many escaping slaves came through Kansas Territory. The success of the Underground Railroad depended on its secrecy.

Ann Clark was an African American slave in Lecompton. She wanted her freedom and had heard stories of people who would help her escape. One day she got away from her master and took shelter at another settler's house. She stayed there for five or six weeks, but the man hiding her was unable to provide her with safe passage on the Underground Railroad. Proslavery men eventually found her and took her back to Lecompton to collect their reward.

When they reached Lecompton, it was evening. Ann went to the kitchen to clean herself up. As it grew darker and darker she studied the situation, trying to plan her escape. The men were busy eating and drinking. Ann noticed that only the women were watching her. Finally, Ann saw her opportunity. She ran out of the kitchen and into a ravine. She hid in thick brush. She could hear the men coming for her, and she lay very still. She lay there until morning.

When it was light, Ann crept out of the ravine to the top of the hill. She could see across the prairie. Southwest of Lecompton she came across a man carrying a book under his arm. Ann reasoned that this must be an educated man. Perhaps he might help her. She approached the man with caution and recognized him to be Dr. Barker, a neighbor of her master. He agreed to take her to his home. After a day or two, he hitched up his horses to the wagon to take Anne to a safe house. Ann crawled inside and lay quietly while he covered her up. Dr. Barker drove Ann to Lawrence. From there she was quietly transported to Topeka, ending up at the home of Mr. and Mrs. Scales.

In the basement of the Scales' home, Mr. Scales had stored a very large barrel that had been used as a shipping crate. He gathered up straw and blankets and placed them into the barrel. This gave Ann a cramped, but more secure, hiding place. During the day, Ann came out of the barrel and helped Mrs. Scales with the housework. After six weeks, a "conductor" on the Underground Railroad came for Ann. His name was John Armstrong. He had borrowed a closed carriage and a team of mules.

It was expensive to transport fugitives north. John had raised nearly $70. John and Ann started north toward Holton. He knew the houses at which they could stop. Still, it was not an easy journey. At one point the carriage became stuck in a creek. John had to ask Ann to leave the safety of the carriage to help him get it unstuck. After three long weeks on the road, they finally made it to Iowa and to freedom.

The Eldridge family owned and lived in the Free State Hotel. The family survived the attack on Lawrence and later rebuilt the hotel.

Bleeding Kansas

The fight over slavery in Kansas Territory eventually erupted in violence. About 50 people lost their lives during the territorial period. Many more were injured or lost property. National attention was focused on the violent confrontations, giving rise to the name "Bleeding Kansas."

Acts of War

The killing of a free-stater started what became known as the "Wakarusa War." Shortly after the killing, proslavery supporters arrested a man attending a free-state meeting. Fellow free-staters came to his rescue. Samuel Jones was sheriff of Douglas County and a Southern sympathizer. He called the rescue of the free-state man a "lawless action." This alarmed the people of Lawrence, a free-state town in Douglas County. The citizens of Lawrence prepared for an attack. Proslavery forces moved in, positioning themselves just outside of Lawrence. For a week, Lawrence was under *siege*. The siege was part of the Wakarusa War.

During the siege, the proslavery forces blocked supplies from reaching Lawrence. However, some Lawrence residents managed to get supplies through the blockade. Two women made a daring attempt. They managed to get through the blockade with ammunition by sewing it into their petticoats. The women were so weighted down with ammunition that when they reached Lawrence they had to be carried out of their carriage. A major attack on Lawrence never came, but the media interest in the Wakarusa War was intense. Newspapers across the country picked up the story and exaggerated it.

The outspoken residents of Lawrence

This flag was carried by a group of South Carolinians who participated in the raid on Lawrence. The flag was flown over the Free State Hotel and the Herald of Freedom *newspaper offices* before the proslavery men destroyed the buildings.

Sheriff Jones and his men burned the Free State Hotel during the attack on Lawrence.

continued to annoy those who were proslavery. The newspapers of Lawrence were highly critical of proslavery leaders. For this reason, a proslavery grand jury determined the newspapers were nuisances that should be shut down. Sheriff Jones entered the town with a group of armed men and went on the attack. They burned down the two newspaper offices. Businesses were destroyed and the home of Charles Robinson, a well known antislavery advocate, was burned. Two people were killed. Sheriff Jones was quoted as saying, "This is the happiest day of my life, I assure you." The horror of the attack on Lawrence made national news.

Beecher Bibles

The guns carried by proslavery forces were squirrel rifles, heavy buffalo guns, or army muskets. The antislavery forces had access to the superior Sharps carbine rifle. These rifles are sometimes called "Beecher Bibles." Henry Ward Beecher was an abolitionist preacher from Connecticut. His followers founded the Beecher Bible and Rifle Colony. The settlers brought both Bibles and Sharps rifles to Kansas Territory. Some guns were shipped in boxes labeled "books" so they would not be detected.

The Pottawatomie Massacre

Only three days after the attack on Lawrence, John Brown assaulted proslavery settlers. Brown and others were on their way to defend Lawrence when they got word that the siege was over. Brown enlisted the help of some of his sons and a few others in carrying out a brutal attack on proslavery settlers. Five proslavery men were killed near Pottawatomie Creek in Franklin County. The "Pottawatomie Massacre" was denounced by southern, and some northern, newspapers.

Many more skirmishes took place between antislavery and proslavery forces. The violence eventually declined. The last major violent act happened two years later. During the "Marais des Cygnes Massacre,"

11 free-state supporters were kidnapped by a group of proslavery men. Those captured were taken to a ravine and shot. Five were killed, five were wounded, and one escaped by pretending to be dead. National attention on the massacre increased tensions across the country.

What do you think?

National attention was drawn to Kansas Territory because newspapers across the country played up the violence. Sensational stories were written about violent clashes over slavery. Today, people often accuse the media of being sensational. What do you think the role of the media should be in reporting such violent or dramatic events?

Name-Calling!

As tensions grew on the border between Kansas and Missouri, there was name-calling. The name **border ruffians** was given to Missourians who crossed over the border to influence the outcome of the slavery issue in Kansas Territory. These were mainly the men who voted illegally in the early territorial elections.

Bushwhackers were generally thought of as Missourians who jumped over the border to make raids on antislavery settlements. On the other hand, Missourians referred to Kansans who made raids on Missouri as **jayhawkers**. The labels of bushwhackers and jayhawkers lived on into the Civil War era.

These jayhawkers crossed into Missouri to rescue a friend who had been accused of stealing slaves.

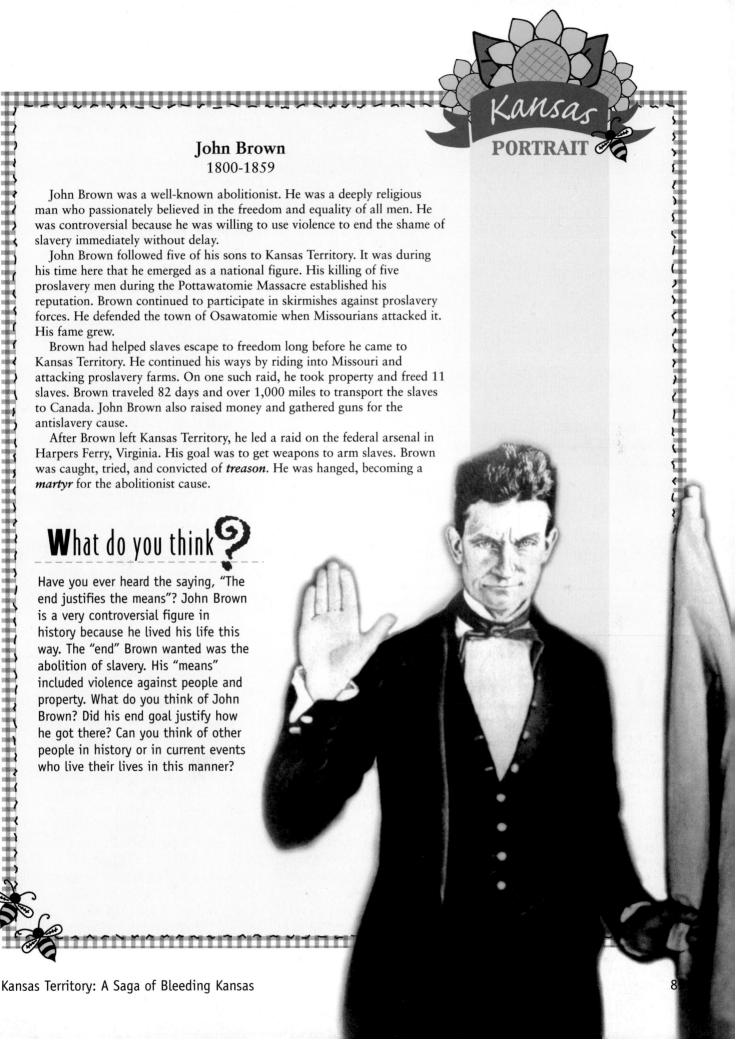

John Brown
1800-1859

John Brown was a well-known abolitionist. He was a deeply religious man who passionately believed in the freedom and equality of all men. He was controversial because he was willing to use violence to end the shame of slavery immediately without delay.

John Brown followed five of his sons to Kansas Territory. It was during his time here that he emerged as a national figure. His killing of five proslavery men during the Pottawatomie Massacre established his reputation. Brown continued to participate in skirmishes against proslavery forces. He defended the town of Osawatomie when Missourians attacked it. His fame grew.

Brown had helped slaves escape to freedom long before he came to Kansas Territory. He continued his ways by riding into Missouri and attacking proslavery farms. On one such raid, he took property and freed 11 slaves. Brown traveled 82 days and over 1,000 miles to transport the slaves to Canada. John Brown also raised money and gathered guns for the antislavery cause.

After Brown left Kansas Territory, he led a raid on the federal arsenal in Harpers Ferry, Virginia. His goal was to get weapons to arm slaves. Brown was caught, tried, and convicted of *treason*. He was hanged, becoming a *martyr* for the abolitionist cause.

What do you think❓

Have you ever heard the saying, "The end justifies the means"? John Brown is a very controversial figure in history because he lived his life this way. The "end" Brown wanted was the abolition of slavery. His "means" included violence against people and property. What do you think of John Brown? Did his end goal justify how he got there? Can you think of other people in history or in current events who live their lives in this manner?

Kansas Territorial Capitals

Nebraska

Missouri

Pawnee●

Topeka●

●Leavenworth

Wyandotte●

Lecompton● Shawnee
Mission

The territorial government moved several times. Not all locations were official "capitals," but all were places the government met.

Politics

The politics of Kansas Territory were chaotic. Election fraud was common. Ten different territorial governors served in seven years. Four different constitutions were written. At one point, two separate governments were operating at the same time. Both the fight over slavery and personal ambitions led to this chaos.

Election Fraud

President Franklin Pierce appointed Andrew Reeder to be the first governor of Kansas Territory. Most people believed he would support slavery in the new territory. What Reeder believed in was popular sovereignty. He wanted the residents of Kansas Territory to decide on the issue of slavery.

Governor Reeder called for the first election shortly after he arrived in the territory. The November 1854 election was to select a delegate for U.S. Congress. John W. Whitfield, a proslavery supporter, was elected. Border ruffians from Missouri had crossed over to participate in the election. It

Governor Reeder developed the initial design of the Kansas Territorial Seal. The motto means "Born of the popular will," which addresses the issue of popular sovereignty.

is believed that over half the votes were illegal. Although the election results were challenged, Whitfield was allowed to serve.

The following spring, Missourians again crossed the border to vote illegally in the first legislative election. This resulted in the "Bogus Legislature." It was called that because the free-staters believed this proslavery legislature was illegitimate due to election fraud.

The First Territorial Legislature

The Bogus Legislature met in Pawnee, near Fort Riley. Governor Reeder picked the town of Pawnee for several reasons. He wanted the legislature to meet far away from the influences of Missouri. Another reason was that Reeder was an investor in the city of Pawnee. When word spread that Pawnee was to be the capital, settlers began to move there. When the proslavery legislature arrived, the building they were to meet in had no roof, floor, windows or doors yet. Although some lodging was available, most legislators stayed in tents.

When Governor Reeder spoke to the first territorial legislature, he identified goals. The legislature was charged with establishing counties, setting up a judicial system, levying taxes, and organizing a militia. The legislators also had to determine a permanent seat of government, create a constitution, and decide if Kansas was to be a free or slave state.

The legislature met for only four days in Pawnee. One of its major actions was to kick out all of the antislavery members. This, of course, angered the free-staters. It was later reported that one antislavery legislator responded, "Gentlemen, this is a memorable day, and may become more so. Your acts will be the means of lighting the watch-fires of war in our land."

The Bogus Legislature passed a bill moving the government to Shawnee Mission near the Missouri border. When the legislature met at Shawnee Mission, Governor Reeder announced that President Pierce had removed him from office. The proslavery legislature passed a slave code making it a punishable offense to speak against slavery in the territory. This so angered the antislavery residents they decided to set up their own government.

Governor Reeder eventually sided with the free-staters, angering the proslavery forces. He also was charged with placing the capital of Kansas Territory at Pawnee for his own benefit. Reeder's enemies charged him with treason, and he was forced to escape the territory in disguise.

With the proslavery state of Missouri next door, Kansas Territory had a tough time making popular sovereignty work. Proslavery Missourians were encouraged to cross the border to vote. Their illegal votes created the Bogus Legislature.

Writing a Constitution

Before Kansas could become a state, the territorial government had to write a constitution, and the U.S. Congress had to accept the constitution. People in the territory felt so strongly about the issue of slavery that there was little room for compromise. Both sides were desperate to win. They believed their very survival depended on it, and they were willing to do just about anything to claim victory. Constitutional conventions took place in Topeka, Lecompton, Leavenworth, and Wyandotte.

The Topeka Constitution

The Topeka movement formed in reaction to the election fraud that created the Bogus Legislature. There were now two separate governments operating in Kansas Territory, one free-state and the other proslavery. Free-state delegates met in Topeka to write a constitution that prohibited slavery. According to the Topeka Constitution, only white males and "civilized male Indians who had adopted

the habits of the white man" would be allowed to vote. While this constitution was anti-slavery, it was not for the rights of black people. A clause was later added that made it illegal for African Americans to live in Kansas.

The Topeka Constitution was approved by a large majority of voters. However, the proslavery supporters had refused to vote. Members of the U.S. Congress questioned if the Topeka Convention even had the legal authority to write a constitution. Even though the Topeka Constitution had some support in Congress, this affected its chances of being accepted.

The Lecompton Constitution

The proslavery Bogus Legislature called for a constitutional convention of its own. While the constitution was being written in Lecompton, a free-state legislature was elected. This made things awkward and confusing. When the Lecompton Constitution came up for a vote there was even more chaos.

People were not allowed to vote on the entire constitution. Instead, residents were asked to vote for the constitution with slavery or for the constitution without slavery. The ballot was worded in a confusing way on purpose. Both choices would make slavery legal because the constitution protected current slave owners.

The antislavery residents were angered with the process. They wanted to vote on the whole constitution. The free-staters saw the election as a fraud and refused to vote. This meant the constitution with slavery won by a large majority.

In the meantime, the free-state territorial legislature called for another vote on the Lecompton Constitution. This time it was defeated. Nevertheless, President Buchanan submitted the Lecompton Constitution to Congress and recommended Kansas be admitted to the Union as a slave state. After much debate about popular sovereignty, members of Congress questioned if the Lecompton Constitution reflected the will of the people. The Lecompton Constitution was sent back to the territory for a third vote, and it was defeated.

Today, Constitution Hall in Lecompton is a State Historic Site.

The Leavenworth Constitution

While Congress wrestled with the Lecompton Constitution, the people of Kansas Territory tried again. Free-state delegates came together in Leavenworth to write a third constitution. The Leavenworth Constitution was antislavery. It also eliminated the word "white" from the document. This meant that all men, including African Americans and American Indians, would have the right to vote. However, the word "male" remained in the constitution, restricting women's rights. The Leavenworth Constitution was put to a vote. The number of people who chose to vote was quite small, but the constitution passed. It was taken to Congress as an alternative to the Lecompton Constitution, but it failed to gain enough support to make it all the way through Congress.

Governor Reeder established the first executive office at Fort Leavenworth.

Kansas
PORTRAIT

Charles Robinson
1818-1894

Charles Robinson led a group of settlers from Massachusetts to Kansas Territory under the guidance of the New England Emigrant Aid Company. He soon became a leader of the free-state movement.

In a speech, Robinson said, "It is for us to choose for ourselves, and for those who shall come after us, what institutions shall bless or curse our beautiful Kansas. Shall we have freedom for all her people, and consequent prosperity, or slavery for a part, with the blight and mildew inseparable from it?"

After voters ratified the Topeka Constitution, Robinson was elected governor. This meant that he would be governor once Kansas became a state under the Topeka Constitution. Proslavery supporters did not recognize the Topeka Constitution and arrested Robinson for treason and conspiracy. Robinson spent several months in jail in Lecompton before he was acquitted.

Charles Robinson was again elected governor after the Wyandotte Constitutional Convention. Once Kansas became a state, he served as the first governor of the State of Kansas.

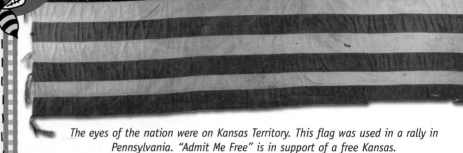

The eyes of the nation were on Kansas Territory. This flag was used in a rally in Pennsylvania. "Admit Me Free" is in support of a free Kansas.

The Wyandotte Constitution and Statehood

A fourth and final constitutional convention took place in Wyandotte. The Wyandotte Constitution made Kansas a free state. The document restricted most voting rights and service in the militia to white men. But it made some improvements in the rights of women.

The people of Kansas Territory easily approved the Wyandotte Constitution, but it did not gain U.S. congressional approval immediately. So divisive was the issue of slavery that Kansas could not gain admittance to the Union until southern states began seceding just prior to the Civil War. Once the balance of power shifted in the U.S. Senate, there were enough votes for statehood.

The Wyandotte Constitution remains the foundation of our state government today.

Constitution of the State of Kansas;

Adopted at Wyandot July 29th 1859.

90

SOUTHERN CHIVALRY — ARGUMENT versus CLUB'S.

The Caning of Senator Charles Sumner

So tense was the nation over the issue of slavery that both Sumner and Brooks became heroes of sorts. Their parties applauded each one's actions.

One of the most dramatic moments in the history of the U.S. Congress was connected to Kansas Territory. Name-calling and violence erupted in Washington, D.C., over whether Kansas should enter the Union as a free or slave state. Senator Charles Sumner was an antislavery Republican from Massachusetts. He addressed the Senate in a long and passionate speech on the "Crime Against Kansas." In this speech, he called out the names of two Democratic senators he believed responsible for the "crime."

Stephen Douglas was in the chamber when Sumner called him a,"noise-some, squat, and nameless animal...not a proper model for an American senator." Douglas's crime, according to Sumner, was opening up the issue of slavery in Kansas Territory through the Kansas-Nebraska Act. Sumner also verbally attacked another senator, Andrew Butler of South Carolina, for his support of slavery.

Sumner's personal attack on fellow senators was believed by some to be ungentlemanly. Representative Preston Brooks from South Carolina found the remarks to be unforgivable. Brooks brought a cane to the Senate chamber and attacked Sumner. He hit him again and again, beating Sumner unconscious. The attack so injured Sumner that he was unable to resume his work in the Senate for three years.

Kansas

PORTRAIT

Clarina Nichols
1810-1885

Most political discussions in Kansas Territory were over the issue of slavery and the rights of African Americans. Some people also worked for women's rights. Clarina Nichols was nationally known as a voice for women's rights. An abolitionist, she came to Kansas Territory with the New England Emigrant Aid Society. Nichols settled near Lawrence, but later moved to Quindaro.

During this time, women had very few rights. They could not vote, and they had limited property rights. They did not have legal rights over their own children. Nichols traveled, giving speeches and gathering petition signatures. She attended the Wyandotte Constitutional Convention, not as a delegate, but as an invited guest. Between debates she spoke to delegates about the rights of women.

Nichols' work paid off. The final version of the Wyandotte Constitution gave women more rights than they had in other states. Women were given rights in child custody and a voice in education. They also gained certain property rights.

Activity

Women's Rights and the Wyandotte Constitution

When Clarina Nichols attended the Wyandotte Constitutional Convention she represented the Moneka Woman's Rights Association. "The Secretary's Book of the Moneka Woman's Rights Association" (1858-1860) is a primary source. The notebook contains the official minutes taken at the association meetings. Within the notes are several resolutions. These address the goals of the group. Look at the list of resolutions adopted by the group in 1858. Compare that list to the Wyandotte Constitution. Make a chart that lists what women wanted and what results women achieved.

From *The Secretary's Book of the Moneka Women's Rights Association*:

Resolved that every woman in Kansas who believes that equal rights belong to women should consider herself a committee of one whose duty it is to do all in her power to convert to her views at least one legal vote.
Resolved that Kansas cannot be truly free while the words "white" or "male" are found within the limits of her constitution.
Resolved to enact such laws.

- *1st As will secure to woman the property which she posses before marriage.*
- *2nd Also a just proportion of the joint property of the husband and wife acquired during marriage.*
- *3rd Also at the death of the husband or wife that the same laws shall govern the widow or widower in the possession and disposal of the estate and children belonging to them jointly.*

From the Wyandotte Constitution:

Article XV—Miscellaneous

SEC. 6 The Legislature shall provide for the protection of the rights of women, in acquiring and possessing property, real, personal and mixed, separate and apart from the husband; and shall also provide for their equal rights in the possession of their children.

Everyday Life in the Territory

Settlers in Kansas Territory built houses and established schools and businesses. They raised crops and tended livestock to provide food for themselves and their families. All people in the territory experienced the hardships of the frontier. Housing was often not of the quality the settlers had left behind. Doctors and dentists were sometimes hard to find. New businesses were usually speculative at best. No one really knew if they would succeed or fail.

The weather was not always a friend to the settlers. Winters were particularly brutal. Settlers were also challenged to survive severe droughts. Some emigrants left the territory. Others endured the hardships. Thaddeus Hyatt, president of the National Kansas Committee, wrote to the president of the United States about the conditions in the territory in 1860.

Thousands of once thrifty and prosperous American Citizens are now perishing of want: winter is upon them: of clothing they are nearly bereft: food they have not to last them through the cold season that is approaching: of over a hundred thousand people upon Kansas soil six months ago, at least one quarter or a third have left: of the remainder it is safe to say that 40,000 at this moment see nothing but exodus or starvation at the end of sixty days now just before them.

"Pike's Peak or Bust" became the slogan for many gold seekers.

There's Gold in Those Hills

The western boundaries of Kansas Territory extended all the way to the Rocky Mountains. Big news travels fast, and there was no bigger news than the discovery of gold on the eastern slopes of the Rockies.

Settlers in Kansas Territory spread the word east through letters to friends. "There is a good deal of excitement out to Pikes Peak. Every one talks of going there in Leavenworth next spring," wrote a Leavenworth resident. Newspapers also promoted the rush for gold. "Later accounts only tend to confirm the first reports, and it is now definitely settled that gold is not only found in Kansas, but that it exists in such quantities as to prove profitable to engage in searching for it," printed the Atchison Freedom's Champion.

Thousands of people came to Kansas Territory to seek their fortunes in gold. Some became quite rich, and others found themselves discouraged and headed back home. Many businesses made small fortunes selling supplies to miners. A stagecoach line between Leavenworth and Pike's Peak delivered fortune seekers to the gold fields for $125. The gold rush lasted only about a year.

Both the northerners and the southerners who came to Kansas Territory brought with them their customs and traditions. Although there were hardships to overcome, life went on. This invitation is for a dance.

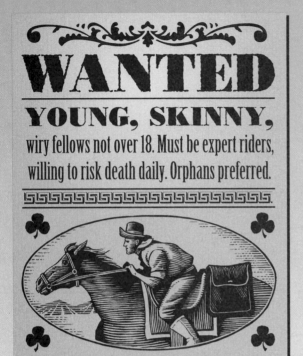

WANTED

YOUNG, SKINNY,

wiry fellows not over 18. Must be expert riders, willing to risk death daily. Orphans preferred.

The Pony Express

If you wanted to get a letter from Kansas Territory to California within 10 days, you used the Pony Express. The Pony Express existed for only 18 months. It ran between St. Joseph, Missouri, and Sacramento, California. Young men rode in relay fashion and carried the mail. A rider left his home station and rode about 33 miles. He changed horses every 10 to 15 miles. When he finished his route, he met up with another rider. The mail was transferred to the new man who would take off on his ride. The entire route was 2,000 miles.

The speed of mail delivery was remarkable. However, it was a very expensive operation. For $5, your letter would be transported by horseback and could be picked up at any of the 11 stations in Kansas Territory. This was very expensive in a time when many people earned less than $1 a day.

The mail was picked up and delivered twice a week. There were almost 200 stations, and the Pony Express employed about 80 riders. At the time of the Pony Express, a *transcontinental* telegraph line was being developed. By the end of the territorial period, some people in Kansas were connected to all parts of the country through the telegraph wire. The expense and the new technology brought an end to the Pony Express.

One of the original Pony Express stations in Kansas is preserved as a state historic site. Hollenberg Station, near Hanover, offered all of the necessary services, such as food and shelter, for both riders and horses.

Chapter 4 Review

What Do You Remember?

1. Why did the Kansas-Nebraska Act repeal the Missouri Compromise?
2. What did popular sovereignty mean under the Kansas-Nebraska Act?
3. Why did the permanent Indian frontier fail?
4. Explain why attempts to organize Kansas Territory were politically difficult.
5. Where did most of the settlers in Kansas Territory come from?
6. How did residents in Kansas Territory obtain cheap land?
7. Why did both the proslavery and antislavery advocates want control of Kansas Territory?
8. What was the role of the New England Emigrant Aid Company in settling Kansas Territory?
9. How did the Underground Railroad work in Kansas Territory?
10. How did Kansas Territory get the name "Bleeding Kansas?"
11. Who were bushwackers and jayhawkers?
12. How did John Brown make a name for himself in Kansas Territory?
13. Why did Missourians cross over the border to vote in territorial elections?
14. What was the Bogus Legislature?
15. Explain ways in which the proslavery and antislavery forces refused to cooperate with each other in writing a state constitution.
16. Under what circumstances was Charles Robinson arrested for treason?
17. What was the conflict between Senator Charles Sumner and Representative Preston Brooks that led to violence?
18. Explain at least one right women were given under the Wyandotte Constitution.
19. What factors put an end to the Pony Express?

Think About It!

1. Many people came to Kansas Territory to make a better life for themselves and their families. Many of the settlers were not interested in the fight over slavery. Was it possible to live in the territory and not have the issue of slavery affect your life? Why or why not?
2. During the territorial period many people were speculating on land and new businesses. Governor Reeder was also investing his money in the new territory. Some people felt he had a conflict of interest in moving the capital to Pawnee. What do you think? Is it right for public officials to use their offices to financially benefit themselves and their friends?

Activities

1. Research how the political careers of Stephen Douglas and Abraham Lincoln are connected. Trace the successes and failures of each. Explain how the Kansas-Nebraska Act helped or hurt their futures.
2. Pretend you live in Kansas Territory. Develop a town map and a brochure that advertises a new town you want to develop. Remember that your map and brochure are meant to attract investors to your project.
3. Review both the U.S. and Kansas Constitutions. Develop a classroom exhibit on the responsibilities given to the federal and state governments. Are there any responsibilities they share?

PEOPLE TO KNOW
Black Kettle
Cyrus K. Holliday
John James Ingalls
James Lane
Abraham Lincoln
Julia Louisa Lovejoy
Sterling Price
William C. Quantrill
Charles Robinson

PLACES TO LOCATE
Colorado
Fort Dodge
Fort Harker
Fort Hays
Fort Larned
Fort Leavenworth
Fort Riley
Fort Scott
Fort Wallace
Fort Zarah
Junction City
Maryland
Medicine Lodge
Paola
Lawrence
Leavenworth
Topeka
Virginia
Washington, D.C.

50 to the Acre

DROUTHY

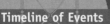
Timeline of Events

96

1861
Kansas becomes a state.
Topeka becomes the
state capital.

1861   1862   1863

1862
James Lane recruits African
American soldiers for the First
Kansas Colored Infantry.

1863
William Quantrill and
other Confederates
raid Lawrence.

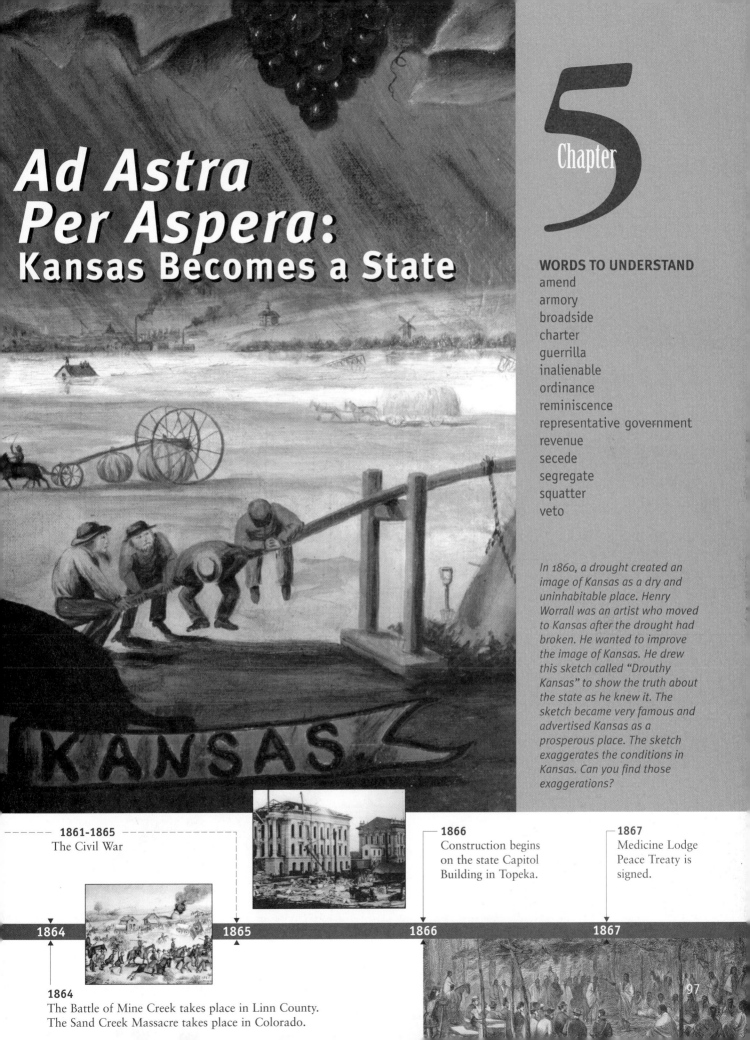

Ad Astra Per Aspera:
Kansas Becomes a State

WORDS TO UNDERSTAND
amend
armory
broadside
charter
guerrilla
inalienable
ordinance
reminiscence
representative government
revenue
secede
segregate
squatter
veto

In 1860, a drought created an image of Kansas as a dry and uninhabitable place. Henry Worrall was an artist who moved to Kansas after the drought had broken. He wanted to improve the image of Kansas. He drew this sketch called "Drouthy Kansas" to show the truth about the state as he knew it. The sketch became very famous and advertised Kansas as a prosperous place. The sketch exaggerates the conditions in Kansas. Can you find those exaggerations?

1861-1865
The Civil War

1866
Construction begins on the state Capitol Building in Topeka.

1867
Medicine Lodge Peace Treaty is signed.

1864   1865   1866   1867

1864
The Battle of Mine Creek takes place in Linn County.
The Sand Creek Massacre takes place in Colorado.

97

Kansas became the 34th state in the Union. This handmade flag dates from when Kansas became a state.

Kansas Becomes the 34th State

On January 29, 1861, Kansas became a state. *The Daily Conservative*, a newspaper in Leavenworth, had the scoop on the story. It became the first newspaper to announce the news by putting out an extra edition of the paper. At the time, *The Daily Conservative* had been in business for only one day.

According to the paper, "the news flew like wild-fire." People on street corners sent up cheers. Even though times were tough in Kansas, people were excited to be citizens of the newest state. The celebrations centered around the future, not the past. *The Daily Conservative* wrote, "Let us forget border wars, drouth, and hard times . . . With the fairest land and sky in our united and glorious Union, who can predict the future wealth, prosperity and grandeur of this, our free State of Kansas?"

A Rough Start

Life in Kansas Territory had been difficult, and things did not change overnight when Kansas became a state. A serious drought took its toll on the people of Kansas. Crops failed, and in some parts of the state, drinking water was scarce. Many Kansans ran out of money.

The Kansas Relief Committee was formed to get help. Some criticized the committee for exaggerating the conditions in Kansas. But people needed help. *Broadsides* and flyers were sent to the East, asking for assistance for starving Kansans.

One such broadside read:

From nearly everyone of our forty counties, comes the wail of distress, and the cry for help. The prospect before us is indeed hard and desperate. The rigors of winter and the horrors of hunger lie across our path. Starving parents are today imploring food and clothing for Starving Children. Acorns have already been used for food, and the bark of trees for clothing. In the name of our industrious but distressed, we appeal to you for help.

Kansas was in financial trouble. However, the country was about to break apart over the issues of slavery and states' rights. The focus of the nation was no longer on the troubles of Kansas, but rather on the approaching Civil War.

What do you think?

The Kansas Relief Committee appealed to the government, churches, and individuals to provide assistance to the starving people of Kansas. When a disaster hits a community, it is common to begin relief efforts. It has long been debated whether the government should assist its citizens when disaster strikes or if relief should be provided by private organizations and individual donations. What do you think? Who should help the people in need?

Celebrating Kansas Day

Every January 29, schools in Kansas celebrate Kansas Day. This date is the anniversary of Kansas statehood. Did you ever wonder how this celebration started? A teacher in Paola wanted to make history come alive for his students. On January 29, 1877, the students of Mr. LeGrande Copley participated in activities and contests on the history and geography of Kansas.

The first Kansas Day was celebrated only 16 years after Kansas entered the Union. In order to prepare for the celebration, Mr. Copley's students researched the history of their very young state. The students interviewed people in their community to gather information. When the day came, the students read quotations from important writers about Kansas. The class also divided into teams to test their knowledge of Kansas history.

Everyone was thrilled with Mr. Copley's Kansas Day celebration. Two years later, he became superintendent of the Wichita Public Schools, and the idea for Kansas Day spread. Within three years, a group of teachers published a small pamphlet containing information on the state. "Kansas Day," as the pamphlet was called, contained ideas about celebrating January 29. An annual celebration was born.

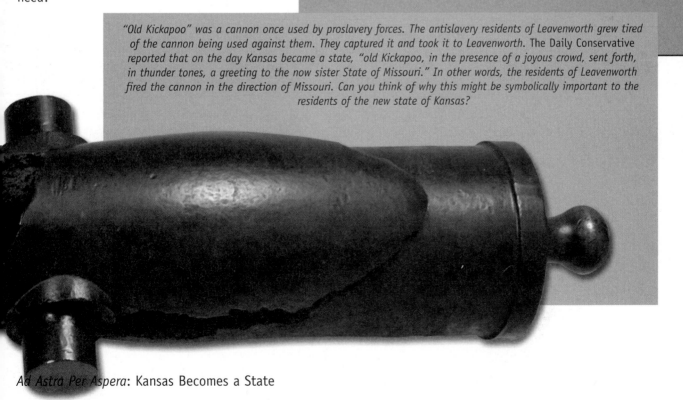

"Old Kickapoo" was a cannon once used by proslavery forces. The antislavery residents of Leavenworth grew tired of the cannon being used against them. They captured it and took it to Leavenworth. The Daily Conservative reported that on the day Kansas became a state, "old Kickapoo, in the presence of a joyous crowd, sent forth, in thunder tones, a greeting to the now sister State of Missouri." In other words, the residents of Leavenworth fired the cannon in the direction of Missouri. Can you think of why this might be symbolically important to the residents of the new state of Kansas?

Establishing a State Government

When Kansas became a state, it had to create a state government based on the Wyandotte Constitution. There was no money in the state treasury, and the state was in debt. There were no guns or ammunition in the state *armory*. To the east, Kansas still had a hostile border with Missouri. Missouri remained proslavery, whereas Kansas was now a free state. To the west was the Indian frontier, where tensions were increasing due to American's push for more land and resources.

Charles Robinson was elected the first governor of Kansas. Robinson wanted the U.S. government to pay for damages in the state that were the result of the Bleeding Kansas struggle. But he was doubtful the U.S. government could help. Robinson felt that the state should help its own citizens who were suffering from the drought. But he knew the state could not afford to do so. It was not a great start for the 34th state.

Ad Astra Per Aspera

The Kansas state motto is *Ad Astra Per Aspera*. It is written in Latin and means "to the stars through difficulty." John James Ingalls proposed the motto while he was secretary to the first Kansas Senate. Ingalls was very familiar with the struggles in Kansas Territory. He had been a member of the Wyandotte Constitutional Convention.

Ingalls also suggested a design for the state seal. He wanted it to be simple and symbolic. He proposed a single

The Kansas state seal contains images of mountains, a river, Indians on a buffalo hunt, a pioneer wagon train, and a farmer plowing his field. Can you see any images that remain from John Ingalls' original idea?

rising star coming out of a cloud. The star would appear moving toward a number of other stars, representing the states of the nation. The rising star represented Kansas' future as it emerged from its stormy creation.

Although Ingalls' idea for the state motto was accepted by the first state legislature, the design for the seal was modified. The legislature added many things to the state seal to represent the state's history.

The State Constitution

The Wyandotte Constitution was patterned after the United States Constitution. The document has a Bill of Rights that spells out those rights we consider to be *inalienable*. These rights are guaranteed and are similar to those found in the U.S. Bill of Rights and the Constitution. Among other things, the citizens of Kansas have the right to assemble in a peaceful manner and bear arms for their defense. They also have the right to freedom of speech and the right to worship according to their own beliefs.

Perhaps the most important idea in the State Constitution is that "all political power is inherent in the people." This means that all of us have an important role in the government. All people are governed by the Constitution. And the Constitution gives all people the responsibility of participating in their own government. Both the State and the U.S. Constitutions may be *amended*. This means that they are living documents and can change over time according to the will of the people.

The U.S. Constitution does not dictate all rights, responsibilities, and privileges. Some matters are left in the hands of the individual states. The Kansas Constitution as it was originally written was different from the U.S. Constitution in several ways. The Bill of Rights in the State Constitution prohibited slavery. The U.S. Constitution did not prohibit slavery until six years after the Kansas Constitution was adopted. In Kansas, women were given the right to vote in school board elections. It took another 61 years for the U.S. Constitution to be amended to give women the vote in all elections.

Activity

The Wyandotte Constitution and Civil Rights

The Kansas Constitution prohibited slavery in the state. But this did not mean that the Constitution provided for the civil rights of all people. In 1859, when the Constitution was written, many privileges were given only to white men over the age of 21. Read the following excerpts from the State Constitution as it was passed in 1859. Analyze the sections to determine who is granted certain rights and privileges, and who is not. Does the Constitution seem consistent or inconsistent to you? Can you explain and support your point of view?

Although Kansas women were given the right to vote in school board elections, they continued to fight for the right to participate in all aspects of political life for many years to come. This famous drawing is called "American Woman and Her Political Peers." It was designed by Henrietta Briggs-Wall and painted by Mr. W.A. Ford, both of Hutchinson, Kansas. The painting was displayed at the World's Columbian Exposition of 1893, in Chicago, where it created quite a stir. The painting depicts those who were not allowed to vote in the 1890s.

Bill of Rights

Sec. 1. All men are possessed of equal and inalienable rights, among which are life, liberty and the pursuit of happiness.

Sec. 2. All political power is inherent in the people.

Sec. 6. There shall be no slavery in this State, and no involuntary servitude, except for the punishment of crime, whereof the party shall have been duly convicted.

Sec. 11. All persons may freely speak, write or publish their sentiments on all subjects.

Article II - Legislative

Sec. 4. No person shall be a member of the Legislature who is not at the time of his election a qualified voter of and resident in the county or district for which he is elected.

Sec. 23. The Legislature, in providing for the formation and regulation of schools, shall make no distinction between the rights of males and females.

Article V - Suffrage

Sec. 1. Every white male person, of twenty-one years and upward, belonging to either of the following classes, who shall have resided in Kansas six months next preceding any election...shall be deemed a qualified elector: First, Citizens of the United States. Second, Persons of foreign birth who shall have declared their intention to become citizens, conformable to the laws of the United States on the subject of naturalization.

Sec. 2. No person under guardianship...or insane, shall be qualified to vote; nor any person convicted of treason or felony, unless restored to civil rights.

Article VIII - Militia

Sec. 1. The militia shall be composed of all able-bodied white male citizens, between the ages of twenty-one and forty-five, except such as are exempted by the laws of the United States or of this State; but all citizens, of any religious denomination whatever, who, from scruples of conscience, may be averse to bearing arms, shall be exempted there from, upon such conditions as may be prescribed by law.

Article XV - Miscellaneous

Sec. 6. The Legislature shall provide for the protection of the rights of women, in acquiring and possessing property, real, personal and mixed, separate and apart from the husband; and shall also provide for their equal rights in the possession of their children.

The Rules of State Government Today

There are levels of government in the United States. The federal, or national, government makes laws and provides services to everyone in the country. State governments also make laws and provide services, but they must follow the laws dictated by the federal government. Counties and cities also have governments. These local governments follow the laws of both the federal and state governments but make local laws called *ordinances*. As citizens, we receive services from all three levels of government.

Our state government is made up of the executive, legislative, and judicial branches. All three branches of government are identified in the State Constitution and have parallel duties to those outlined in the U. S. Constitution.

Governor Kathleen Sebelius is shown driving a combine near Caldwell. The governor was traveling the state surveying the wheat crop. In 2004 half of the wheat was destroyed by drought and late spring freezes. It is important for state officials to know what is happening with the state's farmers. In this case the state was preparing to ask the federal government to declare a disaster so that money would be available to help Kansas farmers who lost their crops.

Executive Branch

The governor is the head of the executive branch. The State Constitution gives the governor the responsibility of administering the laws of the state. The governor is elected by the people and can serve up to two consecutive four-year terms. He or she reviews the condition of the state and makes suggestions about how to improve life for all Kansans. The governor then works with the legislature to find solutions to problems. The governor oversees the budget of the state and represents Kansas at many events.

The people of Kansas receive many services from state government. Most state agencies are under the executive branch. Maintaining and building roads, protecting our food and water supply, providing for a secure and safe place to live, and administering parks and historic sites are just a few of the functions of the executive branch. It is also the job of the executive branch to collect taxes. Tax *revenue* is tied directly to the amount of services the public receives.

The state also has a lieutenant governor who can take over the governor's duties if the governor is unable to serve. The secretary of state is in charge of elections, and the attorney general is the chief lawyer for the state of Kansas. The state treasurer keeps track of the state's revenues. These are all elected offices that are part of the executive branch as written in the State Constitution.

Legislative Branch

The state Senate and House of Representatives make up the legislature. It is their job to make the laws of the state. Each January, senators and representatives come together in Topeka for the legislative session. The state is divided into Senate and

The Kansas Senate and the House of Representatives meet each year in the State Capitol. The Senate chamber was considered very elegant when it was completed. The senators' desks and chairs are hand-made of native Kansas woods.

State Legislature

Senate
40 senators
4 Year Terms
(each represents
approximately
60,000 people)

House
125 representatives
2 Year Terms
(each represents
approximately
19,000 people)

House districts based on population. The people in each district elect members to the legislature. This allows for people in all areas of the state to be represented in state government.

The process of making laws can be complicated. Any member of the legislature can introduce a bill. The State Constitution does not allow a member of the public to directly introduce legislation. Instead, the people must convince their elected officials to introduce their concerns to the legislature. This is called *representative government*.

A legislative bill may allocate the budget of a state program. An example of such a bill would be one that provides money for your school. Sometimes the legislature has to introduce bills that increase or decrease taxes, depending on spending needs. Bills

may also propose new laws or changes to existing ones. For example, the legislature has considered bills that change the requirements for obtaining a Kansas driver's license.

A bill must pass both the Senate and the House of Representatives and be approved by the governor before it can become law. If the governor *vetoes* a bill, it still may be reconsidered by the legislature. If two-thirds of the members of both the Senate and the House of Representatives still want the bill, then the bill becomes law without the governor's approval.

Judicial Branch

It is the job of the judicial branch to interpret the laws. The courts settle disagreements between people, determine if a person broke the law, and answer legal questions about a law.

A criminal case is one that involves a crime. It is the court's responsibility to decide if a person is guilty of that crime and if so what his/her punishment should be. We assume that people are innocent until proven guilty. The courts also hear civil cases. A civil case is between two parties that have a dispute over such things as money or property rights. The court is responsible for settling the dispute in a fair manner.

Juries are a very important part of the court system. Juries are made up of citizens. A grand jury is one that determines if there is enough evidence to take a person to court. Once a case goes to court, the trial may have a jury. It is the job of the jury to determine if someone is guilty or not guilty. It is the responsibility of the judge to make sure that the jury performs its job in a fair way.

The Kansas Supreme Court is the highest court in the state. Today, Kansas has a unified court system. That means that all courts in the state are under the administration of the State Supreme Court. Seven justices make up the Supreme Court. The governor appoints the justices. The Supreme Court interprets the laws to make sure that they are legal under the State Constitution.

What do you think?

The power of the government is held by the people. To have a truly representative government it is important for all citizens to participate in their government. Can you think of ways that you and your family can participate in state government? How might you actively participate in your community?

"Justice" is a very large sculpture in the atrium of the Judicial Center. The bird depicted in the sculpture is a prairie falcon, which is native to Kansas. The message on the wall reads, "Within these walls the balance of justice weighs equal." High school students in the state were asked to submit phrases they thought were important to the concept of justice. This message was the winning entry.

What Does Local Government Do?

Each community in Kansas has a local government. There are city and county governments. Local governments are responsible for making sure that federal, state, and local laws are carried out in their communities. Local governments also provide important services, making sure your community is a safe and desirable place to live.

Many local governments have Internet sites to share what is happening in their community. Read the passage below from Wichita's site to learn what services the local government provides:

Ever wonder what a day in the life of the City includes? We averaged yearly numbers to determine what is done in 24 hours:

- *Central Inspection will review and issue 115 building, electrical, plumbing and mechanical permits for new building construction, remodeling or alteration projects.*

- *Public Works will sweep 150 miles of street, fill 140 potholes, repair 160 sq. yards of pavement and make 20 new street signs.*

- *Parks & Recreation will mow and maintain 25 acres a day, plant 5 trees and host 25 events in their facilities.*

- *The Airport will have 40 departures and 3,400 passengers flying in or out of Wichita and process over 85 tons of cargo.*

- *Every day Housing Services provides housing to over 2,400 low-income families in Wichita, processes 5 loan requests and responds to 150 rental assistance calls.*

- *Law will handle 24 legal matters involving civil litigation, claims for damages, legal service assignments and Municipal Court appeals.*

- *Municipal Court will process 1,329 people and close 11 probation cases.*

- *Police will patrol 100 sq. miles, investigate 68 cases, interview 30 suspects work 14 accidents and give 3 presentations on crime prevention.*

- *Fire will respond to 8 structure fires, 78 medical-related emergencies, investigate the cause of 3 fires and give 2 fire prevention programs for 40 children.*

- *Water & Sewer will operate and maintain 61.7 million gallons of water, operate and maintain 1,850 miles of water line, operate and maintain 53 sanitary sewer lift stations and treat 37.9 million gallons of wastewater.*

- *Transit Services will transport 5,700 people and 600 disabled people in special ADA vehicles to their destination.*

———Activity———

Your Local Government Services

As a class, review the current budget of your city or county government. By examining the budget you can determine what services your government provides. Do all the things your local government does to make your life better surprise you? Are there other services you would like to see from your government? Remember, you must be willing to pay for services. That is why we have taxes.

THE KANSAS

The State Capitol in Topeka stands as a monument to state government. It is where the governor and legislature work. It was also once home to the judicial branch, which now makes its home in a separate building, called the Judicial Center.

The most recent addition to the state Capitol is the statue of a Kansa Indian on top of the dome. For many years the dome was topped with a lone light bulb. The Kansa Indian statue was added in 2002.

Choosing a Capital City

Many cities wanted to be the capital of Kansas. Cyrus K. Holliday, one of the founders of the city of Topeka and the Atchison, Topeka, and Santa Fe Railroad, worked hard to convince people that Topeka was the perfect capital city. His most persuasive argument came in the form of a donation of 20 acres of land upon which the capitol could be built.

The Wyandotte Constitutional Convention made Topeka the temporary capital. The location of the capital was put to the vote of the people. Topeka won, receiving 7,996 of the 14,471 votes. Lawrence came in second with 5,291 votes.

Building the State Capitol

The governor and legislature wanted to build one of the best capitols in the United States. They thought the Kansas Capitol should be as good as or better than the national Capitol in Washington, D.C. This was quite a contrast to the buildings that existed in Kansas at the time. Most people lived and worked in modest buildings. Some were even made from sod.

The state Capitol did not always look like it does today. It was built in stages and took 37 years to complete. The two wings of the building were built first. In the beginning, a covered wooden sidewalk connected the two buildings. It was called the "Cave of Winds."

STATE CAPITOL

Originally, the Capitol was to be built of stone quarried near Topeka. The foundation was laid, but the harsh winter made the stone crumble. This was not a good sign for such an important building. The Topeka stone was removed and replaced with limestone from Junction City.

A Ghost Story

Building the Kansas Capitol was a monumental task. The work was hard and dangerous. Nine men lost their lives building the state Capitol. Sometimes on rainy, windy nights, workers at the Capitol hear strange sounds and echoing footsteps. Neighbors have reported hearing a tapping sound coming from the dome. Some think it is the ghost of a worker who died during construction.

It was the job of one worker to fasten plates on the dome of the Capitol. One day he stretched to reach a bolt, lost his balance, and fell to his death. Because the accident occurred near the end of the month, the worker was never able to collect the pay he had earned. Workers were paid at the end of the month. Legend says the worker returns to the Capitol each night searching for someone to pay him. Sometimes he continues to work, tapping on the dome, working overtime for his wages.

Newspapers at the time praised the style of the state Capitol. They thought it showed strength and respect for government. It was a symbol of something permanent.

The East Wing was the first part of the Capitol built and occupied. A fence surrounded the building to keep cows, pigs, and other animals away from the statehouse grounds.

The exterior of the central portion of the state Capitol was completed 37 years after the East Wing was begun.

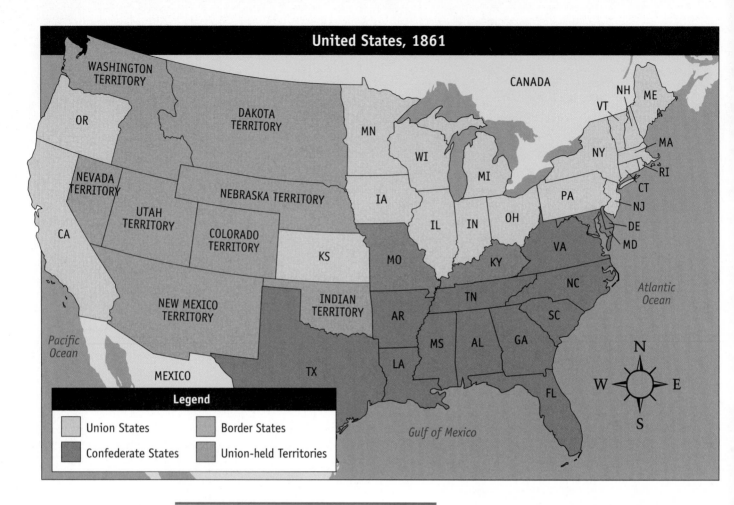

WASHINGTON TERRITORY

OR

DAKOTA TERRITORY

CANADA

NH
VT
ME

MN

WI

NY

MA

NEVADA TERRITORY

UTAH TERRITORY

NEBRASKA TERRITORY

MI

RI
CT

CA

COLORADO TERRITORY

KS

IA

IL

IN

OH

PA

NJ

DE
MD

VA

NEW MEXICO TERRITORY

MO

KY

NC

Atlantic Ocean

Pacific Ocean

INDIAN TERRITORY

AR

TN

SC

MS

AL

GA

MEXICO

TX

LA

FL

Gulf of Mexico

N
W   E
S

Legend

Union States

Border States

Confederate States

Union-held Territories

Kansas and the Civil War

As Kansas was working to become a state, the United States was splitting apart and heading for civil war. The disputes were over slavery and the right's of states to govern themselves. The Confederate, or Southern, states wanted to preserve their way of life, which included slavery. Southern states began to *secede* from the Union. Eventually, violence erupted between the Confederacy and the Union.

The Civil War began less than three months after Kansas became a state. Most Kansans supported the Union. They did not want to see the country destroyed after they had worked so hard to join it. Like President Abraham Lincoln, Kansans wanted to see the Union preserved.

James Lane's Frontier Guard

James Lane was sent to Washington, D.C., as one of Kansas' first U.S. senators. Eight days after he became a Senator,

Southern forces attacked Fort Sumter, and the Civil War began. Washington, D.C., was in a vulnerable position between Virginia and Maryland. Both states were considering seceding from the Union. It became extremely important to protect the capital.

James Lane was known to love a good fight. He arrived in Washington just in time to defend the capital. Shortly after his arrival, he began making speeches on the streets of Washington, D.C. At one such speech, Southerners booed him. But Lane responded saying, "I have a hundred men from Kansas in this crowd, all armed, all fighting men, just from the victorious fields of Kansas!" Northerners cheered him.

Lane organized those Kansans into the Frontier Guard. For a short time, more than 100 Kansas men provided special protection for President Lincoln. For three weeks, the guard camped out in the East Room of the White House. Eventually, the guard was no longer needed as Union troops moved into the U.S. capital.

Activity

The Fort Scott *Democrat*, March 9, 1861

Some Kansans had opposed the election of Abraham Lincoln. But when war broke out, the state remained solidly behind the president. The editors of the Fort Scott *Democrat* were not in favor of the election of the Republican president. However, they published these thoughts a month before the war began. Read the passage, and then answer the following questions:

1. Why have the editors thrown their support behind President Lincoln?
2. What do they want to achieve?
3. Are they leaving behind their belief in the Democratic Party?
4. Which is more important to the editors: loyalty to political party or loyalty to country?

The principles of our party are as dear to us now as ever. . . .But another question has risen, more engrossing and absorbing than all others combined, which overrides party allegiance . . .We have but one duty—that is TO OUR COUNTRY! No party can absolve us from our imperative duty to the Constitution and Union.

We are not willing to give up the Union for 500 parties. . . .We will, therefore, yield a liberal and cordial support to any party, man, or set of men, whose efforts honestly tend to the preservation of our glorious Union.

. . .to Mr. Lincoln, we stand prepared and pledged hereby to support with patriotic zeal and earnestness, and all measures of his administration having in view the restoration of peace to the distracted interest of our country . . .

Peace with our neighbors, and quiet within our own borders we must have; and the Union restored and reconstructed, if within the limits of human possibility.

This illustration was on the cover of the magazine Harper's Weekly *on March 6, 1861. Abraham Lincoln, the newly elected president, was on his way to his inauguration. He stopped in Philadelphia and took part in a celebration welcoming Kansas as a state. He is shown here raising the flag with 34 stars.*

This 1862 photograph shows the men of Company E of the Eighth Kansas Infantry.

The flag of the First Kansas Colored Infantry honors the battles fought by these brave troops. The flag is one of the few remaining artifacts from the regiment. Why is it important to preserve this piece of history?

Kansans at War

When the Civil War started, Kansas had about 30,000 men between the ages of 18 and 45. More than 20,000 men volunteered to fight for the Union in Kansas regiments. Not all of those men were from Kansas, but Kansas made an impressive showing in the Civil War. Nearly 8,500 of these volunteers died as a result of Civil War battles, giving Kansas the highest death rate of any state in the Union.

African American Soldiers

At the start of the Civil War, African Americans could not serve in the Union army. Eventually, the U.S. government changed its mind and welcomed blacks into the military. By the third year of the Civil War, African Americans in the Union army were receiving pay equal to other soldiers. This and other factors made enlisting attractive to African American men. Nearly 185,000 African Americans fought for the Union. About 38,000 gave their lives.

Kansas was the first state in the Union to enlist African Americans as soldiers. James Lane recruited soldiers for the First Kansas Colored Infantry. This was the first African American regiment to engage in battle in the Civil War. Two hundred twenty-five men fought against 500 Confederates in Missouri. The Confederates were defeated.

The First Kansas Colored Infantry was also the first black company to fight alongside white units. The First Colored Infantry gained fame at the Battle of Honey Springs. One Union general wrote, "I have never seen such fighting done as was done by the negro regiment. They fought like veterans, with a coolness and valor that is unsurpassed. . . .Too much praise can not be awarded them for their gallantry. . .They make better soldiers in every respect than any troops I have ever had under my command."

The Civil War Comes to Kansas

During the Civil War, tensions between Kansas and its neighboring state of Missouri remained high. *Guerrilla* warfare took place between the states. Instead of full military battles, both Kansans and Missourians made raids across the border.

Quantrill's Raid on Lawrence

Most of the 3,000 people of Lawrence were asleep at 5:00 a.m. on August 21, 1863. William C. Quantrill, a Confederate guerrilla, and about 400 men rode into Lawrence just as the sun was beginning to appear in the sky. The town had heard rumors of an attack a month before, but nothing had happened. That August morning would be different.

The citizens of Lawrence woke to gunshots. As people came out of their houses to see what was going on, they encountered a violent scene. The Confederate guerrillas were shooting every man they saw on the streets. They also shot into windows as they galloped by on horseback.

As the Confederates approached the center of town, they came upon the campsites of new army recruits. Quantrill's men fired first into the tents of the white recruits, killing many. Next they came upon the African American camp. It was close to deserted since many of the black recruits had escaped into the grasses along the Kansas River.

As Quantrill's men broke into smaller groups, they continued to terrorize the town. The Confederates were determined to burn down the town and kill most of the men and boys in it. To survive, some men hid in wells and under buildings. Others disguised themselves in their wives' clothing because the Confederates were not killing women.

Four hours after the raid began, at least 140 men and boys were dead. Some reported the number to be as high as 200. Only one Confederate had died.

What do you think?

Historians are not certain why Quantrill's men only killed men and boys. What are some reasons you can think of?

Sherman Enderton created this drawing within four hours of the tragedy in Lawrence. This is the only drawing of Quantrill's raid by someone who was in Lawrence that fateful day.

How Do We Know This?

If you had survived Quantrill's raid on Lawrence, do you think you would have strong memories of the event? For many of the survivors, the memories of that morning must have haunted them for some time.

Kate Riggs was in Lawrence on the morning of the attack. She later decided to record her memories so that her grandchildren would know what happened. This is called a *reminiscence*. For Mrs. Riggs, one of the most dramatic moments of that morning was watching a Confederate on horseback shooting at her husband. She remembers how she saved her husband's life by grabbing the horse and turning the Confederate in the opposite direction of her husband.

. . .an inspiration, not a thought, made me spring forward and catch the bridle with both hands, there was a rope in my hands too....your grandfather, thinking the man was upon him, turned to face him. . .He had not known I was near him until he turned and saw me running with the horse, and instead of going across the street, as the [Confederate] intended, we went straight up the street. I saw your grandfather turn just as we passed. We went quite a little distance straight before the man could bring his horse around. . .The man sat on his horse and took deliberate aim at your grandfather. I pulled the horse around so that it faced east, but the man turned himself on the horse and fired the revolver after your grandfather. Up to this time this man had not seemed to notice me any more than he would have noticed a fly that had alighted on his bridle, but now he turned back, and with a fierce oath, he lifted his revolver high in the air to strike me over the hands compelling me to let go.

Battle of Mine Creek

Missouri was a slave state that did not secede from the Union. Yet it was home to many Confederates and Southern sympathizers. After Quantrill's raid on Lawrence, "Order No. 11" was issued by the Union army patrolling the border between Kansas and Missouri. The order cleared all settlers out of four western Missouri counties. The intent was to prevent any more raids across the border. A year later, the border became the sight of a bitter battle between Union and Confederate troops.

General Sterling Price led Confederate troops into Missouri, hoping to capture the state for the South. He had orders to find new recruits. Price also was told that, if he had to retreat, he should exit through Kansas. While in Kansas, he should take cattle, horses, and other supplies.

As Price and his men moved through Missouri, word spread in Kansas that there might be an invasion. The state militia was called out. Price continued to advance toward Kansas City where he was turned away by Union forces. His retreat led him south along the border between Kansas and Missouri. Price had followed his orders and was traveling with supplies he had obtained for the Confederate army. Eventually, Price and his men crossed into Kansas and set up camp.

Price's refusal to let go of the supplies eventually slowed the group down. This allowed the Union army to catch up with him. The two armies engaged in a series of skirmishes. The decisive battle was fought at Mine Creek where less than 2,500 Union soldiers faced down nearly 7,000 Confederates. The fighting was fierce. But in less than an hour, it was all over. The Union had won by launching a cavalry charge that broke the Confederate's line of defense. The defeat at Mine Creek forced Price and his remaining men to abandon supplies and retreat.

At least 200 Confederate soldiers died at Mine Creek. The Union troops also saw casualties. Upon leaving Mine Creek, Price's men purposefully destroyed supply wagons so they could move faster. The Union army continued in pursuit. Three days later Price's army, weakened by their fight at Mine Creek, met their final defeat in Missouri.

Before General Sterling Price and his Confederate troops reached Mine Creek, they fought with Union troops near Kansas City. Fifty Union soldiers were taken prisoner. Among the prisoners was Samuel Reader who managed to escape by posing as a Confederate soldier. Reader walked four days to reach his home just north of Topeka. Upon his return, he recorded his adventure in this painting.

Women and the Civil War

Women were not permitted to serve in the military during the Civil War. However, their contribution to the war effort was invaluable. From the beginning, women organized relief efforts by making uniforms and blankets. Women also took an active role in raising much needed money for the war effort.

By the second year of the war, Union relief efforts were organized under the United States Sanitary Commission. The organization worked with hospitals to recruit nurses and donate food, medicines, and bandages.

Families were torn apart during the Civil War. Keeping in touch with loved ones was important. Manufacturers printed Valentine cards specifically for couples that were apart due to the war. This valentine reads:

FAITHFUL IN DEATH
'To horse!' the bugle
sounds the call,
The foeman rage like
Waves at sea;
If cruel fate should
Bid me fall,
My last fond thought
Shall be of thee.

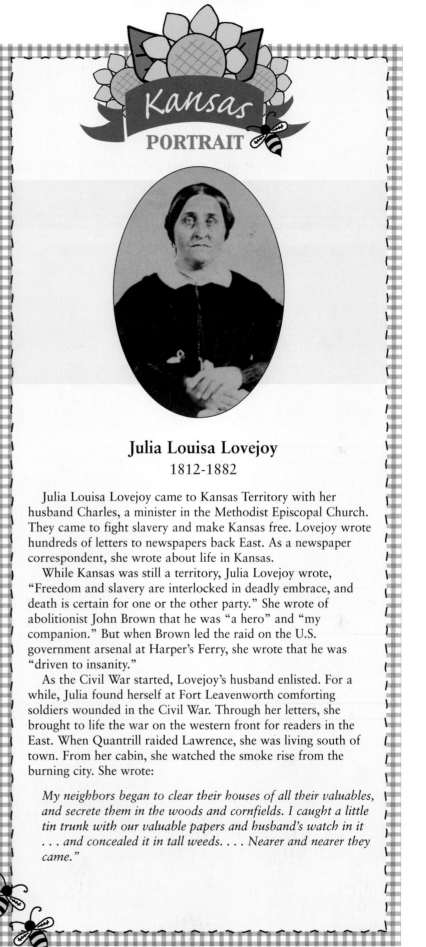

Kansas PORTRAIT

Julia Louisa Lovejoy
1812-1882

Julia Louisa Lovejoy came to Kansas Territory with her husband Charles, a minister in the Methodist Episcopal Church. They came to fight slavery and make Kansas free. Lovejoy wrote hundreds of letters to newspapers back East. As a newspaper correspondent, she wrote about life in Kansas.

While Kansas was still a territory, Julia Lovejoy wrote, "Freedom and slavery are interlocked in deadly embrace, and death is certain for one or the other party." She wrote of abolitionist John Brown that he was "a hero" and "my companion." But when Brown led the raid on the U.S. government arsenal at Harper's Ferry, she wrote that he was "driven to insanity."

As the Civil War started, Lovejoy's husband enlisted. For a while, Julia found herself at Fort Leavenworth comforting soldiers wounded in the Civil War. Through her letters, she brought to life the war on the western front for readers in the East. When Quantrill raided Lawrence, she was living south of town. From her cabin, she watched the smoke rise from the burning city. She wrote:

My neighbors began to clear their houses of all their valuables, and secrete them in the woods and cornfields. I caught a little tin trunk with our valuable papers and husband's watch in it . . . and concealed it in tall weeds. . . . Nearer and nearer they came.

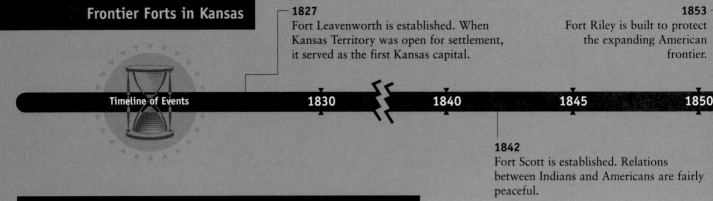

1827
Fort Leavenworth is established. When Kansas Territory was open for settlement, it served as the first Kansas capital.

1853
Fort Riley is built to protect the expanding American frontier.

1830   1840   1845   1850

1842
Fort Scott is established. Relations between Indians and Americans are fairly peaceful.

Kansas Forts

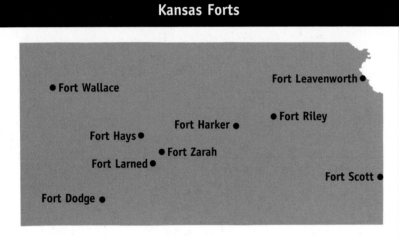

- Fort Wallace
- Fort Leavenworth
- Fort Harker
- Fort Riley
- Fort Hays
- Fort Zarah
- Fort Larned
- Fort Scott
- Fort Dodge

Frontier Forts in Kansas

As America expanded west, the U.S. army built forts on the frontier. It was the job of frontier soldiers to keep the peace between Americans heading west and American Indians who called the West home. Most often, military forts were established to protect Americans, not Indians. But on some occasions, the military was given the role of keeping land-hungry Americans off Indian lands. The differing points of view between the American Indians and the American government were bound to explode into conflict. The conflicts hit a peak during, and shortly after, the Civil War, but the roots of the conflicts started much earlier.

Log cabins served as the first buildings at Fort Scott. Mud was used to fill up the holes between the logs, and the floors were made of dirt.

The Forts and the Trails

The Santa Fe Trail established trade in 1821 between the United States and Mexico. But for some American Indians, the trail was an invasion of their hunting grounds. Soon, the U.S. government sent the military west to protect the trade route.

Fort Leavenworth is the oldest active army post west of the Mississippi River. One of its earliest responsibilities was to protect wagon trains hauling cargo over the Santa Fe Trail. Located in northeast Kansas, the fort was really too far east to carry out those duties. Eventually, the army established Fort Larned for this purpose. Protecting 700 miles of trail was often difficult. Fort Leavenworth was in a much better position to assist families traveling on the Oregon-California Trail.

The Forts and Indian Relocation

When the U.S. government began moving eastern Indian tribes into Kansas, the soldiers at Fort Leavenworth took on new responsibilities. The U.S. army's job was now to protect the Indian lands. Fort Scott was soon established to help with this duty.

1864	1864
Fort Zarah is established to guard commerce on the Santa Fe Trail.	Fort Harker, originally called Fort Ellsworth, is built to protect the Kansas Stage Line and military wagon trains. Soldiers are assigned to protect Americans heading for the Denver gold fields.

| 1855 | 1860 | 1865 | 1870 |

1859	1865	1865
rt Larned is established. ers stationed here escort ail coaches traveling the Santa Fe Trail.	Fort Wallace is established. The soldiers provide military escorts for travelers on stage routes.	Fort Dodge is established as a supply center, and troops secure the area for the U.S. government. Fort Hays is established. The troops at the fort protect workers building the Union Pacific Railroad.

In eastern Kansas, conditions were difficult for both emigrant Indians and tribes native to the region. Sometimes conflicts broke out among tribes, and it was the army's job to keep the peace. It was also the responsibility of the soldiers to keep Americans from illegally settling on Indian lands.

The Army and Manifest Destiny

The role of the army on the frontier changed again. As America began to think it was its destiny to take over all lands to the Pacific Ocean, the U.S. government made the army more of an invading force. The objective became to conquer the land on behalf of the United States.

Fort Leavenworth became the jumping-off point for soldiers going to both the Oregon Territory and the Southwest, which was controlled by Mexico. If the United States was to conquer more land, it needed more forts. Supplies and new recruits were shipped up and down the established trails. Fort Riley was established. From its location troops could be sent to either the Santa Fe or Oregon-California Trails.

The Civil War and the Frontier Forts

When the Civil War broke out, many of the soldiers stationed in Kansas left. Those from the South returned home to fight for the Confederacy. Many of the remaining soldiers were reassigned in the eastern United States to protect the Union.

The Civil War brought about changes in the relations between the army and the American Indians. Many of the forts were staffed with state volunteer troops. These men were not regular army men and felt less obligated to the federal government. The volunteers came from states like Kansas, Illinois, and Iowa. Because of the difficulties of life on the frontier, they may have felt more aggressive toward American Indians.

These officers are stationed at Fort Wallace. Many forts operated for some time with temporary buildings and tents. Wood for buildings had to be brought in from other regions. At the time of this photograph, five stone buildings had been built at Fort Wallace.

Little House on the Prairie

The well-known author, Laura Ingalls Wilder, wrote about her family's experience living in Kansas in her book *Little House on the Prairie*. The Wilder family actually lived in Kansas when Laura was three years old. The land they built their cabin on belonged to the Osage and was not available for settlers. Americans who lived on Indian lands were called **squatters**. Laura writes that her family was told by soldiers they had to move off the land they were illegally occupying. In one of the last chapters in *Little House on the Prairie*, Laura describes the evacuation of the Americans who had squatted on Indian lands.

Tensions Increase

After the Civil War, the U.S. government took control of the military units in Kansas once again. As tensions increased, new forts were established to assert control. The army tried to maintain peace, but by this time neither side trusted the other.

Medicine Lodge Peace Treaties

The United States wanted to make peace with the Indians on the plains. However, the peaceful end the government wanted was to place the Indian tribes on reservations. Reservation life meant that the Indians would be dependent on the Americans for food and housing. This was not what the Indians wanted.

The Plains Indians considered Medicine Lodge to be a sacred area. The Medicine Lodge River was thought to have healing powers. There were no American settlements nearby and no army posts. More than 5,000 Cheyenne, Arapaho, Kiowa, Apache, and Comanche met with a commission appointed by the U.S. Congress at Medicine Lodge. Many speeches were made. Satanta, a Kiowa Chief, spoke asking why the Kiowa should trust government agents for food. He also called the building of homes for them "nonsense."

The U.S. government promised to

protect the Indians from whites, provide them with schools and farming tools, and give them food. The treaties also opened up the area for American settlement and the railroad. The treaties were signed, but they did not bring peace. Some tribes chose to live on the reservations, while others chose to remain free. Treaties and promises were broken. Fighting between the U.S. army and the Plains tribes continued for several years.

Medicine Lodge Peace Treaty Speech, Comanche Chief Ten Bears

The following speech was given by Comanche Chief Ten Bears at the Medicine Lodge Peace Treaties. He uses language well to make his points. Can you pick out some analogies he uses? From his perspective, who started the conflicts? How would you feel in his situation?

My people have never first drawn a bow or fired a gun against whites. There has been trouble on the line between us, and my young men have danced the war dance. But it was not begun by us.

It was you sent out the first soldier, and it was we who sent out the second. Two years ago I came up upon this road, following the buffalo, that my wives and children might have their cheeks plump, and their bodies warm. But the soldiers fired on us, and since that time there has been a noise, like that of a thunderstorm, and we have not known which way to go. . . .

The Comanches are not weak, and blind, like pups of a dog when seven sleeps old. They are strong and farsighted, like grown horses. . . . But there are things which you have said to me which I do not like. They were not sweet like sugar, but bitter like gourds. You said that you wanted to put us upon reservations, to build us houses and to make us Medicine lodges. I do not want them.

This illustration of the Medicine Lodge Peace Treaties appeared in Harper's Weekly *on November 16, 1867. During the 1800s, news from the West reached people in the East several weeks after the event had occurred. Today, news is spread around the world in an instant. How do you think this change in the way the news is reported affects people?*

The Sand Creek Massacre

One of the most tragic events in western history took place one month after Union troops beat back the Confederate invasion of Kansas at Mine Creek. The trail from Kansas to the gold fields of Colorado ran directly through the lands of the Cheyenne and Arapaho. The hunting grounds of the Cheyenne and Arapaho extended along the Arkansas River from Kansas to Colorado.

Some Indian leaders wanted to make peace with the Americans, others wanted to resist the American intrusion. Cheyenne Chiefs Black Kettle and White Antelope went to Washington, D.C., to work for peace. They met with President Lincoln, who gave Black Kettle a large American flag and White Antelope a peace medal. Attaining peace was not easy. Tensions continued, and Black Kettle and other Cheyenne and Arapaho chiefs met with the Colorado governor and the military commander of one of the Colorado Volunteer Regiments.

Black Kettle left the meeting believing that all was well. Black Kettle and his people traveled south and set up camp near Fort Lyon, Colorado. Thinking it was safe, Black Kettle raised the American flag that President Lincoln had given him on a large pole in front of his tipi. He also raised a white flag signaling that he was not there to fight.

The military commander, with whom Black Kettle had met, betrayed him. About 700 soldiers surrounded Black Kettle's camp. As the sun rose in the east, the troops attacked the peaceful Indians. A horrible massacre took place. More than 150 Indians were slaughtered. The troops killed men, women, children, and babies. White Antelope died wearing the peace medal President Lincoln gave him. Black Kettle and his wife survived, but she was shot in the back nine times.

The volunteer soldiers returned to Denver, exhibiting items that they had stolen from the Indians. News of the Sand Creek Massacre spread among Plains Indians. The massacre accelerated the distrust that was already building. It was very difficult for the Indians to trust the Americans again.

Many short railroad lines were given charters in Kansas, but only a few were actually built. A 50-mile line was built from Manhattan, to Alma, to Burlingame in the 1870s.

Buffalo Soldiers

Shortly after the Civil War, the U.S. army began allowing African Americans to serve in the peacetime army. They served in *segregated* regiments, under the command of white officers, in two black cavalry units.

The 9th Cavalry recruited African American men out of Louisiana and Kentucky. They were originally assigned to protect stage and mail routes in Texas, but the unit was transferred to Fort Riley. In Kansas, these soldiers were given the job of evicting squatters who attempted to settle on Indian lands.

The 10th Cavalry was formed at Fort Leavenworth. Unfortunately, the fort commander openly opposed blacks serving in the military. This made life uneasy at Fort Leavenworth. The 10th Cavalry requested a transfer. They were stationed at several forts around Kansas, engaging in the conquest of the West.

The 9th and the 10th Cavalries were referred to as Buffalo Soldiers. No one knows for sure where the name came from. One story says that the Kiowa named the 10th Cavalry Buffalo Soldiers because they were worthy opponents.

The End of the Frontier

It was only a matter of time before the railroad pushed its way through Kansas. During Kansas Territory, the legislature had given *charters* to 51 railroad companies. The approaching Civil War stopped construction. During the Civil War, President Lincoln approved the Pacific Railroad bill. Three feeder lines were authorized to be built in Kansas. Before long, the railroad would connect Kansas to the rest of the country, and life in Kansas would change forever.

The 10th Cavalry was one of the most honored regiments in the army.

The Kansas Journey

Chapter 5 Review

What Do You Remember?

1. Why do Kansans celebrate Kansas Day?
2. What challenges did the new state government face in Kansas?
3. Name at least one difference between the U.S. Constitution and the Kansas Constitution at the time of statehood.
4. What are the three branches of state government and what is the purpose of each?
5. Why did Topeka become the state capital?
6. What is one thing the Frontier Guard did in Washington, D.C.?
7. Who was William C. Quantrill?
8. What was "Order No. 11," and what did it hope to prevent?
9. Describe what happened at the battle of Mine Creek.
10. Name at least two purposes for establishing forts in Kansas.
11. Describe what happened at the Sand Creek Massacre.
12. What did the government want and what did they promise the Indians in the Medicine Lodge Peace Treaties?
13. Name at least two tribes that participated in the Medicine Lodge Peace Treaties.
14. Who are the Buffalo soldiers?
15. What brought an end to Kansas as a frontier?

Think About It!

1. There are many levels of government. Compare and contrast the purposes of the national, state, and local governments. Why do you think it is important to have these levels of government? What is the benefit for a community?
2. Kansans volunteered in large numbers to fight for the Union in the Civil War. Why do you think Kansans made such a strong showing in the Civil War? Was Kansas' patriotic response surprising after the turmoil over slavery in Kansas Territory?

Activities

1. Mr. LeGrande Copley showed his civic engagement when he started Kansas Day. What is civic engagement? Can you think of people in your community who are engaged in making your community a better place to live? Interview someone in your community who is engaged in community action. As a class, use your interviews to create a wall of community "heroes."
2. Women were not allowed to serve in the military during the Civil War. Today, women serve in all aspects of the military. Research when the military began to accept women. What were their roles? Develop a timeline that compares racial and gender integration into the military. On the timeline include when women and African Americans were given the right to vote.
3. Research what daily life at a frontier fort was like. Pretending you are a soldier at the fort, write a letter to your parents about your day.

PEOPLE TO KNOW
Ernest de Boissiere
Abbie Bright
Philip Bright
George Grant
Flora Moorman Heston
Benjamin "Pap" Singleton

PLACES TO LOCATE
Clark County
Clearwater
Franklin County
Harper County
Lindsborg
McPherson County
Nicodemus
Victoria
Volga River (Russia)
Wakefield
Wichita

Trees were scarce in parts of Kansas. Homesteaders built houses out of the materials they could find. This photograph taken in Ford County around 1890 shows a family living in a dug out. The interior of the dug out shows all of the family's possessions brought from the East.

Welcome to Kansas:
"Her Light Shall Shine"

1841-1891
The Preemption Act

1865
The Civil War comes to an end.

1869
Wakefield is founded as an English settlement.

1840   1860   1865

1862
The Homestead Act provides the opportunity for many settlers to get land in Kansas.

1868
The First Swedish Agricultural Company of McPherson County is organized.

1869
Silkville is founded as a French cooperative settlement.

WORDS TO UNDERSTAND
barbed wire
bigotry
chain migration
class system
communal
depression
draft
dug out
emancipation
famine
irrigation
pacifist
sections
sod house
tenant

1873-1891
The Timber Culture Act

1873
George Grant establishes the community of Victoria.
The Mennonites send an official committee to study settlement in Kansas.
African Americans establish the first of a series of colonies in Kansas.

1875	1880	1885	1890	1895

1877
African Americans establish
the community of Nicodemus.

1874
Grasshoppers
invade the
Great Plains.

1876
The first large group of Germans
from Russia arrive in western Kansas.

1879
Exodusters
come to Kansas.

1887
Runnymede is established
to attract the sons of
wealthy Englishmen.

121

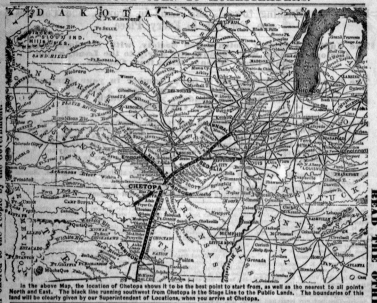
Welcome to Kansas

After the Civil War, it seemed like everyone wanted to come to Kansas—and almost everyone was welcome. Kansas opened its lands to settlers from the East and immigrants from foreign countries. The exception was American Indians who were pushed out to make way for new farms and growing communities.

Years before, Stephen Long had labeled Kansas "The Great Desert." This image was supported when many settlers in Kansas Territory struggled with the lack of rainfall. But the drought was soon over. When living space in the East became more and more crowded, the appeal of Kansas land grew.

The Junction City newspaper, *The Union*, wrote on April 29, 1865:

> The idea that the Central and Western portion of the State is a Desert is exploded. The early and the later rains on the extreme headwaters of Kansas river, the fields of wheat and corn and luxuriant grapes, show this idea to be a false one. Tens of thousands of settlers can find choice lands and homes in Central and Western Kansas. The field is wide and inviting, and there is nothing in the way.

Broadsides advertised the availability of Indian lands to settlers. Chetopa is in the southeast corner of the state. The broadside claims the lands were bought by treaty from the Creeks, Seminoles, Choctaws, and Chickasaws. American Indians often had no choice but to sign treaties with the U.S. government.

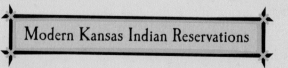

Iowa Indian Reservation
Sac and Fox Indian Reservation
Kickapoo Indian Reservation

Potawatomi
Indian Reservation

Modern Kansas Indian Reservations

Most American Indians were forced to move off their lands in Kansas. After the Civil War, only four reservations remained in Kansas.

Let Our Light Shine

After the Civil War, the population of Kansas increased dramatically. Most of the settlers moved from other states like Ohio, Illinois, and Indiana.

Kansas did more than welcome its new settlers. Our government and businesses recruited many new residents to the state. The state commissioner of immigration asked Kansans to encourage others to move here. He said, "It would not be characteristic for Kansas to be hid under a bushel. Let us see that her light shall shine."

The federal government also did its part to attract new settlers to Kansas. New legislation allowed individuals and families to obtain land at little or no cost. The U.S. government's encouragement of the railroad industry also resulted in increased settlement in Kansas.

Kansas Population Growth	
1860	107,206
1870	364,399
1880	996,096
1890	1,428,108

What was the percentage of population growth from 1860 to 1890?

The Homestead Act

Horace Greeley, a newspaperman in the East, advised "Go West, young man, go West!" After the Civil War, the West became a symbol of new opportunities. The Homestead Act nurtured the idea of land ownership. It successfully motivated thousands of people to move to Kansas.

The requirements to get land seemed simple enough. Any individual over the age of 21 could claim up to 160 acres of public land. The homesteader had to be a citizen of the United States or intend to become one. In order to obtain the land, settlers had to pay a $10 fee, as well as live on and cultivate the land. If, after five years, a homesteader could show improvements to the claim, then he or she would be given clear title. If the settler wanted to buy the land before the five years were up, the price was $1.25 per acre.

For those who were successful, the Homestead Act offered great opportunities. States like Kansas saw a dramatic increase in population when land became available to homesteaders.

Tenant Farming

The Homestead Act encouraged the small family farmer. Although the land was "free," starting a farm was not free. A successful homesteader needed between $500 and $1,000 to start the farm. This was a lot of money, and many settlers came to Kansas with far less. If a homesteader had a difficult first year, he or she might be wiped out almost immediately. When settlers failed they could either go back home or become *tenant* farmers.

A tenant farmer cultivated someone else's land as a renter. By 1890, almost one third of Kansas farms were being run by tenant farmers. Some became tenant farmers first by choice, believing that it would give them opportunities to homestead later. Other farmers found tenant farming as a last option when their own homesteads failed.

The well-known Civil War photographer Alexander Gardner was hired to be the official photographer of the Union Pacific Eastern Division Railroad. Gardner took this photograph at a Kansas ranch on Clear Creek in 1867.

Welcome to Kansas: "Her Light Shall Shine"

In order to survive in Kansas, the whole family often worked together. In this photograph a Riley County family is milking their cows.

Other Ways to Get Land

The Homestead Act was not the only way settlers could obtain land in Kansas. There were several ways the federal government encouraged settlement in the West.

The Preemption Act was designed to give settlers rights to the lands they already occupied. A squatter could take up residence on public lands and buy the land from the U.S. government after 14 months. Up to 160 acres could be purchased for as little as $1.25 an acre. The advantage to the squatter was the opportunity to purchase the land before it went up for public sale. This eliminated any competitive bidders. It also protected the improvements settlers had already made.

The Timber Culture Act allowed settlers to enlarge their land holdings. On the Great Plains, forests were scarce. By increasing the number of trees, settlers would have more firewood and building lumber. Up to 160 acres of land could be claimed, but a large number of trees had to be planted on a portion of the land. There was no requirement that the claimants live on the land. If the claimant successfully followed the

This map of Clark County, Kansas was published in 1886 in The Official Atlas of Kansas. Notice how the sections are laid out in the county to form a grid.

Surveying the Land

Public lands in Kansas had to be surveyed before they could be legally claimed. The grid system of surveying land in the United States dates back to the Continental Congress. Under this system land is divided into one-mile square parcels called *sections*.

Most of Kansas had been surveyed by the 1880s. Measurements were made as accurately as possible with the equipment that was available at the time. Monuments or markers were placed in the ground to designate section borders. These measurements are still in use today in legal documents that describe land boundaries.

Without a land survey it is impossible to establish the exact location of a specific piece of property. We continue to survey land today. When you buy a new home, a land survey is done to establish your property lines.

The Kansas Journey

regulations, after several years the land could be purchased for $1.25 an acre.

Public lands could also be purchased through an auction. They were sold to the highest bidder. If the land did not sell at auction then it could be purchased for $1.25 an acre.

Coming to Kansas

The majority of the people who came here after the Civil War did not have to cross an ocean or learn a new language. They were American-born and saw great economic and social opportunities here.

What was life like coming to Kansas and living on a claim? Not every person experienced the same successes and challenges in Kansas. Not all communities prospered or struggled in the same way. But to paint a picture of what life was like, we can look to the stories of individuals.

American-Born Settlers and Their State of Origin

State	1860 Number of People	1860 Percent of Kansas Population	1870 Number of People	1870 Percent of Kansas Population
Ohio	11,617	12.29%	38,205	12.094%
Missouri	11,356	12.02%	20,775	6.57%
Kansas	10,997	11.64%	63,321	20.04%
Indiana	9,945	10.52%	30,953	9.80%
Illinois	9,367	9.91%	35,558	11.25%
Kentucky	6,556	6.94%	15,918	5.04%
Pennsylvania	6,463	6.84%	19,287	6.10%
New York	6,331	6.70%	18,558	5.87%
Iowa	4,008	4.24%	13,073	4.41%
Virginia	3,487	3.69%	9,906	3.13%
Tennessee	2,569	2.72%	6,209	1.96%
Wisconsin	1,351	1.43%	4,128	1.31%
Massachusetts	1,282	1.36%	2,894	0.92%
North Carolina	1,234	1.31%	3,612	1.14%
Michigan	1,137	1.20%	4,466	1.41%

The Letters of Flora Moorman Heston

Flora Moorman Heston came to Clark County in the spring of 1885. She traveled from Indiana by train with her three children. Her husband Sam arrived in Kansas about six months earlier to establish a claim. Flora wrote many letters to her family back home in Indiana. She was full of hope about her family's future in their new home. She wrote, "I am so glad we came west, for this country is bound to make its mark."

In this letter, Flora describes one of the challenges facing the new settlers. The land where she was living had been surveyed wrong. The boundaries of their land, and that of their neighbors, were incorrect. What are the consequences of this? Observe what the family lost and gained. How would you feel if this happened to you?

Sunday Morning, Apr. 27th, 85

DEAR FOLKS AT HOME

Our garden is growing nicely. We have onions, peas, beans, radishes & cabbage up, but Alas, they are on another mans farm. The survey that we were all located by here has proven to be wrong, and the settlers held a meeting, appointed Sam as chairman, and concluded to have the County surveyor come & survey again, so they appointed Sam to go & see him, he did so, was gone two nights but got the surveyor. He commenced this morning & by the old government stones laid 19 yrs. ago, the survey moves us west & south so that we only own about 40 acres of our original claim. We were awful blue awhile but feel better now. We really get better land (120 acres of bottom land) but it doesn't lay near so pretty, but we have a nicer building place. We lose our house, but get a well 75 ft deep, & a frame house, but of course they will move the house, & Sam will help the man, Mr. Thomas, dig another well, oh but it has caused a racket here, but can't be helped. Nearly everybody lose their houses. Milt Smiths was nearly done & looses it, but gets a better farm.

The Story of Abbie Bright

Abbie Bright was born on her parent's farm in Pennsylvania. She grew up with three brothers and three sisters. By the time she was 12, the nation was in turmoil. With the outbreak of the Civil War, all three of Abbie's brothers enlisted in the Union army. Two were wounded and the third became seriously ill. But, all survived. The four girls spent their time helping their mother with her hospital aid work.

At 15, Abbie enrolled in a nearby college and soon began a teaching career. By the time she was 20 years old, she was making $16 a month for a three-month school year. Two of Abbie's brothers had moved west, one to Indiana and the other to Kansas. Abbie wanted to see the West.

Abbie Bright was born in 1848. She was not a typical young woman, as Abbie chose to travel to Kansas on her own. Yet, her story is similar to many other families that moved west after the Civil War.

Abbie Comes to Kansas

In April 1871, Abbie wrote a letter to her brother Philip. Philip was living on a claim near Clearwater, close to Wichita. The letter informed him that Abbie was coming to Kansas. A week later, without knowing if the letter had ever reached him, Abbie set out for Kansas. Alone and full of adventure, she traveled by train at first.

Arriving in Kansas City at 8:00 a.m., Abbie prepared to change trains. In Topeka, she changed trains again, heading south towards Emporia. It was 6:20 p.m. when she finally reached the end of the line at Cottonwood. Abby gathered her belongings and crossed the track to the hotel in Cottonwood Falls, a mile away. The hotel clerk put her in a room with another young woman who had arrived on an earlier train. The two women were strangers, but they soon became acquainted.

Afraid they would miss the morning stage, the two young women kept the lamp burning all night. Abbie was up in time to enjoy breakfast, her first full meal since leaving Indiana. By 5:30 a.m. there were two stagecoaches waiting for passengers. Each was pulled by a team of four horses. Abbie, and two other women were given the back seat of one of the coaches. It was pretty crowded.

Stagecoach Ride

Soon they were off. Every ten or twelve miles they stopped to change horses. The ride was rough. Every once in a while Abbie's head would bang against the top of the stage. When the ride became exceedingly difficult, the driver would yell out "Make yourself firm." Upon hearing his cry, Abbie would grab on to the side of the stage to keep from getting hurt.

At each stop, passengers departed. From El Dorado to Augusta there was only one large stagecoach pulled by six horses. Fifteen passengers were on board, and Abbie was the only woman. After the stage passed Augusta, they had to cross the Whitewater River. Abbie had never experienced anything like it before. The recent rains had made the river deep, and water came pouring into the coach,

Perhaps Abbie rode in a stagecoach like this one. This sketch is by Kansas artist Albert T. Reid.

The Kansas Journey

soaking her skirt.

Arriving in Wichita

After crossing the river, the passengers rode for a long time, seeing nothing but prairie. Finally, the lights of Wichita appeared in the distance. Abbie got off at the first stop, not knowing if she was in the right place. She wondered how and when she would see her brother. The clerk at the nearby hotel told Abbie her brother's place was still 20 miles away, along the Ninnescah River.

Abbie took a room and slept through the night. The next morning she discovered the letter she had sent her brother sat unopened at the Wichita post office. It was suddenly clear to Abbie that Philip would not be coming for her, since he had no idea she had made the journey.

Abbie decided to take matters into her own hands and hired a young boy to drive her to the Ninnescah River. A pair of mules pulled the open wagon as it crossed more prairie and more streams. There were few houses on the prairie, but Abbie delighted in watching the prairie dogs.

The driver stopped at a supply house to ask about Abbie's brother. The owner told Abbie her brother's claim was across the river and about two miles up. But he warned her the river was too high to cross that day. He suggested she stay with his wife and directed her to small dug out. The man's wife was delighted to see Abbie, for she had not seen another woman to talk to in some weeks.

In the morning, Abbie was excited to see they were taking wagons across the river one at a time. One of the men offered to take Abbie in his wagon. As they reached the other side of the river, the driver took Abbie to a log cabin that served as a frontier store. The driver and the storekeeper convinced Abbie she could not walk the two miles to her brother's place. In an act of kindness, the storekeeper gave Abbie a pony to ride.

Abbie's excitement grew as she pulled herself onto the pony. She had only to ride north a little while and go around a strip of trees. She had come so far. Soon she would see her brother.

How Do We Know This?

We know a great deal about Abbie Bright's experiences in Kansas because she left a detailed diary. Why do you think Abbie kept a diary? Do you think she knew that more than 100 years later, people would be reading about her experiences?

The following excerpt from her diary is dated May 8, 1871. Abbie has decided to stay in Kansas and take a claim in her own name, near that of her brother. She writes about preparing the land to grow a garden. In this excerpt she talks about two ways to prepare the land. What tools are used for each method? How are the settlers obtaining food before their gardens have grown?

Philip . . . has broken some land, and planted corn. He and some men have selected my claim, and when he goes to W[ichita] he will "file on it." Then no one can file on the same land.

He selected a suitable place, and plowed it for a garden, not having a harrow, he hitched the oxen to big brush and dragged it back and forth until it was well raked. . . . I have no hoe yet, but with the help of a stick, I have managed to plant a number of seed. . . . I hope they will grow.

One day when going to the garden, I saw three antelopes and a coyote. There are three deer around, the men see them and I see their tracks in my garden. There is a heard of buffalo twenty miles out. The boys have promised to take me along when they go again. The last time they were out, they brought in a lot of meat, and that is what we are using now. Provision is scarce—potatoes $3, a bushel. The railroad 100 miles away, and the men on claims raising their first crop. Native cattle are very scarce, and the Texas cows are so wild they cannot be milked. Nevertheless, I get along very well and will stay here until I get tired. There is a Scotch man living acrost the river, A Mr. Ross—he was telling me that 'this is such a healthy country, if they want to start a grave yard, they would have to shoot some one.'

They have been breaking sod near here with yoke of oxen. One man drives, one plows—and one followes with an ax—he chops into the upturned sod, and drops corn in the cut, puts his foot on the place, and takes a step and repeats. I will watch that piece, and see what it amounts to. We live on buffalo, fish, bread, molasses and coffee. All have good appetites. I don't drink coffee—but we have good water.

Adapting to the Plains

Western Kansas presented new challenges to settlers. Trees could be found in eastern Kansas, but there were not many in the west. The amount of water found in rivers and streams varied from season to season and year to year. The short grasslands of the west were harder to plow. But settlers on the Plains adapted to the environment.

Hardships

The economic cycles of the nation affected Kansas settlers. During the late 1800s, there were times when the economy went into a *depression* and times when the economy was healthy. These economic cycles affected all Americans, but they were particularly hard on settlers who were trying to start a new life.

Periods of drought made it very difficult to grow crops. Just as devastating as lack of rain were other harsh weather conditions such as blizzards. In some years, grasshoppers were more than a nuisance, invading the plains in large numbers. It seemed like nature was working against the settlers. If they could not successfully grow crops, then they had little chance of economic survival.

Adaptation

Settlers on the plains found new ways of doing things to survive. When wood was not available to build houses, the settlers used earth to create shelter. Some people

During a ten-year period in the late 1800s, American use of barbed wire went from 300 tons to 130,000 tons as settlers moved west.

These settlers are living in a sod house in Lane County. Sod was cut into bricks to build the house. Most sod houses had roofs made of wood and paper covered by a layer of sod.

lived in *dug outs* and others in *sod houses*. The lack of wood in western Kansas also created a shortage of fuel. Some settlers used bundled hay or corncobs for fuel. People soon discovered that dried manure from buffalos and cows would make a good fire. These were called buffalo chips or cow chips.

The lack of trees created another challenge. People needed fences to keep livestock contained. It was too expensive to bring lumber in from the east just to build a fence. The invention of *barbed wire* had a big impact on settlers in western Kansas. Barbed wire was fairly inexpensive, lasted a long time, and was easily connected to fence posts. In much of the state, wooden fence posts were used, but in the central portion of Kansas, limestone fence posts became common.

The lack of surface water also presented a challenge for settlers. To tap into underground water, settlers dug deep wells. They often used windmills to pull the water to the surface. The wells supplied drinking water for both humans and animals. Some windmills also provided water for *irrigation*. People pumped groundwater into a pond. From there, the water went through ditches to reach thirsty crops. Windmill irrigation only worked on small farms.

In southwest Kansas, settlers used the ever-present wind to pull water out of the ground. Beginning in the 1880s, Kansas was home to 50 different companies that manufactured windmills.

This famous photograph was taken near Lakin in 1893. Ada McColl and her brother, Burt, are gathering buffalo chips for fuel. Their mother took this photograph. Burt is wearing a dress, which was common for both young boys and girls.

Gathering Chips

Early settlers had to get over any disgust they might have toward handling buffalo or cow chips. Fuel was a necessity, and without anything else to burn, gathering chips became important work. The newspaper editor of the *Pearlette Call* in Meade County explained it this way on April 15, 1879:

"Most of us burn chips—buffalo chips we call them... These chips make a tolerable fair fire, but of course burn out very rapidly; consequently to keep up a good fire you must be continually poking the chips in and taking the ashes out. Still we feel very thankful for even this fuel.

It was comical to see how gingerly our wives handled these chips at first. They commenced by picking them up between two sticks, or with a poker. Soon they used a rag, and then a corner of their apron. Finally, growing hardened, a wash after handling them was sufficient. And now? Now it is out of the bread, into the chips and back again—and not even a dust of the hands!"

Built in the 1880, the John Summers farm was part of the colony of Dunlap in Morris County. The Tennessee Real Estate and Homestead Association founded the town. Benjamin "Pap" Singleton was the founder of the association.

Benjamin "Pap" Singleton was an ex-slave from Tennessee who promoted migration to Kansas. He distributed posters throughout the South speaking of the virtues of Kansas. "Pap" Singleton helped many African Americans leave the South, and he also made money as a promoter and land speculator.

African American Migration to Kansas

When African Americans were free from slavery, they still faced discrimination and oppression. Many southern whites resented the *emancipation* of the African Americans. This sometimes led to violence against blacks. In the South, many black farmers rented farmland to make a living by growing cotton. As tenant farmers, they paid rent by giving the landowner half of their crops. The percentage of crops owed to the landowner was fixed. It did not change with the fluctuating prices of cotton. With this type of agricultural system it was very easy to go into debt. Although it was terribly difficult to get ahead, some African Americans managed to do so. After more than a decade of freedom, however, very few southern blacks owned land.

Many African Americans found economic, political, and social reasons to leave the South. Kansas came to symbolize the Promised Land. The struggle against slavery in the state, the symbolism of John Brown, and the possibility of land ownership made Kansas an attractive place for southern African Americans. So, "Ho for Kansas!" became the cry, despite the fact that things were not perfect in Kansas either.

African American Settlements

African Americans planned several migrations to Kansas. Black settlements were established in Cherokee, Graham, Hodgeman, and Morris Counties. The best known of these communities was Nicodemus in western Kansas.

Like many towns in Kansas, Nicodemus was developed through land speculation. This meant that undeveloped land was purchased, and a town site was planned before anyone lived there. The city lots, or parcels of land, were sold to people recruited to come there. In order to make money, the town speculators had to advertise for residents.

Freed slaves from Kentucky settled Nicodemus. The town was named for a slave who was believed to have purchased his own freedom. The first year in Nicodemus was difficult. The settlers came prepared to farm, bringing with them teams of horses and farm equipment. The promoters, however, were concerned with selling the land, not with timing, and the first settlers were brought to Kansas too late in the year to plant crops.

The Kansas Journey

This photograph of Nicodemus was taken in the 1890s.

The distance between Nicodemus and the more populated areas of the state also created problems. Many settlers wanted to find work, but they were too far away from cities to do so. Another challenge was the physical environment of western Kansas. The settlers were used to the forests of Kentucky and found the plains to be less than welcoming.

Some of the settlers returned to the South. But those who stayed managed to survive. During the first harsh winter, some of the settlers surrounding Nicodemus provided help. Eventually, Nicodemus proved to be a successful settlement. For a time, it was one of the largest communities in northwest Kansas.

Benjamin "Pap" Singleton
1809-1892

Kansas PORTRAIT

Benjamin "Pap" Singleton was born into slavery in Nashville, Tennessee. He became a skilled carpenter. Escaping slavery several times, he eventually settled in Michigan. While living in Detroit, he helped other escaped slaves live in secret in a boarding house he managed.

After the Civil War, Singleton returned to Tennessee with the idea of helping African Americans improve their economic and social status. He wanted to buy land in Tennessee and reserve it for black farmers. This plan failed when Singleton could not get the land for a fair price. He turned his attention to Kansas.

In Kansas, "Pap" Singleton became a land speculator and promoter. He encouraged hundreds of African Americans from Tennessee and Kentucky to move here. Topeka saw so many new settlers from the South that a section of town became known as "Tennessee Town." Within "Tennessee Town," Singleton organized the United Colored Links. The purpose of the group was to encourage African Americans to own their own industries and factories. Singleton never gained enough capital to make this happen.

When conditions for African Americans did not change quickly enough for Singleton, he began encouraging blacks to leave the country. He first promoted the island of Cyprus, as a good place to immigrate and then later encouraged African Americans to return to Africa. Although not successful in these later ventures, Benjamin "Pap" Singleton left his mark on Kansas.

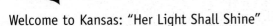

Welcome to Kansas: "Her Light Shall Shine"

Exodusters

A second wave of African Americans came to Kansas from the Deep South. They were called Exodusters, after the Bible story of the exodus from Egypt. Unlike the first wave of black settlers, Exodusters were generally poor. They had heard about African Americans coming to Kansas, and they wanted to come too.

Exodusters came by the thousands, often traveling by steamboat up the Mississippi and Missouri Rivers. Unprepared for the journey, many became sick and some died before reaching Kansas. Upon reaching Wyandotte, the Exodusters stepped off the boats onto the riverbanks of Kansas. At one point the city of Wyandotte decided it could not take in more poor people, so the city paid to move some of the settlers upstream to Atchison.

The Exodusters had no place to go and were stranded in the cities along the Missouri River. The communities along the river were overwhelmed and did not know what to do. Governor John St. John was sympathetic to the Exodusters and formed the Freemen's Relief Organization. Eventually, many of the Exodusters were moved to cities around the state where they could find work.

People from all over the country sent money to help the Exodusters. The well-known women's suffrage advocate Susan B. Anthony sent a letter and a contribution.

The Kansas Journey

Foreign Immigrants Come to Kansas

In the 25 years following the Civil War, Kansas saw its population increase by more than a million people. Most new Kansans were Americans migrating from eastern states. But Kansas also attracted immigrants from overseas. German and English immigrants were the largest of the foreign-born population.

Immigrants left their homelands because something "pushed" them away. While at the same time something was "pulling" them to Kansas. All immigrants experience this "push/pull" factor. But the reasons involved are as different as the individuals and groups who made their home in Kansas.

The state, as well as the railroads, actively recruited immigrants to come here. The Kansas State Bureau of Immigration published pamphlets and other materials promoting settlement opportunities in the state. Although information was provided to all potential immigrants, the Bureau targeted those from England, Germany, and Scandinavia.

The railroad advertised special sleeping cars for people migrating west. This brochure includes the following description: "These cars are built by the Company, and arranged with special reference to the comfort and convenience of families moving from east to the West, with which class of travel they have become especially popular. The general plan of the Emigrant Sleeping Car is similar to that of the first-class sleeping car."

Foreign-Born Population in Kansas

	Czechs	English	Germans	Irish	Mexicans	Russians	Scots	Slavic	Swedes	Welsh
1860	—	1,400	4,318	3,888	—	13	377	—	122	163
1870	105	6,228	12,775	11,009	—	56	1,598	—	4,953	1,088
1880	2,468	14,183	28,034	14,993	—	8,032	3,788	—	11,207	2,088
1890	3,022	18,086	46,423	15,870	68	9,801	5,546	394	17,096	2,488

German Settlers

Germans were the largest European group who settled in Kansas. Not all German immigrants came directly from Germany. They also came from Russia, Switzerland, Austria, and even other parts of the United States. Germans settled in all counties in Kansas, but their influence is particularly seen in the central portion of the state. The German language was so common in Kansas that the state has had more than 60 newspapers published in the language.

Like other immigrants, Germans had many reasons for settling in Kansas. Some families came for economic reasons; others came for political or religious reasons. The earliest German immigrants to Kansas were from Hanover in northern Germany. They were tired of war and were not happy with the leader of their country. Many chose Kansas because it offered economic opportunities. Germans were particularly proud of their success in farming. But they also helped build the railroads and start new businesses.

Many German immigrants wrote letters back to the their families in Europe. They told about the opportunities in this new land. News from Kansas often inspired other people to emigrate. This is called *chain migration*.

Germans From Russia

Catherine the Great was a German who married into the Russian royal family. Concerned with developing Russia's economy, she wanted to see the land along the Volga River cultivated. She encouraged German farmers to move to Russia by promising free land, religious tolerance, and exemption from taxes and military service.

By the time Kansas became a state, more than 250,000 Germans were living in more than 100 villages along the Volga River. Over time they lost the special privileges granted to them by Catherine the Great. The Germans became subject to the military *draft* and lost their right to keep their German-language schools.

Out of frustration, many Germans in Russia began to look for a new home. At the same time, American railroad companies were encouraging settlement in Kansas. Mennonite, Lutheran, and Catholic German Russians immigrated to Kansas. They were attracted to Kansas for many of the same reasons their ancestors had been drawn to Russia. Land was available to be farmed, and there was freedom of religion. The Kansas Constitution exempted those with pacifistic beliefs from serving in the state militia. Many of the Germans from Russia, especially the Mennonites, were *pacifists*.

The plains of Russia are similar in geography to the Great Plains region of the United States. This gave Germans from Russia an advantage in farming. Their knowledge of farming methods helped make Kansas a productive wheat-growing state.

This Mennonite family is living in Marion County. Large numbers of Mennonites were recruited by the Atchison, Topeka & Santa Fe Railroad. In Kansas, Mennonites made their homes along the Santa Fe lines.

German immigrants formed the gymnastics team of the Topeka Turn Verein. In 1908 the team competed in Frankfurt, Germany, with other turnverein teams from around the world.

The Topeka Turn Verein

Germans brought many of their traditions. The establishment of turnverein clubs was one such tradition. Turnverein is a German word meaning gymnastics club. These clubs, which served as both social and athletic clubs, brought together Germans of all ages.

The Topeka Turn Verein was established in the early days of the town's development. The club established its residence at Turner Hall. The hall housed Topeka's best bowling alley and a well-equipped gymnasium. Books in both English and German filled a reading room. The club employed professional athletic coaches and musical directors. Its members participated in gymnastics and other athletic competitions. Club members also valued choral and instrumental music.

The Topeka Turn Verein played an important role in the social and economic lives of its members. The club provided financial assistance to the sick and needy. It also provided money for funerals. The club supported the Topeka community, giving aid to outside charities such as the Topeka Orphan's Home.

The first Turner Hall in Topeka was on the second floor of a building in downtown Topeka. The hall housed the activities of the Topeka Turn Verein. Later the club had its own building with Willkommen (meaning welcome in German) written over the door.

Welcome to Kansas: "Her Light Shall Shine"

Settlers from the British Isles

The Industrial Age in Great Britain had forever changed the British landscape. Areas devoted to agriculture gave way to more and more industrial cities. The cities were becoming overcrowded. It was customary in Britain for children to follow in the footsteps of their parents. For this reason, young men often went into the same trade or work as their father. This helped reinforce a very strong *class system*. This meant that opportunities for advancement were limited.

Many British citizens heard stories about Kansas. One immigrant wrote, "I heard a lecture in England telling about the wonderful Republican river and the steam boats that docked at Wakefield—and about the fish, prairie chickens, quail, buffalo, deer, and wild fruits— grapes so large you had to open your mouth to get one in."

The Kansas Pacific Railroad took an active role in recruiting British immigrants to Kansas. The railroad had a special relationship with the Kansas Land and Emigration Company in London. The land company bought land from the railroad and sold it to British immigrants. This type of promotion helped found the British settlement of Wakefield in Clay County. Most of the residents of Wakefield immigrated to Kansas as families. However, a group of orphaned young men was sent from London to Wakefield to make a fresh start.

Runnymede

An unusual British settlement survived for five years in Harper County. Runnymede was the idea of an Irishman named F.J.S. Turnly. For a $500 fee, he offered to teach the sons of the British upper class how to farm. The young men who came to Runnymede came with a good deal of money and very little interest in agriculture. Instead of working, they staged horse races and hunted foxes, living in the style they were accustomed to in England. After a short time, the British families got fed up with the partying of their sons and brought them back to England.

The French Settlement of Silkville

Ernest de Boissiere was an upper class Frenchman who, despite his wealth, believed in the equality of all men. After Napoleon came to power in France, de Boissiere fled to America. He arrived first in New Orleans, where he gained wealth operating a line of merchant ships. Still believing in the equality of all human

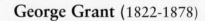

Kansas PORTRAIT

George Grant (1822-1878)

George Grant was a Scottish silk merchant who immigrated to Kansas in 1872. He came with the knowledge that there was growing demand for beef in Britain. Grant hoped to make a profit by recruiting others to raise sheep and cattle in western Kansas. To follow this dream, he bought land in Ellis County from the Kansas Pacific Railroad.

In Ellis County, he founded the town of Victoria, named after the Queen of England. He convinced the railroad to give him special privileges. Grant then went about trying to convince both Englishmen and Americans to buy into his vision. He was only moderately successful at finding investors. But he was very successful at breeding both sheep and cattle.

George Grant died deeply in debt six years after he arrived in Kansas. Perhaps his greatest success was gaining publicity for himself and his vision of Kansas as a major cattle producer. Some of the British settlers Grant recruited to Kansas stayed. Shortly after Grant's death, Germans from Russia successfully settled Victoria.

Ernest de Boissiere brought silk production to Kansas. The number of French immigrants living and working in Silkville varied over time. Estimates range from 40 individuals to two families. This photograph was taken at Silkville at Christmas. De Boissiere is the man with the long, white beard.

beings, he donated a substantial sum of money to an orphanage for African American children. This was not popular among his southern white neighbors.

De Boissiere once again fled his home. Discouraged by the **bigotry** he had encountered, he looked for a place that he believed would be more tolerant of his views. De Boissiere came to Kansas in 1869 and purchased land in Franklin County. He wanted to build a self-sufficient community. Organizing the Prairie Home Association, he hoped to establish a **communal** settlement. For $200, a person could buy a membership in the Prairie Home Association. All members would live together and share the work.

The business of the cooperative became the production of silk. De Boissiere planted mulberry trees and imported silk worms from France and Japan. He helped skilled workers from France immigrate to Kansas. The community became known as Silkville. The workers produced up to 300 yards of silk fabric a day. The silk was of high quality. But eventually the labor costs for the silk became too expensive to compete in the world marketplace.

Swedish Immigrants

Soon after Kansas became a state, people in Sweden began suffering from **famine**. Most Swedes were farmers. The Swedish countryside had become overpopulated. To get more food, forests were cleared and replaced with crops. The soil was poor, and the Swedish farmers became dependent on growing potatoes.

In the late 1860s, extreme weather ruined many of the crops in Sweden. First came the rains, which rotted the potato crops in the fields. Next came drought and then famine. Without enough food to eat, Swedes began immigrating in large numbers to the United States.

In Kansas, Swedes became the third largest immigrant group. Many Swedes came with the encouragement of Swedish land companies. The First Swedish Agricultural Company of McPherson County was organized in Chicago. To encourage Swedish settlement, the Agricultural Company bought 13,000 acres of land from the Kansas Pacific Railroad. In letters to their families, Swedes told about *framtidslander*, meaning the land of the future.

A group of nearly 100 Swedish immigrants settled the town of Lindsborg. These immigrants had another reason for coming to Kansas— religious freedom. The Lutheran church in Sweden had discouraged their beliefs. They wanted to practice a Lutheran faith that they saw as pure. They felt Kansas was the place to do just that and at the same time find economic opportunities.

Immigrants from Denmark and Norway came to Kansas, but the largest group of Scandinavians to settle here were the Swedes. Swedes in Kansas have continued to practice their traditions. The community of Lindsborg celebrates its Swedish heritage through crafts, parades, and festivals.

Marijana Grisnik grew up in Strawberry Hill in Kansas City. She paints the traditions of her Croatian neighborhood. On the Hill, family and friends gather to make large amounts of food for weddings.

Immigration Continues to Kansas

Celebrating Tet, or Vietnamese New Year, is important to Vietnamese immigrants in Kansas. Dragon Dancers perform, while onlookers "feed" money to the dragon for good luck.

Many other groups have immigrated to Kansas. Kansas became home to many Bohemians from what was to become Czechoslovakia. The Bohemian settlers usually did not come directly from Europe. Instead, they settled in larger cities in the eastern United States before moving to Kansas.

Families from Italy settled in southeastern Kansas to work in the coal mines. The area became known as "little Balkans" because of the immigrants from southeastern Europe. Croatians, Serbians, and Slovenians came to Kansas City to work in the meat-packing industry.

Mexican immigrants came to Kansas to escape poverty and the revolution in Mexico. They arrived after much of the land was already settled. They were looking for jobs, and many found work with the railroad. Railroad companies recruited Mexican men to maintain the railroad lines throughout Kansas. They often returned to visit their families in Mexico, keeping their ties to the homeland. Eventually, many of the Mexican railroad workers brought their families to live in Kansas.

Mexican immigrants also came to Kansas to work in agriculture. In the late 1900s, they came to work in the meat-packing plants. The packing plants recruited Mexican workers, like the railroad had earlier in the century.

By the end of the 20th century, the meat-packing industry also was recruiting immigrants from Southeast Asia. With the political turmoil in the 1970s in Vietnam, Cambodia, and Laos, many Southeast Asians immigrated to America. In the early 1980s, the world's largest beef-packing plant opened near Garden City. The work attracted large numbers of Southeast Asians.

Immigrants from the Middle East also came to Kansas. In the early 1900s, Lebanese immigrants came to southern Kansas. Many became peddlers, making a living selling needles, lace, and other goods door-to-door. Wichita became the center of this activity, providing wholesale goods for salesmen who traveled between farms. Eventually, many Lebanese families came to own grocery or other retail stores.

The Kansas population continues to change. Today, immigrants from all over the United States and the world make Kansas their home.

The Kansas Journey

Chapter 6 Review

What Do You Remember?

1. How did the Homestead Act encourage settlement in Kansas?
2. Why is surveying the land important to establishing land ownership?
3. Where did most of the new settlers to Kansas come from?
4. According to the story about Abbie Bright, what kind of transportation was available for settlers coming to Kansas?
5. The western portion of Kansas has few trees. What were the consequences of this for new settlers? Name one way the settlers adapted.
6. What did settlers on the plains use for fuel?
7. What impact did the invention of barbed wire make on the settlement of the west?
8. What is the purpose of windmills on the plains?
9. What are some of the reasons African Americans left the South after the Civil War?
10. Why did the Exodusters at first have a more difficult time in Kansas than the first wave of African American settlers?
11. Name some of the reasons foreign-born settlers were "pushed" away from their homelands.
12. What was the "pull" that brought new settlers to Kansas?
13. What immigrant group came to Kansas in the largest numbers?
14. How did the class system in England affect English immigration to Kansas?
15. Why did silk production in Silkville eventually decline?
16. What caused Swedish immigrants to leave their homeland?
17. Name at least three additional immigrant groups who have settled in Kansas.

Activities

1. Chart or graph the population of Kansas from 1860 to the present. Research the state's population through the U.S. census records. Illustrate the period of greatest population growth. Based on recent population statistics, can you make a prediction of where the Kansas population might be in 10, 30, and 50 years? Illustrate what factors lead to population growth or decline.
2. Review the story of Abbie Bright coming to Kansas. Place the locations in her story on a map of Kansas. Now trace the route Abbie took through Kansas to reach her brother's homestead.
3. Interview someone in your community who has immigrated to Kansas. Ask them what "pushed" them away from their homeland, and what "pulled" them to Kansas.

Think About It!

1. Settlers on the plains had to adapt to a harsh physical environment. Think about your needs and wants. Prioritize your needs. What do you need to survive? What if your top two needs could not be met in the way you are used to? Are there ways you could adapt? If you could not adapt, what would happen?

Railroads, Cattle, and Agriculture

Timeline of Events

1859
The Elwood and Marysville Railroad becomes the first railroad to begin construction in Kansas.

1862
President Lincoln signs the Pacific Railroad Act.

1860   1862   1864   1866   1868

1860
The first train to enter Kansas crosses the Missouri River by boat.

WORDS TO UNDERSTAND
depot
dispatch
incentive
monopoly
obsolete
plat
quarantine
residential
retail
subsidy
subsistence
surplus
yield

Crossing rivers could be difficult for railroads. In the 1860s, the Leavenworth, Lawrence & Galveston Railroad built a bridge across the Kansas River near Lawrence. What is different about this bridge compared to bridges we see today?

1867-1885
Cowboys drive Texas cattle across our state.

| 1872 | 1874 | 1876 | 1878 | 1880 | 1882 | 1884 | 1886 |

1872
Farmers in Hiawatha organize the first Grange in Kansas.

1876
The first Harvey House Restaurant opens in Topeka.

As towns sprang up across Kansas, so did businesses. The J. Muellers Shop was in Ellsworth in the 1870s. Boot shops appeared in cowtowns across the state to provide high quality handmade boots for cowboys.

Growing the Kansas Economy

As the population of Kansas grew, so did the economy of the state. A strong economy is based on having a population that is ready and able to buy the goods and services produced. A successful economy also requires a skilled and trained work force.

As more and more settlers moved to Kansas, towns and cities grew at a rapid pace. Large industries, such as the railroad, prospered. Small businesses brought life to communities, and ranching and farming became staples of the Kansas economy.

The Cattle Industry Begins

At one time, beef had to be served fresh or preserved by drying. Today, we process beef close to where cattle are raised, and we can ship frozen meat to all parts of the world. At the time of the Civil War, cattle had to be moved closer to where people lived, so that meat could be sold fresh.

After the Civil War, there was a shortage of beef in the eastern United States. But demand was high. During the war, cattle in Texas were allowed to run wild because eastern markets were unavailable to Texas cattlemen. This resulted in dramatic increases in the number of cattle in Texas. It is estimated that the herds grew to almost 5,000,000.

Soldiers returning home to Texas after the Civil War found the Texas economy in decline. There were few jobs available. It became profitable for veterans to round up the wild cattle, and even more profitable to take the cattle east. In Texas, a longhorn cow was worth $4. In the East, the price was $40 to $50.

Getting the cattle to eastern markets was a challenge. There were no railroads in Texas that could take the cattle east. But cattle could be herded north to the railroad lines in Kansas. This resulted in what became known as cattle drives. The distance traveled on cattle drives averaged 750 miles, and most drives lasted more than 30 or 40 days.

Between 1867 and 1885, people drove cattle between Texas and Kansas. This period in history created the myth of the American cowboy.

Cattle Trails and Railroad Lines

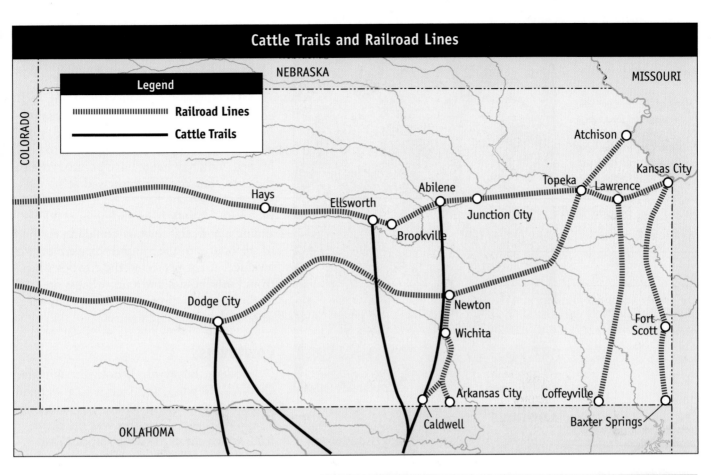

Legend

‖‖‖‖‖‖‖‖‖‖ Railroad Lines
———— Cattle Trails

COLORADO

NEBRASKA

MISSOURI

Atchison

Topeka   Lawrence   Kansas City

Hays

Abilene

Ellsworth   Junction City

Brookville

Dodge City

Newton

Wichita

Fort Scott

Arkansas City   Coffeyville

Caldwell   Baxter Springs

OKLAHOMA

The Chisholm Trail

The cattle drives from Texas to Kansas generally followed Indian trading routes or pioneer trails. It was important that a route offer grass for the cattle to eat and plenty of water. The Chisholm Trail was the most famous route. It was named for Jesse Chisholm, who marked portions of the original trail. The trail went from San Antonio, Texas, to Abilene, Kansas. It became a major transportation route for cattle delivered for shipment on the Kansas Pacific Railroad.

Abbie Bright lived near the Chisholm Trail. On Sunday, June 4, 1871, she wrote in her diary:

The heavy rains raised the river, and a heard of cattle in crossing, stampeded, and 15 or 20 were drownded. Every week 7 to 10 thousands of Texas cattle are driven north over the trail. If the cattle stampede, and don't want to cross the river, the hearders yell and fire off their revolvers.

Sometimes we hear them here, and it sounds —as I suppose a battle does. It is the cattle that keep the trail worn smooth.

"The Old Chisholm Trail"

"The Old Chisholm Trail" is a popular cowboy folksong. There are so many stanzas that some people joke that the song is as long as the trail itself. Here are a few stanzas. What does the song say about the work on the trail?

Oh come along, boys, and listen to my tale,
I'll tell you all my troubles on the ol' Chis'm trail.

Chorus:
Come a-ti yi youpy youpy ya youpy ya,
Come a-ti yi youpy youpy yay.

I'm up in the mornin' afore daylight,
An' afore I sleep the moon shines bright.

It's bacon and beans most every day,
I'd as soon be eatin' prairie hay.

I woke up one mornin' on the Chisholm trail,
'With a rope in my hand and a cow by the tail.

Railroads, Cattle, and Agriculture

Many of the cowboys who worked the long cattle drives were African American and Mexican. The work was hard, but the wages were good.

This circular was used to attract cattlemen to Wichita. During the mid-1870s, Wichita was in competition with Ellsworth and Dodge City for the cattle trade.

Cowboys

Most cattle were driven north under a contractual agreement. A team of cowboys was promised a specific amount of money to get the cattle to the railroad. Cowboys, who were usually in their early 20s, made a good wage of $24 to $40 a month. The trail boss, the man in charge, made more money, but he was held responsible for lost cattle.

It took about eleven men to handle a herd of 3,000 cows. In addition to the trail boss, there were eight men to work the cattle, one man to cook, and still

another to be in charge of the horses. The men needed about 60 horses on the trail. To prevent horses from becoming overworked, cowboys continually changed horses.

Cowboys required special clothing and equipment. A good saddle was a necessity because a cowboy spent 18 hours a day on a horse. A good pair of boots was also needed. Cowboy boots have pointed toes so they can slide easily into the saddle's stirrups. They also have a high heel to keep the cowboy's foot from sliding out. While roping a cow, the cowboy could dig the heel of the boot into the ground to give him leverage. A hat protected the cowboy's head from both the sun and rain. Chaps, or leather leggings, protected the cowboy's legs as he rode through tall brush.

Cowtowns

Abilene, Ellsworth, Brookville, Wichita, Caldwell, Newton, and Dodge City were all cowtowns. Cowtowns had to be located on a railroad line because this was the point from which the cattle were shipped east.

All of the Kansas cowtowns courted the cattle trade. Each town wanted to prove it was the best site for selling and shipping cattle. After all, there was money to be made. Cowboys were generally paid at the end of the trail, so that was usually where they spent most of their money. Local businessmen also made money by buying and selling cattle. It was an important marketplace and a profitable business.

Not everyone in town supported the cattle trade. Local ranchers and farmers usually led the opposition. Sometimes the Texas cattle destroyed local crops. Other

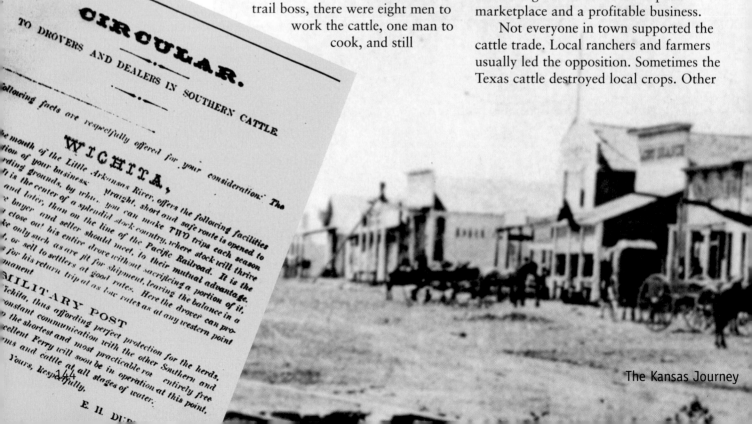

times, the Texas cattle brought diseases that infected the local cattle. The opposition often led to disagreements between the people who lived in the city and those in the surrounding rural areas. The cattle trade made money for the townspeople, but it sometimes caused a loss of money for the farmers and ranchers.

What Ended the Cattle Drives?

Kansas eventually made laws that kept the cattle drives out of the state. Texas longhorn cattle carried a disease called Texas Fever. Settlers like Abbie Bright did not know what caused the disease, but they knew that the Texas cattle destroyed the Kansas herds. On September 3, 1871, Abbie wrote what she and her neighbors believed to be the cause:

Thousands and thousands of Texas cattle, were driven north this Summer. Some have been allowed to graze on this side of the river before crossing. Texas cattle generate - I think that is the word - in their feet during the long trip, a substance that poisens the grass - This does not hurt them - but if native cattle eat that grass it poisens them and they die of what is called Texas fever.

Today, we know that cattle ticks from southwest Texas caused Texas Fever. When Kansas cattle came in contact with the ticks, many of the Kansas cattle died. While Kansas was still a territory, the legislature passed a law prohibiting infected cattle from entering the state. The law was later amended to restrict all Texas cattle to land west of McPherson. This marked a

quarantine line. It became known as the "dead" line.

As settlers moved west to claim land across Kansas, they fenced in their farms to keep the cattle out. The cattle trails and the settlers had different uses for the same land, and it was impossible for them to share the land. The farmers and ranchers who lived in Kansas had more power with the state legislature. Gradually the state moved the "dead" line to the southwest border of the state

It was the railroads themselves that finally ended the cattle drives. Railroads began to extend their lines into Texas, providing rail lines to locations where the cattle were raised.

By the 1890s, the cattle drives to Kansas had ended. This photograph shows cowboys around the chuck wagon in Texas. Texas cowboys could now ship cattle from places closer to home.

Cowtowns like Dodge City, seen here in 1878, were the points at which cattle were loaded onto railroad cars for the trip east.

Railroads, Cattle, and Agriculture

The Railroad

The railroad industry had an enormous impact on the settlement of the West. In our state, the interest in railroads was further fueled by the national desire to build a transcontinental railroad connecting the East and West Coasts. The first railroad reached the Kansas border during the territorial period.

The Elwood and Marysville Railroad was the first company to actually lay tracks in our state. It planned to extend the railroad all the way to the Rocky Mountains. The first engine to arrive in Kansas was the *Albany*. It was ferried across the Missouri River to Elwood. As other railroad cars followed, the excitement grew. When the engine was attached to the cars, people cheered. Unfortunately, the *Albany* could only travel five miles to the nearby town of Wathena. The dream of extending the Elwood and Marysville Railroad farther west never happened.

Nevertheless, the *Albany* showed that railroads could work, and it ignited railroad fever in Kansas.

Railroad Land Grants

People had long debated the role of the federal government in encouraging the development of roads, canals, and railroads. This debate continued when the U.S. government decided it wanted a transcontinental railroad. It had to find a way to stimulate private industry to build one. Railroad companies were not in the business of taking on unprofitable projects. To promote the expansion of the railroad, the federal government passed the Pacific Railroad Act that provided land grants to railroads.

The government gave public lands to railroad companies in exchange for building tracks in specific locations. As railroads expanded into new territory, people believed that settlers would follow. Then the value of land in that area would increase. The land

The federal government gave more than 4 million acres of Kansas directly to two railroads. The Kansas Pacific received 3,925,791 acres, and the Union Pacific Central Branch was granted 223,141 acres. The federal government also gave land to the state of Kansas to grant to railroads. More than 4 million additional acres were given away in this manner.

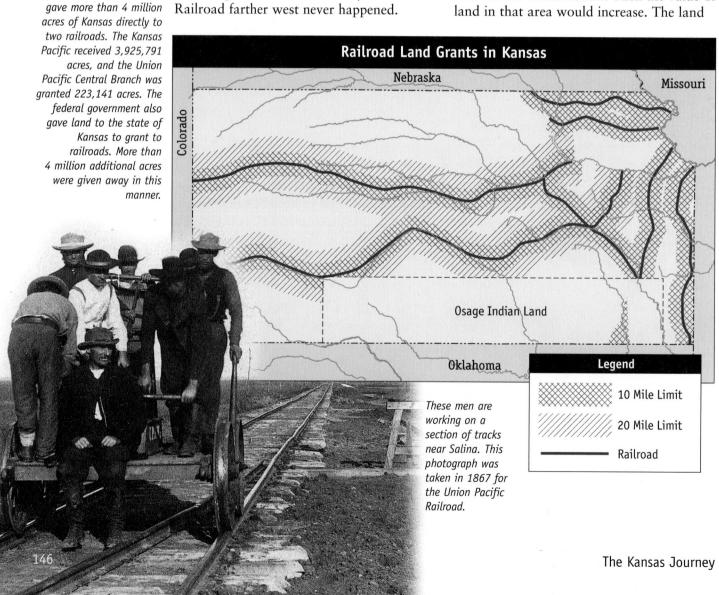

Railroad Land Grants in Kansas

Nebraska

Missouri

Colorado

Osage Indian Land

Oklahoma

Legend

⬚⬚⬚ 10 Mile Limit

/// 20 Mile Limit

—— Railroad

These men are working on a section of tracks near Salina. This photograph was taken in 1867 for the Union Pacific Railroad.

could then be sold, and the railroad company would profit. The federal government assumed any money made by the railroad would help finance further expansion of the tracks.

The U.S. government surveyed the public lands and divided them into one-mile square sections. The land grants gave the railroads every other section. The federal government kept the other sections. These public lands could then be used for homesteading or sold for a profit. Those who supported the land grants believed that everyone would win.

The program of land grants to railroads remained controversial. Since most railroads had a *monopoly* in a specific region, they would eventually make a profit shipping goods to and from communities. Critics of the land grant program felt that the railroads were receiving too much of a *subsidy*. Between 1850 and 1870, 7 percent of the land in the United States was given to 80 railroads. Most of this land was in the west. In Kansas, railroad companies were given one-sixth of the land in our state.

What do you think?

The railroad land grants are not the only time the federal government has provided subsidies to private businesses. Sometimes subsidies are provided through grants or special tax breaks. Oil companies, airlines, real estate developers, and even farmers have received financial help from the federal government.

Some people feel that providing *incentives* to businesses helps us all. Can you think of ways that this might be true? Critics of government incentives for businesses feel that we are giving financial advantages to only a few and that they do not provide enough benefits for the general population. What do you think? Should government provide incentives for businesses?

Kansas PORTRAIT

Cyrus K. Holliday

1826-1900

Cyrus K. Holliday was one of Kansas' most prominent businessmen. Educated as a lawyer, he soon became interested in the railroad. In his home state of Pennsylvania, he helped build a short railroad line and made $20,000. The money helped establish him in Kansas.

Holliday came to Kansas Territory and was active in the free-state cause. As president of the town company that laid out Topeka, Cyrus K. Holliday became a founding father of the capital city. He dreamed of developing a railroad along the old Santa Fe Trail. He wanted to extend the railroad all the way to the Pacific Ocean.

As he tried to interest others in this venture, he was rejected. Finally, he secured a charter for his railroad from the Kansas legislature. He raised money through the purchasing and selling of Potawatomi lands. Eventually, Cyrus K. Holliday had enough money to build the first 20 miles of track from Topeka to Carbondale. His dream was realized when the Atchison, Topeka & Santa Fe Railroad reached the Pacific Ocean.

In addition to being the director of the Atchison, Topeka & Santa Fe Railroad, Holliday also served in the Kansas Senate. His other business ventures included the Excelsior Coke and Gas Company and the Merchants National Bank of Topeka.

"The Best Thing in the West": Selling Railroad Land

The Atchison, Topeka & Santa Fe Railroad received 2,944,788 acres in land grants. In exchange, the company would build a railroad across Kansas to the Colorado border. The company received the grant in 1864, and the railroad line was completed eight years later.

Most of the Atchison, Topeka & Santa Fe lands available for sale to the public were along the line from Emporia to Dodge City. Railroad lands were generally more expensive than lands purchased directly from the government. But railroad lands were situated near railroad lines, making the shipping and receiving of goods convenient. The railroads also offered credit and easy payments for new settlers. This made railroad lands attractive to those moving west.

Like other railroads, the Atchison, Topeka & Santa Fe actively competed for business. It advertised the sale of its lands, as well as the convenience and value of its shipping and transportation services.

This poster to the right was developed in 1874 with the purpose of selling railroad lands in southwest Kansas. Study the poster, and answer the following questions:

1. What clues show you who the poster is trying to attract?
2. Using clues from the pictures, why is the prairie a better place to start a farm than the woodlands?
3. What resources does the poster claim are available in southwestern Kansas?
4. According to the poster, how easy is it to grow trees in Kansas? Is the example given in southwestern Kansas?
5. What crops can be grown in southwest Kansas according to the poster?
6. Do you feel this poster is being truthful about the land in southwestern Kansas?
7. If you wanted to move west in the 1870s, what in this poster would attract you? Why or why not?
8. Create a poster to sell land in your community today. Who would be the audience for your poster? What attributes of your community could you sell in a poster? Might you exaggerate the truth to get people to move to your town?

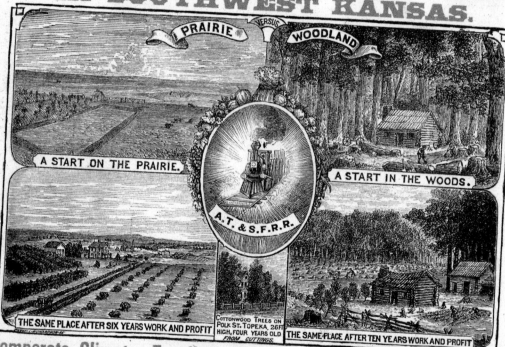

IF YOU WANT A FARM OR HOME

"THE BEST THING IN THE WEST"
IS THE

Atchison, Topeka & Santa Fe
RAILROAD
LANDS
IN SOUTHWEST KANSAS.

PRAIRIE *versus* WOODLAND

A START ON THE PRAIRIE.

A. T. & S. F. R. R.

A START IN THE WOODS.

THE SAME PLACE AFTER SIX YEARS WORK AND PROFIT

COTTONWOOD TREES ON POLK ST. TOPEKA. 26 FT HIGH, FOUR YEARS OLD *FROM CUTTINGS*.

THE SAME PLACE AFTER TEN YEARS WORK AND PROFIT

Temperate Climate, Excellent Health, Pure and Abundant Water.

GOOD SOIL FOR WHEAT, CORN AND FRUIT.

The Best Stock Country in the World.

Or to

For Full Information apply to

_____ *Agent,*

_____

LAND COMMISSIONER,
A. T. & S. F. R. R., Topeka, Kas.

Auskunft ertheilt, C. B. Schmidt, Deutscher Gen'l Agt., Topeka, Kan.

Knight & Leonard, Printers, Chicago.

With the influence of the railroad, small shops like this meat market in Colby were the norm, rather than larger general stores. This photograph is from the 1890s.

Railroads and Town Development

The railroads had a distinct impact on town development in Kansas, especially in the central and western part of the state. The railroads promoted settlement, and they also worked to bring businesses to Kansas. Farmers needed towns where they could do business, and businesses needed people to buy their goods and services. The railroads worked to stimulate this interaction along their lines.

The growth of towns along the rail lines ultimately resulted in profits for the railroad. The closer people lived to a railroad line, the more goods and services they had available to them. Having a railroad station was important to a town's development. The railroad companies controlled where those stations were placed and this gave railroad towns an advantage. By placing stations every seven to ten miles, the railroads discouraged other town promoters.

Town Site Associations

From the earliest days of settlement in Kansas, town site associations were formed. It was the responsibility of the town site association to survey the lands and *plat* the selected town site. To pay for this and other town developments the association sold shares in the town site. Some people who purchased these shares were speculators trying to turn a profit. Sometimes investors bought shares in towns that never developed.

The railroads often hired private town site associations to promote and sell a railroad town. But the relationship between the railroads and the town site associations was often close. In many cases the railroad, or its owners, invested money in the private town site association.

Planning a Town

Once towns were surveyed and platted, the lots needed to be sold. Creating the business section of a town was important. The customary approach to

retail establishments had been the general store. The general store sold a variety of items to the settlers from a single place. It was more profitable for the town site associations and the railroad to encourage several smaller specialized stores, all placed in a central location. One store sold shoes, another hardware, and still another candy. This way more business lots could be sold.

The way towns were platted by the railroad and their town site associations was fairly consistent. Lots for houses were generally 50 feet wide, and *residential* streets were 60 feet wide. Business lots were only 25 feet wide. This encouraged merchants to establish specialty stores. The main streets in a town were 80 to 100 feet wide. The intersection of two such streets was the center of the business district.

The smaller business lots meant that merchants built small narrow buildings. Because most business buildings were the same size and shape, it allowed the retail function of the space to change. If a boot maker went out of business or wanted to move to a new town, he could sell his building to someone in another line of business. The boot shop could become a candy shop. Small buildings were also easier to move. An owner could take his building to another location if he so desired.

This town share certificate was issued by the Geneseo Town Company of Lyons, Kansas. It was issued to S.H. Crikfield, who served as secretary of the town company. The town of Geneseo was located on the Missouri Pacific and Atchison, Topeka & Santa Fe railroad lines.

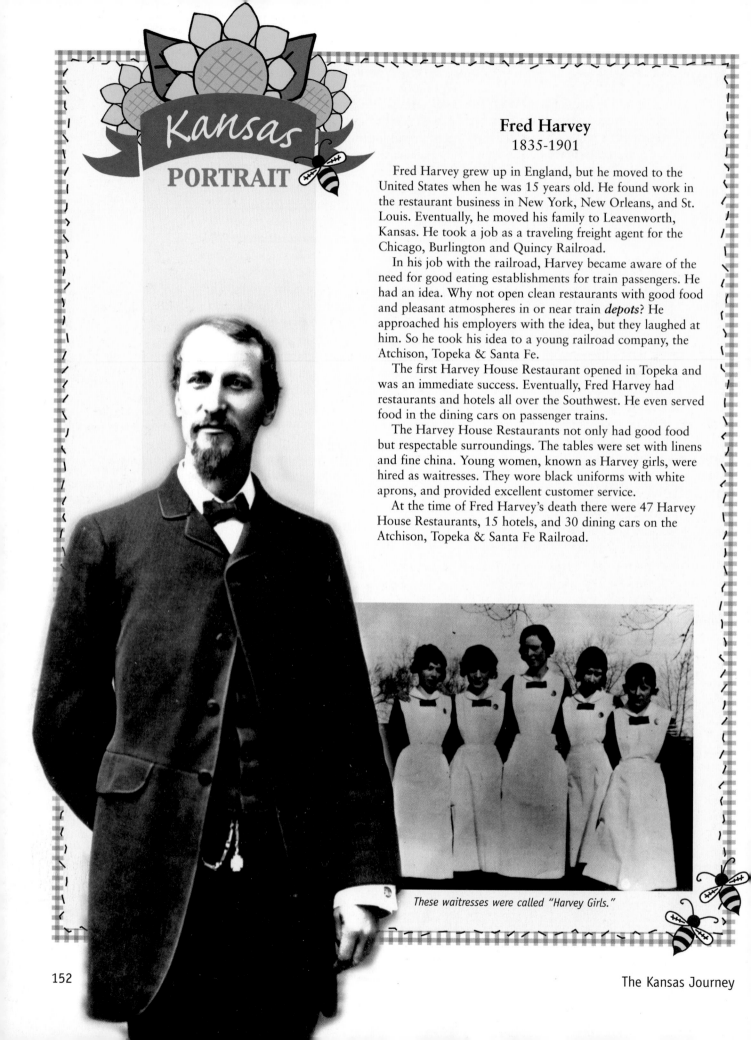

Kansas PORTRAIT

Fred Harvey
1835-1901

Fred Harvey grew up in England, but he moved to the United States when he was 15 years old. He found work in the restaurant business in New York, New Orleans, and St. Louis. Eventually, he moved his family to Leavenworth, Kansas. He took a job as a traveling freight agent for the Chicago, Burlington and Quincy Railroad.

In his job with the railroad, Harvey became aware of the need for good eating establishments for train passengers. He had an idea. Why not open clean restaurants with good food and pleasant atmospheres in or near train *depots*? He approached his employers with the idea, but they laughed at him. So he took his idea to a young railroad company, the Atchison, Topeka & Santa Fe.

The first Harvey House Restaurant opened in Topeka and was an immediate success. Eventually, Fred Harvey had restaurants and hotels all over the Southwest. He even served food in the dining cars on passenger trains.

The Harvey House Restaurants not only had good food but respectable surroundings. The tables were set with linens and fine china. Young women, known as Harvey girls, were hired as waitresses. They wore black uniforms with white aprons, and provided excellent customer service.

At the time of Fred Harvey's death there were 47 Harvey House Restaurants, 15 hotels, and 30 dining cars on the Atchison, Topeka & Santa Fe Railroad.

These waitresses were called "Harvey Girls."

Comparing Jobs of 1875 to Today

Successful businesses serve the needs of their customers. If that need no longer exists, then the business becomes *obsolete.* Changing technology as well as social customs can increase or decrease the need for a specific service or product. This means that some jobs change through time.

In 1875, the Kansas Department of Agriculture published a report showing the number of people who worked in each profession. Some of those professions are listed here. Study the chart, and then answer the questions below:

1. List five types of jobs that were available in Kansas in 1875.
2. List two occupations that are now obsolete.
3. Look through the ads in your local newspaper, and make a list of the jobs that are available today in your community. Compare this list with the chart from 1875. How are jobs alike? How are they different? What jobs do we have today that were not needed in 1875?
4. The State Department of Agriculture also looks at the data in terms of gender. What jobs did women hold in 1875? How are the types of jobs women hold today different from those in the past?

If women worked outside the home, they were often limited to certain types of work. Here women in Junction City do laundry for others.

Occupations in Kansas, 1875

Occupations of Persons 21 +	Male	Female
Agricultural Laborers	14,851	16
Farmers	73,836	1,934
Stock Raisers and Herders	357	3
Barbers and Hair Dressers	223	19
Billiard and Bowling Saloon Workers	370	-
Boarding and Lodging House Keepers	77	70
Domestic Servants	315	2,072
Hotel and Restaurant Keepers and Employees	465	52
Journalists	98	2
Launderers and Laundresses	6	328
Lawyers	888	-
Physicians and Surgeons	1,209	14
Teachers	880	1,489
Clerks, Salesmen, and Accountants (in stores)	2,147	30
Officials and Employees of Railroad Companies	1,450	3
Bakers	151	-
Blacksmiths	1,587	-
Boot and Shoe Makers	708	1
Brick and Tile Makers	63	-
Butchers	463	-
Car, Carriage, and Wagon Makers	361	-
Carpenters and Joiners	2,991	-
Harness and Saddle Makers	384	-
Hat and Cap Makers	16	-
Iron and Steel Workers	158	-
Milliners and Dress Makers	25	688
Miners	631	-
Tailors and Seamstresses	291	370

By the 1880s, Kansas towns were booming. Fort Scott had horse-drawn public transportation by 1886.

Living in Town

When Abbie Bright followed her brother to south central Kansas, she found him living about 100 miles from the railroad. Although she could get basic supplies at a frontier store, Abbie and her neighbors had to rely on their gardens and what they could gather for food. They also relied on meat they could get by hunting.

Food supplies did not always meet the demand in Abbie's world. On September 1, 1871, Abbie wrote, "Brother H[iram] had found some elder berries at the river, enough fore one pie. There were five of us for dinner, so I cut it into five pieces, Mr. Ross [came] while we were at dinner. I treated him to my piece. So I never got a taste of the pie, and there are no more elderberries."

Not all settlers to Kansas were so isolated. In fact, if you lived in town, close to a railroad line, you had access to many of the goods and services available back East.

Activity

The Diary of Ned Beck

Edward S. Beck was born in Indiana and moved to Kansas with his family. When he was 12 years old, he kept a diary of his life in Jackson County. Edward, or Ned as he liked to be called, had a very different experience than Abbie Bright. He was living in a town of about 1,500 people, and his father owned a local drugstore and newspaper. Ned and his brother worked at the newspaper. They served as apprentices, learning the newspaper business.

Twelve-year-old Ned Beck recorded his activities on a daily basis. The entries below talk about the time when his father was waiting for news about the Republican nominee for president. Ned talks about going to the depot several times for *dispatches*. During this time, news was sent by telegraph. On June 8, Ned writes that Garfield has been elected president. He probably meant Garfield had received the Republican nomination in June, as James A. Garfield was elected president in November of 1880.

After reading Ned's diary, answer the following questions:

1. What kind of food did Ned's family have access to?
2. How did Ned's mother wash their clothes?
3. What kind of toys and equipment did Ned have?
4. How fast did Ned and his family get news from the East?
5. Do you feel Ned was isolated living in Kansas in 1880?
6. What role do you think the railroad played in Ned's life?

June 2, Wednesday. Nothing much happened this morning. At school we are reading in the U.S. History. I play ball most of the time at school. Momma borrowed Aunt Floras washing machine and washed...Ed Dilbert [flew] my Kite this evening after school. I pulled weeds a while. I and Will went agate hunting and found a few. We had ice cream for dinner and lemonade for supper. Papa is going to Leavenworth tomorrow to get the dispatch of who was nominated for President as this is the day of the nominations....

June 5, Saturday. This morning Papa said I could stay in the store and help work...I didn't do much in the store but went to the depot 4 times to get dispatches from Chicago. There has been no one nominated for President. There has been 8 dispatches received at Holton...I played ball a while this after noon.

June 8. Tuesday. I got up pretty early and went down to the depot...to see the Excursion from Valley Falls to Garrison. There was a big crowd but not many from Holton....Garfield was elected President of the United States to day.

June 19. Saturday. I helped carry a lot of the things we borrowed back to their places. I finished hoeing the potatoes this morning. After noon I carried around the bills and got 35 cts for it. I got a bow and 2 arrows for sixty cents which was cheap.

A school was an important part of any Kansas community. This is a photograph of the school in Eudora, Douglas County, in 1879. Most children, however, attended one-room schools at this time.

Railroads, Cattle, and Agriculture

Living in the Country

Although people living in town had quicker access to more goods and services, rural folks were not totally isolated. Farm families traveled to and from town on a regular basis. Some farmers actually took part-time work in town. Farming was not always solitary work. Neighbors helped neighbors and sometimes they hired others to help.

Most families who came to Kansas to farm wanted to farm commercially. By the late 19th century, the idea of the farm family living in isolation on a *subsistence* farm was not the norm in Kansas. Farmers usually grew crops to sell, while at the same time they grew gardens to feed their family. Food was also available for purchase, to supplement what was grown.

Rain Follows the Plow

Whether you lived in the country or in town, agriculture was important to Kansas. Much of the state's economy was based on agriculture. The businesses in town were affected by the successes and failures of the state's farmers. If farmers had a bad year, they did not have as much money to spend.

Kansas and other western states had been settled on the belief that "rain follows the plow." It was thought that cultivation of the land could and would change the climate. As the plow broke the sod, the rainfall would increase. Today we know, of course, that this is not true. But this idea gave settlers optimism that encouraged them to find ways to farm on the unpredictable Plains.

Kansas Crops

Tall tales also appeared in altered photographs of the time.

Tall Tales

Tall tales grew up around farming on the Great Plains. Stories exaggerated the successes of farmers. Why do you think such stories became popular? The *Thomas County Cat* of Colby reported the following stories on January 7, 1886:

Cabbage leaves are used for circus tents, and hoop poles are made of timothy stalks. Jack rabbits grow as large as a horse, and the tail feathers of a wild goose make excellent fence posts....A man planted a turnip one mile from the railroad last summer and the railroad company sued him for obstructing their right of way before the middle of July.

Pie plant makes excellent bridge timbers, and pumpkins are in good demand this winter for barns and houses. Pea pods are used as ferry boats on the Arkansas river, and onion seeds are much sought after for wells and terrace work. Rye straw properly connected, makes superior pipe for drainage, and the husk of the berry when provided with rockers, makes unique baby cradles.

Grain elevators, like this one in Abilene in 1880, were used to store grain waiting to be shipped out of town on the railroad. The first grain elevator in Kansas was built in the 1860s. By 1882, it is estimated that there were 125 grain elevators in the state.

When Kansas was first settled, corn was the logical crop to grow. It could be planted with simple tools, and it had a higher *yield* than other grains. Families ate the corn in a variety of ways. Simple stone mills were used to grind it into cornmeal. Corn was used to feed livestock. It was grown not only to sustain the family, but also to be sold in local markets.

People grew oats to use as food for livestock. They also tried growing cotton and tobacco. Due to our state's shorter growing season, these crops proved to be unsuitable. Grains such as rye and barley were grown according to the demands of the market. Flax, castor beans, hemp, and broomcorn were also tried as commercial crops. In parts of Kansas, farmers started grape vineyards and a variety of fruit orchards.

Wheat

Early Kansas farmers also grew some wheat. Wheat, unlike corn, had to be processed into flour in order to be eaten. Once the railroad came to Kansas, grains could be shipped to other markets. This made the production of wheat profitable.

Kansas became known for its winter wheat. Traditional wheat was planted in spring and harvested in late summer. During hot dry summers the wheat would not survive. T.C. Henry operated a large farm near Abilene in the 1870s. He was one of the first to experiment with winter wheat. Henry was also a land promoter. He planted his crop next to the railroad line hoping to attract new settlers to the area. One year after the winter wheat was harvested, grasshoppers attacked, eating all the "spring" wheat and corn. This gave T.C. Henry's winter wheat crop a great deal of attention. Others began planting winter wheat.

Kansans experimented with many kinds of crops. This is a vineyard in Ford County in the 1890s.

The binder cut and tied wheat in one operation. This is a new McCormick binder at Winfield in 1882.

The Grange

The Grange was a national organization that brought farmers together. The name "Grange" came from medieval England and meant the farmhouse or manor of a gentleman farmer.

In Kansas, the Grange was started for social and cultural reasons. It promoted education among farmers. It also offered the chance for farmers to associate with other farmers who might share common concerns. Eventually, the organization became more active representing the political needs of the farmer.

Hundreds of Granges sprang up across Kansas. Leaders of the Grange movement promoted farmers' cooperatives. A cooperative allowed independent farmers to come together to get more buying and selling power. To this end, the Grange developed cooperative stores and grain elevators throughout the state.

This print was given to Grange members to promote farm life.

Technology and Grain Production

Most early farmers settled on 160 acres of land. In western and central Kansas this made the average farm rather large for subsistence farming, but not quite large enough to be fully commercial. Early farms usually produced *surplus* products that could be sold. As farm equipment continued to be mechanized and the market for Kansas farm products increased, farms became more and more like small businesses.

Early on, farmers used pure horsepower to work the fields. It took one full day for a team of horses pulling a plow to break one acre of sod. Plowing the field was necessary to plant the crops. Grain-drilling machines helped farmers to plant seeds. Farmers who could afford such a machine still relied on their horses to pull it.

Grain harvesting equipment had come a long way by the time Kansas became a state. However, the power to run these machines still came primarily from horses. Before mechanization, grain was cut entirely by hand, using a sickle. Later, the mechanical reaper was pulled through the field-cutting the stalks of grain as it passed. Men then tied these stalks into bundles. Mechanized binders soon helped to eliminate this backbreaking work.

At one time, threshing was done by hand. A farmer would usually work alone to separate the grain from the straw. Sometimes older children helped their fathers with this chore. This process was so labor intensive that the farmer was very limited in the amount of grain he could grow. Mechanical threshing came into use about the same time Kansas was being settled.

The mechanization of equipment saved time and resulted in the need for less hired help. However, the farmer's reliance on horsepower limited the farmer's business growth. It was not until the 20th century, and the invention of the gasoline-powered tractor, that Kansas farmers dramatically increased their production.

The Kansas Journey

Chapter 7 Review

What Do You Remember?

1. What was the purpose of the cattle drives?
2. Describe the job of the cowboy.
3. Why would a town in Kansas want to attract the cattle trade?
4. What did a town need to become a cattle town?
5. How and why did the Kansas legislature put a stop to the cattle drives?
6. What were railroad land grants and why were they controversial?
7. Why did the railroads compete to sell land in Kansas?
8. What was the role of a town site association?
9. Why did the railroads encourage small specialized businesses to settle in their towns?
10. Explain the saying, "the rain follows the plow."
11. What were some of the first crops grown in Kansas?
12. Explain the difference between subsistence farming and commercial farming.
13. Name at least one way farm work was made easier by mechanization.
14. What was the purpose of the Grange movement?

Think About It!

1. At one time settlers bought their supplies from a general store. The railroads encouraged the development of small specialized retail stores. What are the trends in business today? Think about what will characterize future trends in retail. What do you think has brought about these changes?

2. Why is it important for a business to meet the needs of its customers? Is it important for businesses to change with their customers' needs?

Activities

1. Locate literature on a new development or neighborhood in your town or somewhere in Kansas. Compare that literature to the flyers developed by the railroad companies to sell their land during the late 19th century. What do the sales pitches have in common? How do they appeal to their audiences?

2. The railroad brought more people and goods to the plains. It also contributed to the end of large buffalo herds. Research more about what happened to the buffalo as a consequence of the railroad. What are the effects on today's buffalo population?

Reform Movements:
"It Happens First in Kansas"

Timeline of Events

160

1861
Kansas women are given the right to vote in school district elections.

1870s - - - - - - - - →
The United States experiences an economic depression.

1873
The Gilded Age is published.

1887
Kansas women are allowed to vote in city elections.

1860   1865   1870   1875   1880

1867
A state constitutional amendment fails that would have granted voting rights to African Americans and women.

1870
The 15th Amendment to the U.S. Constitution gives African American men the right to vote.

1876
The national Prohibition Party is founded.

1887
Susanna Salter of Argonia becomes first woman ma[yor] in the United Sta[tes].

WORDS TO UNDERSTAND
electioneering
foreclosure
inaugural address
industrialization
inheritance
lobby
materialism
moral
Populism
progressive
prohibition
ratify
Socialism
suffrage
temperance
utopian

The People's Party, also called Populists, brought about a national movement associated with farmers. William Jennings Bryan, from Nebraska, was an important figure for the Populists. For a time, the Populist agenda swallowed up the Democratic Party. Bryan was used as a symbol for the Populists in this political cartoon. What other symbols do you see?

1892
Kansas elects a Populist governor, and the party has a majority in the Kansas Senate.

1895
Julius A. Wayland begins publishing the Socialist newspaper, the *Appeal to Reason.*

1919
Emanuel and Marcet Haldeman-Julius purchase the *Appeal to Reason* and begin publishing the "Little Blue Books."

1920
The 19th Amendment to the U.S. Constitution gives women the right to vote.

1890   1895   1900   1905   1910   1915   1920   1925

1893
e United States experiences an economic depression.

1893
Republicans and Populists go to "war" over control of the Kansas House of Representatives.

1896
William Allen White writes the editorial "What's the Matter With Kansas?"

1912
Kansas becomes the seventh state to give equal voting rights to women.

1919
The 18th Amendment to the U.S. Constitution prohibits alcohol.

The Gilded Age

In the late 1800s, the United States saw the rise of *industrialization*. There was a great deal of money to be made in industry, but only a select few benefited. There was no income tax or *inheritance* tax. Wealthy families continued to add to their fortunes. Those with money lived in high style. The rich showed their wealth—often through lavish parties. A Mrs. Stuyvesant Fish of New York was rumored to throw a party in honor of her dog. The dog came dressed in a $15,000 diamond collar.

With so much wealth came corruption—and Kansas was not exempt. The term the "Gilded Age" was born when Mark Twain and Charles Dudley Warner published a novel by that name. It was a satire about the *materialism* and corruption of the time. The novel included a character modeled after a U.S. Senator from Kansas, Senator Samuel Pomeroy.

At that time, U.S. Senators were elected by the state legislature, not by popular vote. When a state legislator claimed that Pomeroy gave him a large amount money for his vote, a scandal exploded. Pomeroy lost his senate seat by failing to win reelection. The fictionalized Senator Dilworthy of *The Gilded Age* experienced a similar fate.

> *On first ballot for U.S. Senator, when voting was about to begin, Mr. Noble rose in his place and drew forth a package, walked forward and laid it on the Speaker's desk, saying, 'This contains $7,000 in bank bills and was given me by Senator Dilworthy in his bed-chamber at midnight last night to buy my vote for him–I wish the Speaker to count the money and retain it to pay the expense of prosecuting this infamous traitor for bribery.' The whole legislature was stricken speechless with dismay and astonishment.*

Three weeks after Senator Pomeroy left office under a cloud of suspicion, Kansas' other U.S. Senator, Alexander Caldwell was forced to resign. He also was accused of bribery and corruption.

Tough Times for Many

Senator Pomeroy never denied giving money to the state legislator, but he claimed it was for a business venture. The accusations of corruption ruined Pomeroy's political career.

Emporia newspaper editor William Allen White observed, "A United States senator . . . represented more than a state, more than a region. He represented principalities and powers in business. One senator, for instance, represented the New York Central [Railroad], still another the insurance interests . . . cotton had half a dozen senators." Whose interests does this political cartoon from 1889 depict?

The nation watched as Kansas reformers worked for prohibition. A National Temperance Camp was held near Lawrence in 1878. The camp lasted a week and drew nearly 50,000 people.

Although the rich were getting richer during the Gilded Age, the poor remained very poor. Only about 5 percent of American families controlled most of the nation's wealth. The average yearly earnings of most Americans fell below the poverty line.

In the 1870s, the United States experienced an economic depression. The country had invested heavily in the building of railroads. There were more railroads and railroad lines than the country could support. When economic troubles from Europe began to reach the United States, the American economy suffered, too. Banks demanded that loans be repaid. Investors sold their stocks. Many banks closed, and thousands of workers lost their jobs. Many of the railroads failed to survive.

An economist of the time reported "a widespread feeling of unrest and brooding revolution." Tough economic times left many people with a feeling of distrust for those with power and wealth. Some people wanted to deal with what they believed were the causes of these problems. Reform movements began.

Kansas and Reform Movements

William Allen White, the editor of the *Emporia Gazette*, once wrote "When anything is going to happen in this country, it happens first in Kansas." White was referring to the many reform movements that have taken shape in Kansas.

What is reform? Reformers want to solve problems and make things better. Reform movements often begin as a minority voice against the establishment. This means that some people are critical of reformers. They do not understand why someone would want change. But despite criticism, reformers continue to fight for their vision of the future.

Kansas has been a leader in reform movements. The abolitionists who came to Kansas Territory were part of a reform movement. They wanted to create a world where people were not enslaved. Kansas was one of the leaders in establishing women's rights. Kansas Prohibitionists led a state and national reform movement to preserve the family through the *prohibition* of alcohol. Kansas farmers joined together to reform government policies in the Populist movement.

164

Prohibition

The abuse of alcohol became a major concern during the Gilded Age. Bars or saloons, as they were called, were not considered places for proper women. Instead, they were places that took men away from their families. Heavy drinking made some people behave badly. Both men and women began to see alcohol as evil and destructive to society. But it was primarily groups of women who took on the fight to eliminate the abuse of alcohol.

There were those who wanted *temperance*. They wanted to see people abstain from the use of alcohol, or at the very least drink it in moderation. Others wanted to prohibit the sale of alcohol in public places. And there were those who wanted to make Kansas a "dry" state through the prohibition of all intoxicating beverages. All of the groups that fought against alcohol were trying to preserve families and create a respectable society.

While Kansas Territory was being settled, emotions began to run high over the drinking of alcohol. The territorial legislature solved the issue by making saloons a matter of local decision. This meant that it was up to each and every community to decide for itself if it wanted to permit public drinking establishments. Six years before Kansas became a state, a group of women smashed a saloon in Lawrence. This violent act against public drinking was a prelude of things to come in Kansas.

Amending the State Constitution

There were early efforts in Kansas to organize a political party around the issue of prohibition. By the mid-1870s, the Kansas Republican Party had taken on many of the values associated with temperance. Kansas voters elected John St. John as governor, a Republican prohibitionist. In his *inaugural address*, St. John spoke against the manufacture and sale of alcohol. He said, "Could we but dry up this one great evil that consumes annually so much wealth, and destroys the physical, moral and mental usefulness of its victims, we should hardly need prisons, poor houses or police."

The state legislature followed the governor's lead and passed a resolution calling for a constitutional prohibition amendment. The question of alcohol was put to the voters of Kansas. It passed, and Kansas became the first state to constitutionally outlaw the manufacture or sale of alcohol. This was 38 years before the United States amended the U.S. Constitution to prohibit alcohol.

Women's temperance groups had worked in Kansas for years. The women of Kansas even helped create a new political party, the national Prohibition Party. The success of prohibition in Kansas gave Governor St. John national attention. He ran for president of the United States on the Prohibition Party ticket, although he did not win.

What do you think?

The Woman's Christian Temperance Union was an active organization fighting for the prohibition of alcohol. Its motto was "Agitate, Educate, Organize." Using these three ideas, members worked to gain support for their cause. Other reform movements have used these same tactics. What do you think? Are the ideas of agitate, educate, and organize useful in changing society today? Can you think of other ways to change people's minds on a particular issue?

Many women in Kansas made quilts to show their support of temperance. The "Double T" was a favorite pattern.

"I CANNOT TELL A LIE--I DID IT WITH MY LITTLE HATCHET!"
Mrs. Nation's Reform Crusade in Kansas, as the Globe Artist Understands It From the Press Dispatches.

Carry A. Nation and the Enforcement of Prohibition

Even though Kansans had voted for prohibition, the state was not "dry." Enforcing the law was harder than it seemed. The constitutional amendment allowed alcohol to be sold for "medicinal" purposes, but many people who were not doctors took advantage of this loophole. Also, Kansans continued to make and use alcohol in their homes.

Saloons continued to operate. In Topeka, the home of the state legislature, a business called the Senate Saloon openly sold liquor. It was one of many saloons in the state capital. The owners of the Senate Saloon continued to operate by paying a monthly fine of $100. Obviously, prohibition did not work quite the way its supporters had hoped. Temperance organizations continued to *lobby* for stronger laws and better enforcement of the

existing law. Some, like Carry A. Nation of Medicine Lodge, decided to take matters into their own hands.

Nation had a reputation as a lecturer, speaking against tobacco and alcohol. When she moved to Medicine Lodge, she helped organize a local Woman's Christian Temperance Union. She also worked with those in prison and the poor and needy. Through her work, Nation came to believe that drinking could rob a man of his money and sometimes push him to a life of crime. She felt she had to do something radical to make Kansas a better place. Motivated by her religious beliefs, Nation began a career of smashing saloons.

At first Nation's followers destroyed saloons by throwing stones and bricks. Eventually she used a hatchet, which became her trademark. As Carry A. Nation's fame grew, small pins in the shape of hatchets were sold to raise money to pay her jail fines.

A supporter presented Carry A. Nation with this stonemason's hammer.

How Do We Know This?

At the age of 10, Carry A. Nation attended a church meeting that stirred her strong Christian beliefs. Her religious faith shaped her life. Eventually, she fell in love with a man who drank. Over her parent's objections, she married him. Two years later, Nation's husband died. She blamed alcohol for his death. Eventually, she married again, but this marriage ended in divorce.

How do we know what motivated Carry A. Nation to begin smashing saloons? In 1908, she wrote *The Use and Need of the Life of Carry A. Nation*. She left clues in her autobiography. What follows is an excerpt from her writings. What role does her religion play in her actions? Why is the cause of prohibition so important to her? What does she want to achieve?

When I found I could effect nothing through the officials, I was sad, indeed. I saw that Kansas homes, hearts and souls were to be sacrificed. I had lost all the hopes of my young life through drink, I saw the terrible results that would befall others. I felt that I had rather die than see the saloons come back to Kansas. I felt desperate. I took this to God daily, feeling He only, could rescue.

On the 5th of June, before retiring, I threw myself face downward at the foot of my bed in my home in Medicine Lodge. I poured out my grief in agony to God, in about this strain: 'Oh Lord you see the treason in Kansas, they are going to break the mothers' hearts, they are going to send the boys to drunkards' graves and a drunkard's hell. I have exhausted my means, Oh Lord, you have plenty of ways. You have used the base things and the weak things, use me to save Kansas. I have but one life to give you, if I had a thousand, I would give them all, please show me something to do.'

The next morning I was awakened by a voice which seemed to me speaking in my heart, these words, 'GO TO KIOWA,' and my hands were lifted and thrown down and the words, 'I'LL STAND BY YOU.' The words, 'Go to Kiowa,' were spoken in a murmuring, musical tone, low and soft, but 'I'll stand by you,' was very clear, positive and emphatic.

I was impressed with a great inspiration, the interpretation was very plain, it was this: 'Take something in your hands, and throw at these places in Kiowa and smash them.' I was very much relieved and overjoyed and was determined to be, 'obedient to the heavenly vision.'

Carry A. Nation became so famous that she received offers to tour the country as a speaker. This poster was created in New York and may have advertised one of her talks. Nation's first name was originally spelled the way it is on the poster. Later in life, she changed the spelling so her name would have a symbolic meaning. Can you explain the meaning of "Carry A. Nation?"

Women's Suffrage

Kansas was a leader in the fight for equal rights for women. It took many years and a series of steps to achieve the goal of women's *suffrage*. Rights for women became an issue as early as the territorial period. While the country watched, Clarina Nichols and other women in Kansas gained property rights and the opportunity to vote in school district elections. It was quite a victory, but not everything that women wanted.

The Fight for Universal Suffrage

Six years after Kansas became a state, an opportunity for universal suffrage put Kansas back in the spotlight. There was a movement to convince the white male voters of Kansas to *ratify* amendments to the state Constitution. These amendments granted voting rights to both women and African American men. This was the first time a state proposed giving women their full voting rights.

Nationally known suffragists, Susan B. Anthony, Elizabeth Cady Stanton, and Lucy Stone, came to Kansas to fight for the cause. They worked side-by-side with Kansas men and women. The reformers traveled the state giving lecturers and participating in discussions. They ate on the run and slept when and where they could. Lucy Stone later wrote of her experiences in Kansas. One night she found herself sleeping in a carriage. As night began to fall, wild pigs surrounded the carriage and began rubbing

Women in Kansas continued to campaign for full voting rights for many years. This photograph was taken in Lawrence in 1912.

The Kansas Journey

up against it. As the pigs scratched themselves, the carriage bounced around all night.

Despite the national attention, the universal suffrage movement failed. The voters of the state defeated the amendments by more than a two-to-one margin. Within a few years, the 15th Amendment to the U.S. Constitution gave African American men the right to vote. Many women reformers felt abandoned, especially by the abolitionist men with whom they had fought to end slavery.

Municipal Suffrage

More and more people in Kansas began to believe that women should have the right to vote. The strategy in Kansas shifted from full suffrage to partial suffrage. Reformers decided to concentrate on municipal suffrage, or the right to vote in city elections. There were those at the national level, including Susan B. Anthony, who did not like this approach. They wanted to settle for nothing less than full voting rights.

A municipal suffrage bill was introduced into the Kansas legislature. Supporters of the bill argued that women were as intelligent as men. Those against the bill argued that politics was no place for a woman. Representative Coleman, a supporter of the bill, summed it up this way:

> [Those against the bill] say that women should not be dragged into the Cesspool of politics; if politics are so degraded, there should be something done to purify and elevate politics. Some purifying influence should be injected into the politics of our country. I believe that woman is the Hercules who will reform the politics of to-day. Will it drag her down? Never!

It took two years in the legislature, but a municipal suffrage bill finally passed with overwhelming support. Women watching the votes being counted cheered in victory when they learned their fate. Kansas was the first state to give women the right to vote in municipal elections.

This illustration of women in Leavenworth soliciting votes was published in Leslie's Illustrated Newspaper *in 1887, the same year Kansas women won the right to vote in city elections.*

Reform Movements: "It Happens First in Kansas"

ROOMS OF THE EXECUTIVE COMMITTEE
STATE IMPARTIAL SUFFRAGE ASSOCIATION
Topeka, Kansas, April 5th, 1867

We are now arranging for a thorough canvas of our State for Impartial Suffrage, without regard to *sex* or color. We are satisfied that an argument in favor of colored suffrage, is an argument in favor of women's suffrage. Both are based on the same principle. It is the doctrine of our fathers, "that governments derive their just powers from the consent of the governed." We "white men" have no right to ask privileges or demand rights for ourselves that we are unwilling to grant to the whole human family. There never has been, and never can be, an argument based upon principle, against colored or women suffrage. *Sneers*, and attempts at *ridicule* are not arguments. Henry Blackwell, of New York, and Mrs. Lucy Stone, are now canvassing our State for *Impartial Suffrage*. Some of the most eminent men and women of the United States have been invited, and promised to visit our State this summer and fall; and we shall succeed; Kansas will be free, and occupy the proudest place, in all time to come, in the history of the world.

We desire to extend our meetings to every neighborhood in Kansas; reach, if possible, the ear of every voter. For this purpose we must enlist every home speaker possible. We shall arrange series of meetings in all parts of the State, commencing about September 1st, and running through September and October. We desire speakers to advocate the broad doctrine of Impartial Suffrage, but welcome those who advocate either. Those who desire colored suffrage alone, are invited to take the field; also those who favor only female suffrage; each help the other.

I am instructed by the State Impartial Suffrage Executive Committee to ask you to aid us, and speak at as many of our meetings as possible. Please answer at once, and let us know how much time you can spend in the campaign, and what part of the State you prefer to speak in.

S.N. WOOD, Corresponding Secretary,
P.O. Box 377, Topeka, Kansas.

Activity

State Impartial Suffrage Association, 1867

The State Impartial Suffrage Association issued the following call for help. The association wanted to convince reformers working toward African American suffrage and women's suffrage to work together. The document uses the term "colored" to refer to African Americans. This was common at the time. After reading the document, answer these questions:

1. What was the strategy of the association?
2. How did they hope to convince voters to adopt universal suffrage in Kansas?
3. List reasons why it is good for people to work together toward a common goal.
4. List reasons why the two groups may not want to work together.

moral issues among the women in the state. Women suffrage groups also sent out literature encouraging women to use their votes. Circulars asked, "Do you not wish to have livestock kept from roaming your streets, breaking your walks and invading your gardens?" and, "Do you not wish to have your money spent as prudently as possible?"

Not only could women vote in city elections, but they could also run for city offices. The same year women received the right to vote in municipal elections, Argonia elected the first female mayor in the history of the United States. Susanna Salter was a member of the Woman's Christian Temperance Union. A group of men in town who opposed the WCTU's influence put Salter's name on the ballot. They thought that no one would vote for a woman, and they hoped it would embarrass the WCTU. They were in for a surprise! Susanna Salter won by a two-thirds majority.

One year later, the city of Oskaloosa elected a woman mayor. The voters of this

How Did Women Voters Change Kansas Politics?

Soon after the passing of the municipal suffrage bill, the Kansas legislature passed a bill to "clean up" polling places. Since women would be voting alongside men, the legislature decided to ban *electioneering* within 100 feet of the polls. Up until then, polling places were filled with men arguing over each other's character and the issues of the day. This law continues today.

For many women in Kansas, alcohol and gambling remained important issues. Women were experienced organizers. Groups like the Woman's Christian Temperance Union began campaigning for northeast Kansas town went even further, electing women to all five city council seats. Kansas politics had changed forever.

The Campaign for Full Suffrage: A Civics Lesson

When people want to change the way the government does something, it takes a lot of hard work and an organized plan. Change is possible, even if those who want the change do not have the power of the vote. The Kansas women's suffrage campaign of 1912 is a good example of civics in action.

Though Kansas women could vote in local elections, they wanted to vote in all elections. The first step toward this goal was getting the state legislature to pass an amendment resolution. The members of the suffrage association contacted every member of the legislature hoping to obtain his support. It worked! The resolution passed both the Senate and the House of Representatives and was signed by the governor. In order for the amendment to become part of the State Constitution, it had to go before the male voters of Kansas in a general election.

The women were organized and had a plan. The suffrage association membership committee made it a goal to contact all of the women of the state and encourage them to join their cause. The education committee pledged to distribute campaign literature, gain endorsements from other organizations, and promote an essay contest in the public schools. The strategy behind the essay contest was that parents would be interested in the work of their children. The press committee's goal was to reach all parts of the state by providing suffrage articles for Kansas newspapers.

One of the greatest challenges suffragists faced was financing the campaign. They had to raise money, and they began with themselves. Each association board member gave money, and they solicited donations from others. Local groups held festivals, bazaars, and teas as fundraisers. The association even printed balloons that said, "Votes for Mother" and sold them. After much work, they were successful in financing their campaign.

The suffrage association sent members on the road to organize communities and bring awareness to their cause. Whenever a politician spoke in Kansas, they contacted him to speak for the vote for women. A Men's League for Woman Suffrage was even organized. During the 10 days before the election, Dr. Anna Howard Shaw, president of the National American Woman Suffrage Association, came to Kansas to campaign. On Election Day, when the votes were being counted, Dr. Shaw sent a telegraph that said, "First authentic returns from suffrage vote in Kansas victorious. The national welcomes the seventh star." Kansas had become the seventh state to give women full voting rights.

Susanna Salter was elected mayor of Argonia in 1887. She was the first female mayor in the United States.

Two years after Kansas gave full suffrage to women, this illustration appeared in the Maryland Suffrage News. By 1914, 12 states and one territory had given women full suffrage. In what sections of the country did women have full voting rights? Why do you think this is so?

Reform Movements: "It Happens First in Kansas"

Populism

Populism was a national movement associated with farmers. Kansas played a significant role in the creation of the People's Party. It was the most successful third-party political movement in the history of the United States. Difficult economic times for farmers and a growing frustration with the inequity of wealth in the country fueled the reform movement. Farmers saw corruption in industries such as the railroads. They wanted the government to eliminate the economic inequities of the country.

"In God We Trusted, In Kansas We Busted"

After the Civil War, farmers found it more and more difficult to make a good living. American agriculture faced changes. The new technology of the industrial era created more advanced farm equipment. The new equipment cut time and labor costs for farmers. This allowed them to plant more acres. However, to do this the farmer had to invest in the new expensive machinery. This often put the farmer in debt. It also meant that farmers could produce more food than the market needed, causing a surplus that made prices fall.

In the late 1880s and early 1890s, Kansas experienced a series of droughts that made it nearly impossible to grow crops. If a farmer had a bad year and carried too much debt, he could lose his farm. Over 11,000 Kansas farms faced *foreclosure*. Many people gave up and left the state. In one year, the population of Thomas County fell from 5,032 to 4,415.

In western Kansas, where drought conditions were particularly bad, people were starving and had no fuel. Letters were sent to the governor asking for help. Mrs. Susan Orcutt from Mendota wrote the following plea to the governor on June 29, 1894:

Dear Governor. I take my pen in hand to let you know that we are <u>Starving</u> to death. It is Pretty hard to do without any thing to Eat....We would have had Plenty to Eat if the <u>hail</u> [hadn't] cut our rye down and ruined our corn and Potatoes. I had the Prettiest Garden that you Ever seen and the hail ruined It and I have nothing to look at. My husband went a way to find work and came home last night and told me that we would have to Starve; he has [been] in ten count[ies] and did not Get no work. It is Pretty hard for a woman to do with out any thing to Eat when She doesn't no what minute She will be confined to bed. If I was in <u>Iowa</u> I would be all right. I was born [there] and raised there. I haven't had nothing to Eat to day and It is three [o'clock]. Well I will close. [Write] soon.

The residents of Dickinson County showed their support of Populism.

The People's Party Platform

The basic question behind the People's Party was who should the government represent: the workers or big business? Farmers were particularly angry at the railroads. They felt the railroads charged them unfair prices to transport their crops. Farmers were also angry at the banks that held their loans for charging them such high interest rates. Populists believed that the government favored the railroads, banks, and other businesses.

The People's Party demanded economic and political reform. How did they propose to change the country? Here are some of their ideas:

- Change the way the United States mints and distributes currency so that enough money is always available.
- Break up monopolies and trusts so that prices are subject to competition.
- Create an income tax where rich people pay a higher percent of their earnings than poor people.
- Limit government revenue so that it does not exceed government spending.
- Give the government ownership of the railroads, telegraph, and telephone.
- Prevent land speculation and ownership of land by people who are not citizens of the United States and do not intend to live on the land.
- Reform elections through the use of the secret ballot, the election of U.S. senators by the people, a method by which the people can initiate laws, and the ability of the people to recall elected officials.

The Music of Protest

Farmers wanted a fair price for the food they grew. They were beginning to think that the United States' economic policies favored industry over the farmer. When industrial workers felt they were being treated unfairly, they joined unions for protection. Farmers began to look for alliances of their own. Many Kansas farmers joined the National Farmers Alliance and Industrial Union.

Labor movements have traditionally used music to bring people together for a common cause. Such music usually says something about the working conditions. "The Kansas Fool" was printed in *The Alliance and Labor Songster* in 1890. What does it say about the problems of the Kansas farmer?

The Kansas Fool
To the tune of "Kansas Land"

We have the land to raise the wheat,
　And everything that's good to eat;
And when we had no bonds or debts,
　We were a jolly, happy set.

Chorus:
Oh, Kansas fools! Poor Kansas fools!
The banker makes of you a tool;
I look across the fertile plain,
Big crops—made so by gentle rain;
But twelve cent corn gives me alarm,
And makes me want to sell my farm.

With abundant crops raised everywhere,
　'Tis a mystery, I do declare,
Why farmers all should fume and fret,
　And why we are so deep in debt.

At first we made some money here,
　With drouth and grasshoppers each year;
And now the interest that we pay
　Soon takes our money all away.

The bankers followed us out west,
　And did in mortgages invest;
They looked ahead and shrewdly planned,
　And soon they'll have our Kansas land.

Mary Elizabeth Lease
1853-1933

Mary Elizabeth Lease was a writer, lawyer, and powerful lecturer. She was one of the best known Populist reformers in the country.

Lease was born in Pennsylvania to Irish parents. She came to Kansas in 1870 to teach school. She married, had four children, and spent 10 years trying to farm in harsh conditions. Eventually, Lease and her family moved to the city of Wichita.

Lease actively campaigned throughout the country for a variety of causes. A North Carolina newspaper said she came into the South "with the declaration that [African Americans] should be made the equal of the white man and that all differences between the sexes should be obliterated...what next from Kansas?"

As a Populist campaigner, Lease would say, "Wall Street owns the country. It is no longer a government of the people, by the people, and for the people, but a government of Wall Street, by Wall Street, and for Wall Street."

In Kansas, Mary Elizabeth Lease became president of the Kansas State Board of Charities, but her aggressive style made enemies. Governor Lorenzo Lewelling, the Populist governor, removed her from the position because she was difficult. She refused to recognize the governor's actions and was reinstated for legal reasons. Eventually, Lease left Kansas for New York to become a political writer.

Annie Diggs
1853-1916

Annie Diggs was a reformer whose first cause was temperance. She also campaigned for equal suffrage and became a well-known champion of the Populist movement. Born in Canada, Diggs moved to Kansas from the East. In Kansas, she married and lived in Lawrence. Through her writings, Diggs combined the ideas of several reform movements. For a while, she served as the managing editor of the *Kansas Liberal*.

Diggs was an early supporter of the People's Party. She said that she "became convinced that the reforms which we sought were after all economical rather than moral questions." Diggs put her writing abilities to good use in a Populist column that was published in several newspapers.

Annie Diggs became known as a great political strategist. She is credited with helping elect Populist politicians. She also influenced Kansas government, ensuring that women were given positions of authority in regard to education and charitable institutions.

Annie Diggs was an important figure in bringing together the issues of the woman's movement with those of Populism.

Populist Players in Kansas

In the election of 1890, the People's Party did very well across the country. Kansans elected 92 Populist legislators, giving control of the state House of Representatives to the People's Party. Five of the seven congressional seats went to Populists. The Republican Party remained in control of the statewide offices. Realizing that change was in the air, the Republican Party in Kansas became friendlier to many of the Populists ideas.

Jeremiah Simpson, a rancher from Medicine Lodge, was one of the Populists elected to the U.S. Congress. He became known as "Sockless Jerry" when he accused his opponent of wearing silk socks. Simpson used the metaphor as a symbol for wealth. He felt his opponent was out of touch with the common person. Simpson claimed he had no silk stockings. This type of speech making got "Sockless Jerry" elected. In Washington D.C., he had the reputation of being one of the best-dressed congressmen, but the nickname stayed with him.

At that time, the state legislature, not the voters, selected U.S. senators. The Populists controlled the Kansas legislature, so they picked one of their own. William A. Peffer, a lawyer and newspaper editor, became the first Populist U.S. senator. Peffer had been chairman of the national conference that organized the People's Party and served as president of the National Reform Press Association. He was such an important reformer that Populism was sometimes referred to as "Pefferism." William Peffer believed "that public functions shall be exercised by public agents," and that government should, "serve all the people, not only a few."

In the next election of 1892, the People's Party in Kansas did even better. Their cause was strengthened when the Kansas Democratic Party supported all of the Populist candidates instead of selecting nominees of their own. The Populists took half the congressional seats. Governor Lorenzo Lewelling and all of the other statewide elected officials were Populists. The People's Party took control of the state Senate and appeared to take the House of Representatives.

"Sockless Jerry" Simpson served three terms in Congress. Here he is shown in a debate in Harper in 1892.

Political cartoons made fun of Kansas Populists. This cartoon depicts U.S. Senator William Peffer and Mary Elizabeth Lease, well-known Kansas Populists.

William Peffer was easy to portray in political cartoons because of his extraordinarily long beard.

From bleeding Kansas's wind-swept plains,
Where whiskers take the place of brains,
You come with all your verbose strength
Of speeches of unending length.
Here, take the hint PUCK gives — resign !
Let Mary be your Valentine.

Legislative War

Election returns were still being questioned when the 1893 legislature came together. In the Kansas House of Representatives, both the Populists and the Republicans claimed they had won the majority. Governor Lewelling stirred emotions when he addressed the legislature and proclaimed Kansas as the "first people's government" in the United States. This made the Republicans angry.

The Republicans and the Populists set up separate Houses. They elected their own officers and began work. This meant there were two different groups of representatives acting as the majority. Both groups occupied the House chambers. Sharing the same space meant they had to out-shout each other. It was chaos. The Populist governor and Senate declared the Populist House the official one, but the Republicans refused to leave.

Stand-off

The Republicans decided to push the issue and charged the chief clerk of the Populist House with disturbing the peace for interrupting the work of the Republicans. This made the Populists angry, and they locked themselves in the House chambers. The next day the Republicans marched to the Capitol and, using a sledge hammer, broke down the doors to the chamber.

The frame of this photograph was made from the doors broken at the State Capitol during the Legislative War.

Governor Lewelling called up the state militia. The Populists took control of the east wing of the Capitol and surrounded the building so no one could enter. The Republicans remained in the House chambers. The Populist strategy was to starve them out. The Populists shut off the heat, the electricity, and the telephones, leaving the Republicans in the dark. The stand-off made national news. The *Kansas City Star* wrote, "The Legislative situation in Topeka suggests a new use for Kansas avenue; too wide for a street and hardly wide enough for a cornfield, it would make a fairly roomy battlefield."

Eventually, the state Supreme Court had to decide who had the legal majority in the House. There were three supreme court justices at the time, and two of them were Republican. This made the Populists unhappy, and they threatened to move the capital to Kanopolis. As expected, the court ruled in favor of the Republican majority. The capital stayed in Topeka. The war was over, and the remaining Populists joined the Republicans and went back to business as usual.

"What's the Matter With Kansas?"

William Allen White was the owner and editor of the *Emporia Gazette*. He became a national spokesperson of sorts for small-town America. His editorials were read and loved by many.

White was a Republican. In the 1890s, he claimed the Populists were "gibbering idiots" who were ruining Kansas. His point-of-view was that of a conservative. One day after a group of Emporia Populists had made him angry, White wrote a powerful editorial against the People's Party. He called it "What's the Matter with Kansas?"

In the editorial, White complained that Kansas had lost people and money. According to White, the Populists made Kansas look foolish to the nation.

> Go east and you hear them laugh; go west and they sneer at her; go south and they "cuss" her; go north and they have forgotten her. Go into any crowd of intelligent people gathered anywhere on the globe, and you will find the Kansas man on the defensive. The newspaper columns and magazines once devoted to praise of her, to facts and startling figures concerning her resources, are now filled with cartoons, jibes and Pefferian speeches.

White used sarcasm in the editorial to belittle Kansans for accepting the Populist point of view. He felt it was wrong for the state to ignore the needs of businesses.

> Whoop it up for the ragged trousers; put the lazy, greasy fizzle, who can't pay his debts, on an altar, and bow down and worship him. Let the state ideal be high. What we need is not the respect of our fellow men, but the chance to get something for nothing.

From his desk at the Emporia Gazette, William Allen White captured national and international attention. He loved Kansas, but he would scold the state when he thought things were not right.

William Allen White's fame grew as "What's the Matter with Kansas?" was reprinted in Republican newspapers across the country. The editorial was so powerful that the Republicans reprinted it in a pamphlet and circulated it to as many voters as possible. The editorial certainly did not help the Populists, but other factors also led to their decline. Eventually, Kansas Democrats decided to pull their support of Populist candidates. More and more internal disagreements helped bring about the downfall of the People's Party.

It was ironic that William Allen White had a role in the decline of Populism. As time went on, White became more and more *progressive* in his point of view. Later, as a Progressive Republican, he began to believe in many of the Populist ideas.

VOL. 20 NO. 503   JUNE 6 1891   PRICE 10 CENTS.

Judge

ENTERED AT THE POST OFFICE AT NEW YORK AS SECOND-CLASS MATTER.   COPYRIGHT 1891 BY THE JUDGE PUBLISHING CO.

A PARTY OF PATCHES.
Grand Balloon Ascension—Cincinnati, May 20th, 1891.

Activity

Drawing Politics: Learning to Read Political Cartoons

Benjamin Franklin drew and published the first American political cartoon, but this way of expressing political views did not catch on until after the Civil War. Political cartoons include caricatures that exaggerate a person's physical characteristics. Political issues are expressed as a set of symbols and slogans.

Political cartoons use images to affect a viewer's opinion. This type of social expression took a serious subject and presented it in a funny way. Even those who could not read well could appreciate political cartoons.

Populism was a frequent target of political cartoons. Study this cartoon to figure out its meaning. Answer these questions:

1. Who are the characters?
2. What do the balloon patches stand for?
3. How are the Populists characterized?
4. What does the artist think of the People's Party?
5. How does the artist of the cartoon hope to influence the reader's opinion?

Socialism

In the Gilded Age, much of the wealth of America was concentrated in the hands of a small number of people. These conditions gave rise to a variety of social and economic reform movements. Among them was *Socialism*. Socialists wanted to see the wealth of the country distributed throughout all economic classes. They wanted the government to take more control. Kansas played a central role in the Socialist movement in America.

Appeal to Reason

The major Socialist newspaper in the country, the *Appeal to Reason*, was published for many years in Kansas. Julius A. Wayland started the *Appeal to Reason*, publishing it first in Kansas City and later in Girard, Kansas. At one point, it had a readership of more than half a million. Compared to other newspapers in the United States, this was an extremely large readership.

Wayland started the *Appeal to Reason* after years in the newspaper business. He grew up poor in Indiana and was forced to get work at an early age to help support his family. Wayland became a printer's apprentice at his hometown newspaper, which he eventually owned. Wayland became a Socialist after reading a number of books on the subject. Before starting the *Appeal to Reason*, he published another radical journal and started a *utopian* colony.

Many well-known reformers wrote for the *Appeal to Reason*. Eugene Debs, Mary "Mother" Jones, Helen Keller, Jack London, Kate Richards O'Hare, and Upton Sinclair were all contributors. Upton Sinclair's well-known novel, *The Jungle*, about immigrant workers in the Chicago meat-packing industry was first published in the *Appeal to Reason*.

The Socialist Platform

Julius Wayland often defended the views of Socialism in the *Appeal to Reason*.

In the midst of plenty you are starving. In the midst of natural wealth and mechanical means...many of you are deprived of employment, while those of whom work is given must toil increasingly for a decreasing pittance. The more you produce, the less you get....That class, which you have enriched, keeps you in poverty. The class, which you have raised to power, keeps you in subjection.

The Socialist Party ran candidates in local, state, and national elections. Although their ideas were too radical for most Americans, the Socialists made significant contributions to the national debate. What

Copies of the Appeal to Reason *were placed at the train station in Girard to be shipped across the country.*

they stood for influenced the direction of the United States. How did the Socialists propose to change America? Here are some of the ways:

- Fair treatment of workers, including a shorter workday, safe working conditions, workman's compensation in case of injury, child labor laws, and equal wages for women.

- Government ownership of the railroads, canals, telegraphs, telephones, and all means of public transportation and communication.

- Abolishment of government land grants.

- Congressional legislation prohibiting the waste of natural resources.

- An income tax structure where the wealthy pay a larger percent of their earnings and the very poor are exempt.

- A free education to all children, including public assistance for meals, clothing, and books when necessary.

- Establishment of a government work program for the unemployed.

- Election reform such as the use of secret ballots, universal suffrage, a method by which people can initiate laws, and the ability of the people to recall elected officials.

- Discontinuation of the United States Senate.

"From the Depths."

What do you think?

This drawing appeared in the *Appeal to Reason* in December of 1906. The illustration uses symbolism to make a point. What do you think the drawing means?

Little Blue Books: Making Literature Available to Everyone

Emanuel and Marcet Haldeman-Julius had very different backgrounds. Emanuel was the son of Russian Jewish immigrants. He lived in New York City and wrote for a Socialist publication. Marcet grew up in southeast Kansas. Her mother was president of the State Bank of Girard, the first woman in America to hold such a position.

Emanuel moved to Girard as an editor for the *Appeal to Reason*. Marcet had left Kansas to become an actress. When her mother died, she was left a large amount of money. In order to claim her inheritance, Marcet returned to Girard for a year. During that year, Marcet and Emanuel met and married. Believing that marriage was an equal partnership, they combined their last names into one. They both used the new name, Haldeman-Julius.

The two purchased the *Appeal to Reason* and became publishers. At the request of a literature professor at the socialist college in Ft. Scott, the two developed an inexpensive book series. The purpose of the "Little Blue Books," as they were called, was to make literature affordable for everyone. From 1919 to 1951 their company published more than 6,000 titles.

Millions of the inexpensive books were produced and sold by Emmanuel and Marcet Haldeman-Julius.

Kate Richards O'Hare
1876-1948

Kate Richards O'Hare became a well-known Socialist reformer. Born in Ottawa County, O'Hare later wrote about her early days in Kansas. "[They] gave me health and strength and love of freedom, taught me to depend on myself, to love nature, to honor rugged strength of mind and body and to know no shame in life."

O'Hare eventually moved to Kansas City and became an apprentice machinist and joined the International Order of Machinists union. Deeply religious, she became involved in the temperance movement. After hearing a speech by "Mother" Jones, O'Hare became more and more interested in Socialism.

While attending the International School of Social Economy, sponsored by the *Appeal to Reason* in Girard, she met her husband. The two spent their honeymoon organizing for the Socialist Party. She spent most of her career writing and organizing for Socialist causes. She also entered politics as a Socialist. O'Hare was the first woman in the United States to run for the U.S. Senate. Although she did not win the election, she continued in leadership positions for the Party.

Kate Richards O'Hare traveled throughout the country speaking against the United States' entrance into World War I. After the United States entered the war, O'Hare's protests resulted in her indictment under the Espionage Act. She was one of the few women to go to prison for her anti-war activity. Ultimately, she received a full pardon from President Calvin Coolidge. O'Hare spent her later years working for prison reform.

Kansas
PORTRAIT

Chapter 8 Review

What Do You Remember?

1. What was Kansas Senator Pomeroy accused of during the Gilded Age?
2. What happened as a result of the depression of the 1870s?
3. Why was alcohol a big problem during the Gilded Age?
4. What gave Governor John St. John of Kansas national attention and helped him run for president of the United States?
5. In what ways did Kansas fail to enforce its own prohibition laws?
6. Why did Carry A. Nation become famous?
7. What did the fight for universal suffrage involve?
8. What does municipal suffrage mean?
9. Name at least one issue that was of interest to women voters in Kansas.
10. Who was Susanna Salter?
11. How did Kansas women achieve full suffrage?
12. What is Populism?
13. Name at least three things the People's Party wanted to accomplish.
14. Compare and contrast the work of Mary Elizabeth Lease and Annie Diggs.
15. How did "Sockless Jerry" Simpson get his nickname?
16. How was William Peffer able to become a U.S. senator from Kansas?
17. What caused the Legislative War?
18. What was William Allen White saying in his editorial "What's the Matter with Kansas?"
19. What was the importance of the newspaper the *Appeal to Reason*?
20. Name at least three things the Socialists wanted to accomplish.
21. Who was Kate Richards O'Hare?
22. What was the purpose of the Little Blue Books?

Think About It!

1. Why did Mark Twain and Charles Dudley Warner coin the term The Gilded Age? Why do you think it is, or is not, an appropriate term for the time period? What conditions would need to exist for another "Gilded Age" to happen in the United States?
2. What made farmers angry during the Gilded Age? What did farmers have in common with industrial workers? Do you think farmers saw themselves as workers or business owners? How might their views on this issue change how they viewed the economic conditions of the time?

Activities

1. There are people in every community who are motivated to make their neighborhood, town, or state a better place. Ask someone who has made a difference in your community to speak to your class. Ask them to discuss what motivated them and how they achieved their goals.
2. As a class, think of a change you would like to make in your community or in Kansas. Create a detailed plan of how you might go about achieving your goals and objectives.

PEOPLE TO KNOW
Walter Chrysler
Samuel Crumbine
Frederick Funston
Peggy Hull
Albin K. Longren
Charles Sheldon
William Allen White

PLACES TO LOCATE
Abilene
Chanute
Dodge City
El Dorado
Fort Riley
Freedom
Girard
Goodland
Hutchinson
Iola
Junction City
Marysville
Neodesha
Philippine Islands
St. Louis, Missouri
Topeka
Wichita

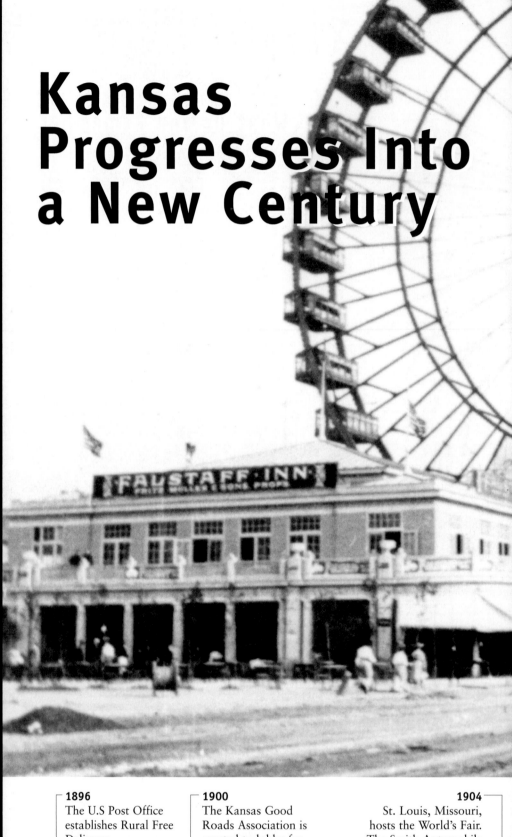

Kansas Progresses Into a New Century

One highlight of the St. Louis World's Fair was the enormous Observation Wheel. It had 36 cars—each was the size of a streetcar and could hold 60 people. An unusual wedding took place on the ride. Dollie Coffman, from Kansas, and her fiancé, a rider in a wild west show at the fair, rode their horses into one of the cars and married at the top of the ride.

Timeline of Events

1896
The U.S Post Office establishes Rural Free Delivery.

1900
The Kansas Good Roads Association is created to lobby for improved roads.

1904
St. Louis, Missouri, hosts the World's Fair. The Smith Automobile Company originates in Topeka.

1896   1898   1900   1902   1904

1897
Charles Sheldon publishes *In His Steps*.

1898
The United States declares war on Spain, resulting in the Spanish-American War.

1905
Dr. Samuel Crumbine becomes secretary of the Kansas State Board of Health.

Chapter 9

WORDS TO UNDERSTAND
capital
consumer
contaminated
credit
diversified
epidemic
extraction
horticultural
lobbyist
neutrality
quota
refinery
regulation
rural
Rural Free Delivery
specialization
trade
tuberculosis
underdog
urban

1905
Kansas adopts a comprehensive child labor law.

1909
Kansas outlaws the common drinking cup to control the spread of tuberculosis.

1911
Albin Longren builds the first successful Kansas airplane.

1914-1918
World War I

CLEAR THE WAY
BUY BONDS
FOURTH

1906   1908   1910   1912   1914   1916   1918

1907
Kansas passes a Food and Drug law and a Water and Sewage law.

1913
The Sixteenth Amendment legalizes a federal income tax.
The Seventeenth Amendment provides for the direct election of U.S. Senators.

1915
The oil fields near El Dorado are opened.

1917
The United States enters World War I.

Kansas showed its pride at the St. Louis World's Fair in 1904.
It was a time of prosperity.

The Beginning of the 20th Century

Kansas entered the new century with great optimism. The United States was recovering from difficult economic times. The future looked prosperous. Kansas was emerging as a leader in agriculture. Farm products steadily increased in value. More than half of the state's population worked in agriculture.

By 1900, more than 20 percent of Kansans lived in cities. *Urban* areas were growing across the country. Kansas City, Topeka, Wichita, and Leavenworth were the largest cities in Kansas. Atchison, Pittsburg, Lawrence, Fort Scott, and Galena were growing larger.

Electricity was a new invention that changed lives in urban Kansas. *Rural* Kansans generally did not get electricity until later. Families living on farms welcomed *Rural Free Delivery*. This allowed them to receive mail at home, rather than at the post office in town. By the beginning of the 20th century, Kansas had 200 rural mail routes. This was also the beginning of the popularity of mail order catalogs. Farm families could order goods, such as clothing and household items, and have them delivered right to their doors.

"Meet Me in St. Louis"

Nothing captured the optimism of the times better than the St. Louis World's Fair. It celebrated the 100th anniversary of the Louisiana Purchase. Everyone wanted to go to the fair! The country was singing the popular song "Meet Me in Saint Louis" long before the fair even opened.

People from all over the world found their way to the biggest world's fair in history. Most traveled by train, boat, or horse and carriage. Fifty foreign countries and 43 of the 45 states contributed exhibits to the fair. Nine hundred buildings were constructed at a cost of 15 million dollars. This was the same amount the United States paid France for the Louisiana Territory 100 years earlier.

The St. Louis World's Fair captured the mood and the values of the times. Americans valued education as the key to the future. Education was a major emphasis of the fair. New technologies and innovations were also featured. Americans entered the 20th century believing that all problems could be solved through scientific discovery and invention. It was an age of progress, and Americans saw no limits to the possibilities.

People came to the fair to have fun and see new

products and inventions. Electricity was so important to the fair that Thomas Edison, the inventor of the light bulb, supervised the electrical displays. The newly available automobile was featured, as were experimental flying machines. Electric clocks, coin changers, and x-rays were all introduced at the fair.

Kansas at the World's Fair

Kansas, like most of the others states, participated in the St. Louis World's Fair. It was an opportunity to promote the state and its economy. The records of the Kansas *Horticultural* Society reveal the state's thinking about the fair:

> *Kansas, as the center of the Union, and a successful, rustling, vigorous chunk of the Louisiana purchase, should be prominent. Kansas, as a neighbor and supporter of Missouri, should do all she can to show that this is no longer the great American desert, but the fruit-garden of the continent.*

Kansas contributed to the success of the fair in many ways. The fancy exteriors of many of the fair buildings were made of plaster. The plaster contained limestone mined in Kansas. The Kansas State Board of Agriculture bragged that, "Each time a visitor paused to admire vast palaces . . . and other buildings, or gaze in wonder . . . he was reminded that Kansas contributed more materials for the construction of this incomparable memorial than any other state or country."

Kansas built its own state building. Some called it the most welcoming and comfortable of all the buildings at the fair. The large rooms welcomed guests, encouraging them to relax in the ladies' parlor or the men's reading room. Kansas parents were allowed to leave their youngest children in the nursery. Paintings by Kansas artists covered the exhibit walls.

Kansas was also present in other buildings at the fair. The state's agricultural products were prominently displayed. A Kansas mining exhibit included coal, oil, salt, and bricks.

Filipinos made this village at the World's Fair.

American Interest in the Philippine Islands

World travel was a luxury, available only to the very wealthy. The St. Louis World's Fair gave many Americans their first look at other cultures. The largest foreign exhibit was from the Philippines. Native villages populated by 1,100 Filipinos occupied a large section of the fair grounds. Why such interest in the Philippines? The answer can be traced to the Spanish-American War. It was during this conflict that Cuba won its independence from Spain. Spain also lost control of Puerto Rico, Guam, and the Philippine Islands. They all became territories of the United States.

Four Kansas volunteer regiments were recruited for the Spanish-American War. The 23rd Kansas Volunteers was an African American unit and the first led by black officers. It served in Cuba. The 20th Kansas Volunteers were under the command of Frederick Funston from Iola. This regiment was sent to the Philippines after Spain surrendered. Its mission was to put down the resistance of Philippine residents to American control of the islands. After several months, the "Fighting Twentieth," as it was called, returned to Kansas. Funston returned to the Philippines and became famous as the man who brought an end to the resistance.

By the time of the St. Louis World's Fair, Americans disagreed about the United States' involvement in the Philippines. Some people opposed America ruling a country so far away. Others felt that the United States had a new Manifest Destiny to control the islands of the Pacific Ocean. The Philippine exhibits at the fair were intended to make Americans more comfortable with their role in the Pacific. The American government saw itself as bringing progress to another part of the world.

The Progressive Movement

The Progressive movement was about building a better society. It was not a political party, nor was it a single movement. Instead it was a series of movements all desiring to make the United States a more equitable place. Both Democrats and Republicans were associated with the Progressive movement. It was about progress and moving forward.

William Allen White, a leader in the Progressive movement, described it as, "a middle-class revolt against the injustice of our society." The Progressives wanted to help out those who could not always help themselves. This was different from the Populists, who saw themselves as *underdogs* and were fighting to change their own lives. In time the Progressives took on many of the same issues as the Populists, including election reform, government *regulation* of businesses, and the establishment of an income tax.

The Progressive leaders in Kansas were followers of President Theodore Roosevelt. William Allen White, a good friend of the president, is seen here with President Roosevelt at a 1910 political rally.

The Progressives in Kansas wanted to make a better place for all of the state's citizens. They fought for the following reforms:

- Election reforms, including establishing statewide primary elections and allowing the public to initiate laws and recall elected officials.

- Government reforms, including instituting measures to better control funding of state programs, establishing a tax on inheritance, requiring *lobbyists* to register, and establishing a juvenile court system.

- Labor reforms, including child labor laws and workman's compensation for injured workers.

- Business reforms, including controlling railroad ticket prices, establishing public utilities, and requiring all companies to be truthful in *consumer* information.

- Economic reforms, including guaranteeing the safety of all bank deposits.

- Public health reforms, including food safety and anti-cigarette laws.

The Progressives in Kansas achieved many of their goals. Laws were passed that made government and businesses more accountable to the people. Kansas consumers were given protections under the law. The state provided more and more protections for Kansas children.

Kansans were demanding good roads as the automobile became more common. This 1914 photograph shows residents near Beloit coming together to build a road. Five years earlier, Progressive Kansas governor Walter Stubbs called for the establishment of a state highways department. Eventually, the state took over public highways, using tax money to improve roads.

Farm families did not want to see laws that prohibited their children from working on the family farm. This 1912 photograph shows a young girl feeding the chickens on the farm.

Protecting Kansas Children

In the early days of our country, most children worked, just like their parents. Children were an important part of the agricultural economy. Many worked on the family farm. Many were also hired out to work for other farmers. Young boys often began to learn a *trade* between the ages of 10 and 14.

During the Industrial Age, more children began to work in factories. Machinery allowed children to take over jobs that were previously done by adults. By the age of 10, many children found themselves working to help support their families. Working conditions in some industries were unsafe and unhealthy. Work hours were long.

By 1900, over 10 percent of Kansas children between the ages of 10 and 15 went to work each day. Most worked in agriculture, manufacturing, and domestic service. Some Kansans were against children working, but others did not want the government regulating what they believed was a family matter. Kansans valued education, and the law required that all children between the ages of eight and 14 had to go to school for at least 12 weeks a year. Not everyone agreed about where children belonged.

Right before the turn of the century, Kansas passed a law to protect the morals of children. This law restricted children from working at certain jobs. No one under the age of 14 could be employed as an acrobat, circus rider, rope walker, beggar, or street musician. Within a few years, Kansas adopted its first major child labor law. Children under 14 could not be employed in factories, meat-packing houses, or in mines. To work in any occupation that was considered dangerous, you had to be 16 or older. When this became law, nearly 2,000 Kansas children were taken out of the factories and placed in schools.

Activity

Reading a Law:
1905 Child Labor Law

The state legislature adopts bills that are signed into law by the governor. What follows is the text of the 1905 law that prohibited child labor in certain occupations. This law started as a bill in the state senate. All laws are open to interpretation. Sometimes laws are legally challenged, and then the courts must interpret the law. This is the responsibility of the judicial branch. In reading this law, can you guess what parts of it might be open to interpretation?

Make a chart that has five sections. Summarize each section of the law using the following questions.

Section 1:	Meaning
Who does the law effect? What are the restrictions?	

Section 2:	
How will the law be implemented? How must employers prove that they are following the law?	

Section 3:	
Who is charged with enforcing the law? What must they do if the law is violated?	

Section 4:	
What are the penalties if someone violates the law? Who is punished?	

Section 5:	
When does the bill become law? What has to happen for the law to go into effect?	

CHILD LABOR PROHIBITED IN CERTAIN EMPLOYMENTS

Senate bill No. 86.

AN ACT concerning child labor, prohibiting the employment in factories, packing-houses and mines of persons under fourteen years of age, and regulating the employment in other occupations or places of persons under sixteen years of age.

Be it enacted by the Legislature of the State of Kansas:

Section 1. No child under fourteen years of age shall be employed at any time in any factory or packing-houses or in or about any mine. No person under sixteen years of age shall be employed at any occupation nor at any place dangerous or injurious to life, limb, health, or morals.

Sec. 2. All persons, firms or corporations employing children shall be required first to obtain a certificate of the age of such children, where possible, from the school board, principal of school or teacher of the school in district or city wherein such children reside....When it is impossible to secure the certificate...the firm, person or corporation employing such child shall secure a statement of the age of such child, which statement shall be verified under oath before some officer authorized to administer oaths. Such certificate shall be sufficient protection to the employer of any child as to the age of such child, except when such employer has actual knowledge of the falsity of such certificate; and all such certificates shall be kept constantly on file in a convenient place, and shall at times be open to the inspection of the proper authorities, as provided in this act.

Sec. 3. It shall be the duty of the state factory inspector, state inspector of mines and their deputies to inspect the certificates hereinabove provided for, to examine children employed in factories, mines and packing-houses as to their age, and to file complaints in any court of competent jurisdiction to enforce the provisions of this act, and it shall be the duty of the county attorney of the proper county to appear and prosecute all complaints so filled.

Sec. 4. Any person, firm or corporation employing any person or child in violation of any provisions of this act, or permitting or conniving at such violation, shall be deemed guilty of a misdemeanor, and upon conviction thereof shall be fined in a sum not less than twenty-five dollars nor more than one hundred dollars, or by imprisonment in county jail not less than thirty days nor more than ninety days.

Sec. 5. This act shall take effect and be in force from and after its publication in the official state paper.

Approved February 22, 1905.
Published in official state paper February 28, 1905.

So important was Crumbine's campaign against the fly that some communities gave prizes to the students who could kill the most flies.

Dr. Samuel Crumbine and Public Health Reform

Have you ever seen a brick that says, "Don't Spit on the Sidewalk?" Do you know how and why the fly swatter was invented? Have you ever thought about why you have screens on your windows? Do you know the meaning of the slogan "Ban the Public Drinking Cup?"

These and other public health campaigns were the ideas of Dr. Samuel Crumbine. Before Crumbine led the way, most Americans did not know where germs came from and how diseases could be prevented. Crumbine, a doctor from Dodge City, became secretary of the Kansas State Board of Health and a national figure for public health reform.

The idea that diseases were caused by germs was new to the scientific and medical communities. Dr. Crumbine led the way in taking this knowledge to the people. His interest was in disease prevention. He felt education was the key to getting people to change their behavior. Crumbine also saw value in expanding the state's legal authority over unsafe practices.

Crumbine championed laws that provided for pure foods and drugs. He launched a major campaign called "Swat the Fly." The military discovered that flies carry bacteria to open containers of food. A Kansas teacher gave Crumbine a ruler with a wire screen attached. Crumbine named it the "fly swatter." Communities across Kansas began putting screens on their windows to keep out unwanted flies.

Next, Crumbine went after the public drinking cup. Before drinking fountains, if you wanted a drink in a public place, you used a cup that everyone shared. Crumbine saw this as a health hazard and banned its use. This was part of his fight against the

The April 1910 Bulletin of the Kansas State Board of Health said, "We hate the house fly. Not personally, but because scientists have assured us he is a disease breeder, carrying germs from affected to healthy communities." Crumbine used cartoons, as well as words, to make his point.

spread of *tuberculosis.* For the same reason, he wanted people to stop spitting in public. He asked Kansas brick makers to print "Don't Spit on the Sidewalk" on their bricks to get people's attention.

Clean water was another public health issue. Crumbine took a canoe trip down the Kansas River and sampled the water at various points. His research proved that the water contained bacteria. One-fourth of the rural wells in Kansas were also found to be *contaminated.* Crumbine became an advocate of sewage treatment to prevent the dumping of sewage directly into streams and rivers. Before he left the State Board of Health, Crumbine initiated a "save the baby" campaign. To reduce infant deaths, Crumbine wanted to make sure babies were cared for in clean environments.

The Legacy of Progressive and Reform Politics

Many things that we take for granted today were issues brought to the forefront by the reform movements of the late 19th and early 20th century. Child labor laws, workman's compensation, and the eight-hour workday all came about because of the attention paid to labor reform.

Government regulations of industries and utilities for the good of the people were part of reform politics. Reforming government was also successful. Today, we hold primary elections and vote directly for U.S. Senators. The graduated income tax and the inheritance tax remain controversial, but they came about during this time. These taxes required those who could afford it to pay more. Laws protecting consumers and the environment have their roots in these reform movements.

During their time, Populism, Socialism, and Progressivism were distinct political movements. But they wanted many of the same things, and in the end many of their reforms became part of our lives today.

Activity

"The Chuckling Socialist," June 26, 1913

In 1913, William Allen White, the editor of the *Emporia Gazette,* wrote the following editorial about the relationship between the reform movements. After reading it, answer these questions:

1. What has happened to the Socialist agenda according to White?
2. What evidence does he use to make his point?
3. Why did White think the political mood of the country had changed?

Kansas City, Kansas, voted to construct a municipal electric lighting plant. Yesterday, Judge Hook, of the federal circuit court, approved a plan looking to the municipal ownership of the Kansas City street car system. Last week Attorney John Dawson declared that ice, being a public utility, should be controlled by the state. Last month a bill favorably considered by a committee of Congress provided for the construction of a government railroad in Alaska, and for government ownership and lease operation of coal mines. All these things have happened in the past thirty days.

If you were a Socialist, wouldn't you hunt a cool shady spot between two buildings where air poured through and sit down in a kitchen chair and chuckle and chuckle and chuckle?

The really interesting part of the situation is that about half of the American Socialist platform for 1904 is now on the statute books of one third of the states, and much of it is in the platforms of at least two of the great parties.

The Socialists are getting too conservative for this country. They will have to get a move on themselves or they will be without an issue in 1916. For the Bull Moosers have stolen the Socialists thunder, and the progressive Republicans declare they are just as progressive as the Bull Moosers, and the Democrats say they are more progressive than the Progressives. Unless the Republicans and Democrats are lying about how progressive they are, and unless the Bull Moosers are as short-lived as their enemies declare they are, the Socialists might as well go out of business, for all the great parties will be swiping the Socialist planks.

Which is funny. But it indicates that the people have begun thinking along economic lines, and the politicians are trying to capitalize the popular tendencies.

Charles Sheldon
1857 -1946

Charles Sheldon came to Topeka to become the pastor of the Central Congregational Church. He was interested in the needs of the poor. He became very involved in the section of Topeka called Tennessee Town. It was a place where many former slaves lived. He started kindergartens, libraries, and neighborhood clean-up campaigns. Sheldon also found ways to provide the community with free medical and legal assistance.

Sheldon was part of the social gospel movement. The idea was to take the ideals of social justice from the Bible and apply them to one's own community. This was how some clergy applied the ideas of the Progressive era.

In order to attract young people to his church, Reverend Sheldon turned his Sunday evening sermons into stories, always ending in a "cliffhanger." This kept people coming back each Sunday to hear the end of the story. One of Sheldon's stories became very famous. It was called "In His Steps" or "What Would Jesus Do?" It was a series of stories about people who choose to live their daily lives as they thought Jesus would. This best-selling book remains popular today.

Sheldon also experimented with the idea of "good news." For a week, the publishers of the *Topeka Daily Capital* gave Sheldon the chance to edit the newspaper. He cut out stories that were negative and refused advertising from theaters and tobacco sellers. This experiment was so famous that special editions of the paper were printed in New York, Chicago, and London. Sheldon donated his earnings to charity.

Applying the ideas of social justice found in the Bible, Reverend Charles Sheldon founded a kindergarten for African American children in Topeka. This photo shows the school's band.

The Kansas Economy Progresses

The Kansas economy grew through the use of science and technology. Farmers in Kansas began to practice "scientific" agriculture. They began testing soils, introducing new seeds, and finding new ways to get water to crops. New technology also brought industrial advancements to Kansas. Science allowed Kansas to find rich oil and natural gas deposits. New technologies allowed for the creation of *extraction* industries, which removed precious natural resources from under the ground. Science also created new forms of transportation, including automobiles and airplanes. Kansas was not only progressive in its politics—the state's economy also progressed.

Agriculture

The availability of new machinery changed farming in Kansas. Steam and gasoline-powered engines were replacing the horse, which had provided power to earlier farms. Tractors allowed farmers to plow, plant, and harvest much faster. This increased the number of acres a farmer could work and eventually led to larger farms.

Gasoline-powered engines enabled farmers to pull more water out of the ground, allowing for better irrigation. New powerful machines also led to new practices in dry farming. Dry farming used water stored in the soil to nurture crops. This meant that a farmer must work his soil after every rain. This required the ability to work quickly, and new machines helped the farmer do just that. Dry farming also required the use of crops that needed less moisture. Wheat was the ideal dry farming crop.

New technology also led to more *specialization* in farming. Earlier farms were more *diversified*. Farmers raised, processed, and stored their own food. They grew grains, vegetables, and fruits and also raised all types of livestock. With increased technology, farmers could produce more, which resulted in surplus products for the marketplace. Once farmers began producing for the marketplace, it became easier to specialize. For example, a farmer might concentrate on growing one type of crop and sell that crop to someone else to store and process.

The agricultural college at Manhattan and organizations like the Kansas State Board of Agriculture used scientific principles to help Kansas farmers increase their crop and livestock production. During this time, pigs and chickens joined cattle as important to the Kansas agricultural economy. Sorghum, sugar beets, and broom corn became important Kansas crops. Wichita even became known as the broom corn capital of the world when local factories began turning the straw into household brooms.

The Kansas State Fair

Fairs in Kansas have always been linked with agriculture. Fairs provide an opportunity to showcase Kansas' best agricultural products. They also create educational opportunities to exhibit new methods of cultivation and new varieties of seeds and livestock.

Shortly after Kansas became a state, the Kansas State Agricultural Society considered holding a state fair. They rejected the idea because the nation was engaged in the Civil War. Within a few years, the Society began to sponsor an annual state fair. Cities competed to host the fair. Local and regional fairs were also held throughout the state. The fair as we know it today began in 1913, with Hutchinson becoming the fair's permanent home.

Hutchinson held state fairs even before it became the home of the official Kansas State Fair. This photograph shows horses being judged in 1906.

Oil and Gas

From the beginning of statehood, Kansans knew there was oil in eastern Kansas. It took another 30 years before the first big oil strike in Neodesha opened the Mid-Continent Oil Field. So productive was the well that Standard Oil Company, run by John D. Rockefeller, opened an oil *refinery* in Neodesha. This caused an oil boom in the region.

The new technology of the age created a whole new economy for Kansas. In Chanute, they were pumping both oil and natural gas. The city controlled 21 gas wells and provided its citizens with inexpensive natural gas for heating. It was said "it is . . . cheaper to keep warm in Chanute than it is to freeze to death." In 1900, Chanute had a population of 4,200. In three years, that population jumped to 7,115. The more than 30 oil and gas companies that made Chanute their home caused this population increase.

Within a few years, Standard Oil controlled much of the oil economy of southeast Kansas. Independent oil drillers and producers became angered at Standard Oil's power over prices. Standard Oil Company not only drilled the oil, but it refined crude oil and transported it, giving Standard Oil a monopoly. During this period of progressive reforms, the state legislature decided to place regulations on Standards Oil's operations. Kansas even considered running a state-owned oil refinery using prisoners as labor. But the courts struck down this idea. These attacks on Standard Oil had their consequences, and the company pulled out of Kansas.

Many people were scared that Kansas' oil days were over. But soon the most productive oil field in the United States was discovered in El Dorado, using scientific geological methods. Oil workers and their families poured into El Dorado by the thousands. Most were experienced workers from the oil fields in the East. They worked 12-hour shifts with only one day off a year. The money was good, but the work could be dangerous. Businesses in El Dorado grew rapidly to keep up with the increasing population. Many stores and services were open 24 hours a day to serve the needs of the oil workers.

The discovery of oil in the El Dorado Field had an enormous impact on Kansas and the United States. The Kansas economy diversified, and many people were making a lot of money. Kansas was pumping so much oil that during World War I, the United States never had to ration oil. The richness of the El Dorado Field inspired further exploration of oil in western Kansas. The availability of oil also helped to accelerate farm mechanization.

Company oil towns sprang up in Butler County. Oil workers were paid $30 a week. They paid only $5 a month to the company for housing.

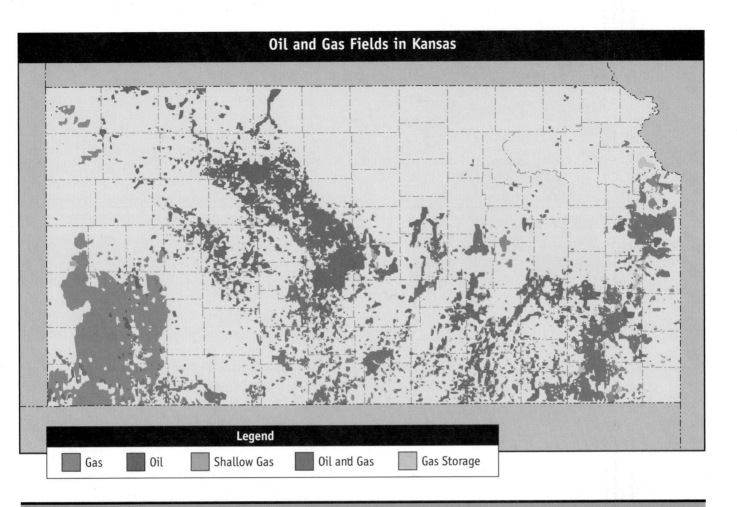

Legend

Gas   Oil   Shallow Gas   Oil and Gas   Gas Storage

Discovery of Rock Salt

Do you remember reading about the Permian Sea? This great inland sea left Kansas with many natural resources. Limestone, coal, oil, natural gas, and salt are just a few of the resources the sea left behind.

Salt has been produced in Kansas throughout the state's history. Salt was obtained through evaporation. Wells were dug into pockets of salt water. When the water evaporated, salt was left behind. Salt was obtained this way in Miami, Republic, and Dickinson Counties.

An oil company digging near Hutchinson discovered rock salt. This salt deposit is one of the largest in the

This advertisement from 1892 claims that the Hutchinson Salt Company is the largest manufacturer of salt in the United States.

world. At first, the salt was extracted by pumping water into the wells to dissolve the rock salt. Salt was then harvested through evaporation. Underground salt mines were eventually used to extract the rock salt in much the same way that coal is taken from the ground.

Kansas Progresses Into a New Century

Kansas
PORTRAIT

Walter Chrysler
1875-1940

Have you ever wanted to take something apart to see how it works? That is exactly what Walter Chrysler did with his first car. He took it apart and put it back together many times, teaching himself how the automobile worked.

Chrysler first learned about engines from his father, who was an engineer for the Union Pacific Railroad. Chrysler was born in Wamego, Kansas, but grew-up in Ellis. As a young boy, he was fascinated with model train engines. He was a hard worker. He delivered milk produced by the family's cows to people around town. His mother let him keep a penny for every quart of milk he sold. As a teenager, he delivered groceries in town, earning two pennies an hour.

As an adult, Chrysler took a job cleaning up the Union Pacific Railroad shops for $1 a day. He worked his way up to the job of locomotive mechanic. Chrysler eventually left Kansas, working for a variety of railroads. After attending an automobile show in Chicago, he became fascinated with cars. He was so interested that he borrowed money to buy an expensive car just so he could take it apart.

Chrysler went on to have a distinguished career in the automobile industry. As president of the Buick Motor Company, he increased production from 45 cars to 600 cars a day in less than 10 years. He also ran the Maxwell Motor Company, introducing a new car called the "Chrysler." It was very popular with the public, and Chrysler renamed the company after himself.

The Chrysler Corporation came to include both Dodge and Plymouth models. The Chrysler Building in New York City is probably one of the most recognizable buildings in the world and a tribute to this Kansan's success.

Kansas Automobiles and the Good Roads Movement

In 1900, only one out of every 9,500 Americans owned a car. The majority of these were powered by steam or electricity. Only about 20 percent of the cars were powered by gasoline. In four more years, the United States would become the number one producer of automobiles in the world using the gasoline engine. The development of gasoline-powered cars was tied to the growing oil industry.

Kansans were involved with the early manufacturing of automobiles. In Topeka, the Smith Automobile Company made cars with powerful engines. Its most popular model was the Great Smith touring car. It was very expensive, costing $2,650, not including "accessories" such as a top and a windshield. In contrast, a Ford Model T could be purchased for around $850.

There were at least three other automobile manufacturers in Kansas. Small companies in Wichita, Parsons, and Hutchinson did not have the *capital* to compete with the larger American car companies. Without the money to improve their production efficiency, smaller automobile manufacturers simply went out of business.

As automobiles became increasingly more common in Kansas, they began to change rural life. Cars made it easier for farm families to go to town by decreasing travel times. Car trips became something to do in leisure time. This made touring cars, like the Great Smith, popular among those who could afford them.

Most rural roads were dirt. Farmers used those roads to get their products to town. Maintaining roads was not the job of the state or federal government at this time. Instead, local governments and individual landowners were responsible for maintaining their roads. The Kansas Good Roads Association encouraged communities to maintain their roads. One pamphlet argued, "Rough and muddy roads cost the average farmer more than his taxes. If each farmer will, at the proper time, do a little dragging on the road in front of his land, the State's bad roads will largely be made good roads."

This Wichita automobile manufacturing company was one of four in Kansas. Here workers install wiring at the Jones Motor Car Company.

Automobile Club of Wichita, Kansas, 1909-1910

At one time, road maps were not common. Highways did not have numbers. How did motorists find the way from one town to another? They used guidebooks with written driving directions.

This is an excerpt from a guidebook published by the Automobile Club of Wichita. These directions take the driver from Winfield to Wichita. Use a modern road map to trace the approximate route that the guidebook is suggesting. What would the directions be today? Compare your modern directions with these. Which are easier to follow?

The Hockaday Motor Cycle Co. is advertised in the 1909-1910 Automobile Club of Wichita guidebook. Hockaday, a Wichita automobile dealer, launched a campaign to mark Kansas auto routes. In 1918, he published a road map showing 33 marked highways in the United States.

Route No. 8A
Winfield to Wichita

Mileage

0	WINFIELD. Go west 7 miles bearing 1 mile north in last mile.
7	KELLOGG. At west side of town turn north, crossing two R.R. tracks. Continue north to
16	UDALL. Turn west through Udall. In west part of town near stand-pipe, north short distance to first section line - then west to first section line.
17	Turn right, go north 6 miles to
23	COUNTY LINE. Go west 6 miles to center of
29	MULVANE. North out of center of town 3 miles (R.R. track near town. Dangerous crossing.)
32	West 1 mile.
33	North 11/2 miles.
34.5	West 1/2 mile to south end of Main street of
34.6	DERBY. North 21/2 miles from south side of town. At north part of town bear to west few rods, then north.
34.7	West 1/2 mile.
38	North.
42.5	COUNTY POOR FARM, on right.
44	West 1 mile on Harry street.
45	North 11/2 miles on Hillside avenue to Douglas avenue.
46.5	West on Douglas avenue to center of
48.5	WICHITA. (Corner Lawrence avenue.)

The Hunt rotary aircraft was built in Jetmore in 1910. Can you see why this invention could not fly?

Kansans Experiment with Flight

Three years before Wilbur and Orville Wright made their famous flight in North Carolina, at least one Kansan was already dreaming of air travel. Carl Dryden Browne built a commercial airplane factory and a prototype airplane. Browne had gained some fame as the Chief Marshall of "Coxey's Army," a group of unemployed workers who marched on Washington, D.C., in 1894 to protest the lack of jobs.

Browne came to Kansas to participate in a utopian worker's community, established in Freedom. He wanted to build flying machines to provide work for the unemployed. His plan was to sell the flying machines at such a low price that they would take the place of bicycles in most families. Browne never tested his flying machine, and the factory was closed within two years.

After the Wright brothers flew, all kinds of people began tinkering with flight. A socialist lawyer by the name of Henry Call has been credited with building the first airplane west of the Mississippi River.

Financed primarily by J. A. Wayland and readers of the newspaper *Appeal to Reason*, Call started the Aerial Navigation Company in Girard. The first plane was named the "Girard Airship" by Call. The townspeople called it "Mayfly" because "it may fly!" It never got off the ground. In fact, the first six planes Call built did not fly. The seventh flew for less than a mile before crashing and giving the pilot a black eye.

Kansans also experimented with rotary-wing flying machines. These were early types of helicopters. A Jetmore blacksmith named A. E. Hunt built one out of pipe and iron. The principle of using rotors to move and hold up the aircraft was right, but the materials were wrong. The pipe and iron Hunt used weighed more than three tons. The aircraft would not move. In Goodland, two railroad machinists, Charles Wilson and William Purvis, built a two-story aircraft with two sets of blades that spun in opposite directions. Wilson and Purvis demonstrated their invention on Thanksgiving Day 1909, but it never flew.

Flying High

Albin K. Longren built the first successful Kansas airplane. Longren was a Topeka mechanic who enjoyed working with machinery. With the help of his brother and a friend, he set out to build an airplane. They began creating their new machine on the second floor of a building.

Building a plane on the second floor soon proved impractical, and Longren and his team moved the airplane parts to a field southeast of Topeka. Each night one of the three men took turns watching over their invention. When the plane was complete, Longren gave it a test flight. It worked! Several days later, he flew over downtown Topeka, introducing people to his new invention. Can you imagine the town's reaction?

Longren took on the nickname "Birdman." He traveled across the state showing off his new flying machines. In fact, he made 1,372 exhibition flights with only one serious accident. Longren dreamed of building airplanes to replace automobiles. In his mind, he saw a small airplane in every garage. As with most early aircraft companies, Longren eventually went broke.

Albin K. Longren, along with his brother and a friend, established the first airplane manufacturing company in Kansas. This photograph was taken in 1916.

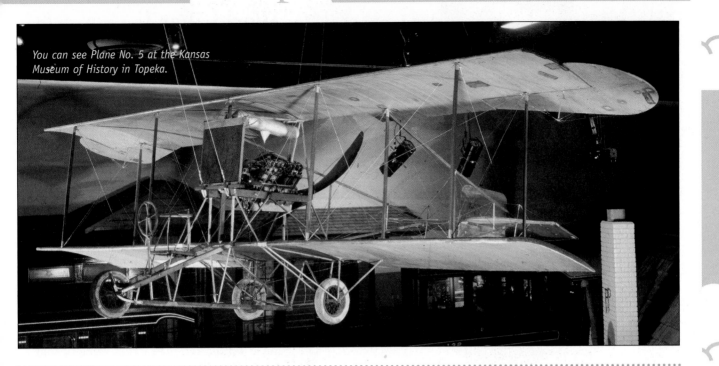

You can see Plane No. 5 at the Kansas Museum of History in Topeka.

How Do We Know This?

Museum curators do not just collect artifacts—they study them. Artifacts are the things people from the past leave behind. They can tell us how someone lived or help us trace the development of technology. Albin K. Longren's airplane does just that.

What do we know about this artifact, and how did it get into a museum? "Plane No. 5," as it was called, was built in 1914. Early aviators often used parts from older aircraft to build new ones. The engine and the radiator in Plane No. 5 were recycled from Longren's very first plane. Plane No. 5 was used for exhibition flights. Early aviators would "barnstorm" the countryside. This meant they would fly their planes while crowds of people watched.

Early aviation was very dangerous. One day in Abilene, a strong wind brought down Plane No. 5. It crashed into the ground, seriously injuring Longren's leg. Eventually, Longren rebuilt the plane and sold it to Phillip Billard. Billard used the plane until World War I, when the army sent him to France. Unfortunately, Billard was killed in an aviation accident. Plane No. 5 remained in the family's garage for the next 20 years. Billard's brother understood the historical value of the plane and donated it to the Kansas State Historical Society in the 1930s.

By examining Plane No. 5, we can learn a lot about early aviation. The plane's propeller is mounted in the rear of the plane. This means the aircraft was "pushed" from behind. The plane has a pedal accelerator much like a car. From its placement, we know that the pilot's right foot operated the accelerator. We also can tell that the pilot steered the aircraft with a wheel, just like one found on an automobile.

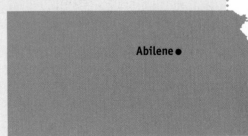

Abilene●

Kansas
PORTRAIT

Peggy Hull
1889-1967

Peggy Hull was the first woman war correspondent accredited by the United States government. She reported on the military for 31 years, following American soldiers around the world. Her newspaper articles were popular back home because she focused on the personal side of war. Her stories were about the lives of the soldiers.

Hull was born on a farm near Bennington but grew up in Marysville. She attended high school in Junction City, where her family moved when she was 15. Hull's teachers recognized a talented young writer. After she left school, Hull decided she was interested in journalism and applied to work at the *Junction City Sentinel*. She began her newspaper career as a typesetter. Two weeks after she was hired, a fire broke out in town, and no reporter was available to cover the story. Hull got her chance and so impressed the editor that she became a writer for the paper.

At 18, Peggy Hull left Kansas to work on a variety of newspapers. During the Mexican Revolution, American troops were called into duty along the border. Peggy Hull was sent to cover the story. She wore an army uniform, carried her own equipment, and slept on the ground, all so she could write about soldiers' lives.

When the United States entered World War I, Hull went to France. Male reporters were uncomfortable with her presence, and they convinced the army to send her away from the front. The men claimed that Hull did not have official status from the U.S. government. This did not stop Peggy Hull. Instead, she convinced the officials in Washington, D.C., to give her accreditation.

World War I

World War I began in Europe. The Allies (Russia, France, and Great Britain) were at war with the Central Powers (Germany, Austria-Hungary, and Turkey). Eventually, the "Great War," as it was called, spread beyond Europe. World War I saw the first use of chemical weapons and the first air attacks on civilians.

Most Americans had little interest in entering a war so far from home. President Woodrow Wilson issued a proclamation of *neutrality*. This meant that the United States intended to stay out of the war, but the war still had an effect here at home.

One consequence of the war was that agricultural production was interrupted in Europe. This increased interest in Kansas farm products. Farmers began growing more wheat, and the market value of that wheat rose. The generosity of Kansans was demonstrated through wheat donations to Belgium, a country that had been defeated by Germany.

Germany eventually launched attacks on American ships, and the United States could no longer remain neutral. As the United States ended its official ties to Germany, many Kansans began to change their minds about the war. Governor Arthur Capper became concerned about the food supply and asked Kansans to grow gardens and conserve food.

The United States declared war on the Central Powers. Needing men to fight the war, the United States instituted a military draft. Kansas exceeded its *quota* of enlistments. Almost 80,000 Kansas men joined the armed forces. With so many new men going into the service, there was a need for a training facility. Camp Funston was established at Fort Riley for that purpose.

At and near Fort Riley, people set up ▶ temporary hospitals to treat the flu victims. By the end of 1918, it is estimated that 12,000 Kansans had died as a result of the epidemic.

The Flu Epidemic of 1918

The worst *epidemic* in world history may have started in Kansas. Fort Riley was a very active army base during World War I. It housed about 26,000 men and thousands of horses and mules. These animals produced a large amount of manure that was disposed of by burning. One day in March, a dust storm came out of the Kansas sky. The dust mixed with the burnt ash of the manure and created a yellow haze. Some people believe that may have been the start of the worldwide flu epidemic.

Two days after the dust storm, an army cook at Fort Riley reported he had a bad cold. By noon that day, over 100 men were sick with the same symptoms. The flu spread like wildfire throughout the camp. An 18-year-old girl working in the laundry wrote about the flu epidemic years later. "We lost lots of them," she recalled, referring to the soldiers. "We'd be working with someone one day, and they'd go home because they didn't feel good, and the next day they were gone. Every day we wondered who was going to be next."

Eventually, the soldiers at Fort Riley were shipped overseas to fight in World War I. They took with them the flu virus, as did other soldiers. The flu spread to Europe, Russia, North Africa, India, China, Japan, the Philippines, and New Zealand. It was soon worldwide, affecting one fifth of the world's population.

Many people were caught by surprise by the seriousness of the flu epidemic. People had faith in science and believed that it could solve all problems. When medical science was unable to control the disease, many people turned to home cures, such as garlic and onions. But nothing seemed to help. Many people died, especially young people. It is estimated that 675,000 Americans died. This is 10 times more than the number of Americans that died in the battles of World War I.

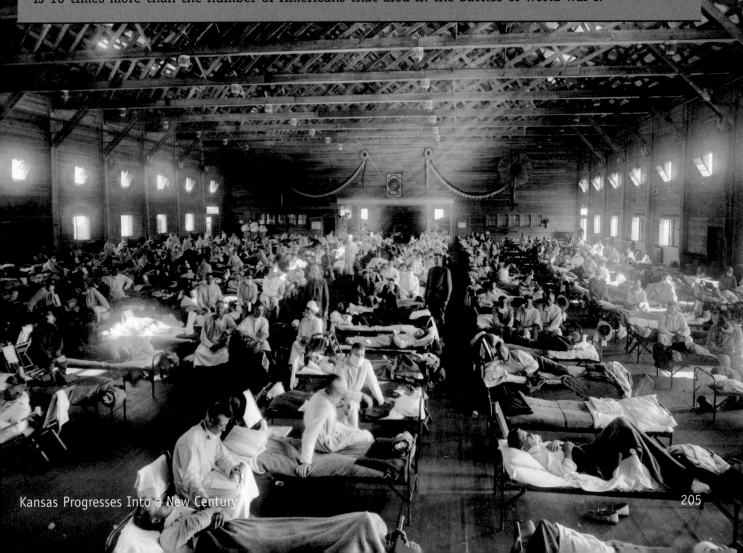

Women in Seneca volunteered their time to the Red Cross. They made bandages for the war effort.

"Win the War with Wheat"

Even after war was declared, maintaining the food supply continued to be of great importance in Kansas. Farmers were asked to grow more food. High school students were asked to do their patriotic duty and help with the harvest. Women formed canning clubs to preserve food. Since there was a worldwide demand for Kansas wheat, farmers were asked to grow other crops for home use. Corn became an important part of the Kansas diet during World War I.

The *Topeka Daily Capital* on July 19, 1917, ran a front-page story called "All Kansas into Fight to Win the War with Wheat."

'Win the War with Wheat.' That is the Kansas slogan. It is a battle cry that is heard in every home of the state. . . . a determined and patriotic people have enlisted in a great industrial army to fight the battle for bread as truly and as bravely as our soldiers will fight for liberty and humanity on the battle fields of Europe. . . .

In letters from western Kansas to the state council of defense and to the governor, it is stated that the streets of towns and villages are deserted. Every available man is in the fields, helping to prepare the soil for the 10,000,000 acreage and a 200,000,000-bushel wheat crop next year that will help win the war. Hundreds of young men have given over their places in offices, stores, and other business enterprises to girls and young women and have gone out to help in the fields.

In Kansas homes, some foods were rationed. Sugar and cornstarch were conserved. Kansans participated in national programs such as "meatless Tuesdays" and "wheatless Saturdays." The state faced a coal shortage. Some businesses, like theaters, were asked to reduce their hours of operations. Women joined the Red Cross, making bandages and helping raise money for the war effort.

The Federal Land Bank of Wichita, 1917

One thing that helped Kansas "Win the War with Wheat" was the creation of the first federal land bank. The year before the United States entered World War I, President Woodrow Wilson signed into law the Federal Farm Loan Act. This provided long-term loans to farmers and ranchers to increase their land holdings.

The first Federal Land Bank was established in Wichita. It was to serve farmers and ranchers in Kansas, Oklahoma, Colorado, and New Mexico. The bank provided affordable *credit*. This was something farmers had been wanting for a long time. It allowed them to purchase additional acreage during the war years. This in turn allowed Kansas farmers to increase their wheat production.

High school students from Scott City helped with the war effort. Cut stalks of cane were run through a press to make syrup. What type of power are the students using to run the press?

Patriotism and Discrimination on the Home front

Although many Kansans were reluctant when the United States entered World War I, the state responded to the president's call to arms. To raise money for the war effort, the United States government increased taxes. But more money was needed, and the sale of Liberty Bonds was begun. Each state was assigned a quota of bonds to sell. In turn, each Kansas county was expected to sell a certain number of bonds to reach the quota. Kansas easily exceeded its quotas. However, not all Kansans felt comfortable with the program.

Many Kansans had immigrated here because of their pacifist beliefs. Mennonites and others held religious beliefs that did not allow them to support war efforts. Many of these people were native German speakers. Since America was at war with Germany, this made them the target of suspicion. The Liberty Bond program was voluntary, but you were considered unpatriotic if you did not participate. Many Kansans with pacifist beliefs felt they could not participate.

Local newspapers published the names of people who did not buy Liberty Bonds. Those who were considered disloyal were turned over to citizen-run Loyal Leagues, where they were put on "trial" for their beliefs. Mennonite churches were vandalized

Posters encouraged citizens to buy Liberty Bonds. By purchasing a bond, citizens could lend the government money to fight the war. At the same time, people could expect to earn interest and eventually be paid back.

and painted yellow. Pacifist farmers had their cattle stolen and sold for the war effort.

What do you think❓

The United States is home to people with different beliefs and values. Our government is based on the will of the majority of the people, yet the U.S. Constitution protects the rights of minorities. This means that those who have a different point of view than the majority are protected under the law. Many people think that this freedom of thought is what makes the United States such a powerful nation. In times of stress, such as war, differing opinions often come into conflict. Is it important to allow for diverse opinions even in times of war? Why or why not?

The War to End all Wars Finally Ends

Kansans were glad when World War I ended. Approximately 2,500 Kansas men died in the war. Like most Americans, Kansans felt World War I had been "the war to end all wars." The decade had begun with a faith in science and technology and was ending with the belief that another world war was not probable. This mind-set was one reason Americans ignored problems that continued in Europe. Eventually, these problems would lead to another world war.

The residents of Chanute celebrated the end of World War I in 1918. The Kaiser was the leader of Germany. What symbolism is used to show the end of the war?

Chapter 9 Review

What Do You Remember?

1. What was Rural Free Delivery?
2. Why did Americans have an interest in the Philippine Islands at the turn of the century?
3. Name at least three things the Progressives wanted to change in Kansas.
4. How was the 1905 Child Labor Law enforced?
5. Why did Dr. Samuel Crumbine campaign to ban the public drinking cup?
6. What is an extraction industry? Give an example.
7. How did steam and gasoline-powered engines change agriculture in Kansas?
8. Why was the discovery of oil in El Dorado so important to Kansas?
9. How is salt extracted from under the ground?
10. Why did automobile manufacturing companies in Kansas go out of business?
11. What made Walter Chrysler famous?
12. Retell the story of one early pioneer in Kansas aviation.
13. List one of Albin K. Longren's accomplishments.
14. Why did the market value of wheat increase during World War I?
15. How did the flu spread during the epidemic of 1918?
16. Who was the first female war correspondent?
17. What does the slogan "Win the War with Wheat" mean?
18. Why was the Federal Bank of Wichita important to farmers?
19. In what way were the Mennonites discriminated against during World War I?
20. Why was World War I called "the war to end all wars"?

Activities

1. During the Progressive era "truth in advertising" laws and public health legislation protected Kansans. Research a current consumer protection or public health issue, and develop a tabletop exhibit that addresses the problem and possible solutions. Use a historical perspective.
2. Research the editorials of William Allen White. Find an editorial that reflects an idea from the Progressive era. Write your own editorial addressing the same issue, either agreeing or disagreeing with White.

Think About It!

1. The St. Louis World's Fair characterized America at the beginning of the 20th century. It was all about progress and the promise that science and technology could solve all problems. Do you think that this type of faith in science and technology was valid? Defend your answer by giving examples.
2. The Standard Oil Company had a monopoly in the oil industry in Kansas. The state legislature passed laws to break the monopoly. Give arguments that would support both Standard Oil's and the state legislature's positions. Were there other ways to resolve the conflict?

THE TIME
1919–1937

PEOPLE TO KNOW
Henry Allen
Walter Anderson
Olive Ann Beech
Walter Beech
Arthur Capper
Clyde Cessna
Glenn Cunningham
John Steuart Curry
Charles Curtis
Frank Marshall Davis
Aaron Douglas
Amelia Earhart
Minnie Johnson Grinstead
Coleman Hawkins
Alexander Howat
Langston Hughes
Martin Johnson
Osa Johnson
Walter "Big Train" Johnson
Birger Sandzen
Lloyd Stearman
William Allen White

PLACES TO LOCATE
Atchison
Chanute
Crawford County
Elkhart
Graham County
Kansas City
Lawrence
Lindsborg
Seward County
Shawnee County
Wichita

Time Line Events

210

1919
The Eighteenth Amendment prohibits the making, selling, and consuming of alcohol. Minnie Johnson Grinstead becomes the first woman to serve in the Kansas legislature. Coal miners in southeast Kansas go on strike.

1920　　　　1922　　　　1924　　　　1926

1920
The Nineteenth Amendment gives women the right to vote in all elections. The Negro National League is formed.

1921
The first White Castle restaurant opens in Wichita.

1922
Workers across the country go on strike against the railroads.

Good Times, Bad Times

WORDS TO UNDERSTAND
arbitrate
bankrupt
censor
collective bargaining
cooperative
discrimination
disincentive
fuselage
improvisation
installment
racism
speculation
stock
union

Families during the 1920s and 1930s gathered around the radio to listen to the news or a variety of entertainment. The radio was also an important way for politicians to get their messages into Kansas homes.

1929
The stock market crashes, leading to the Great Depression.

1930
The Prairie Print Makers are founded at the Lindsborg studio of artist Birger Sandzen.

1933
Franklin Roosevelt becomes U.S. president. The Soil Erosion Service helps those affected by the Dust Bowl.

1937
John Steuart Curry begins work on the murals in the Kansas Capitol.

1928   1930   1932   1934   1936   1938

1925
Walter Beech, Clyde Cessna, and Lloyd Stearman form Travel Air Manufacturing Company.

1931
Kansas and the Great Plains experience severe drought and dust storms.

1932
Amelia Earhart becomes the first woman to fly solo across the Atlantic.

1935
President Roosevelt creates the Rural Electrification Administration.

1936
Glenn Cunningham wins a silver medal at the Olympics. Alf Landon, Kansas Governor, runs for U.S president.

America After World War I

Americans were tired of war and international politics at the conclusion of World War I. They wanted to return to a normal, stable life. They worried more about the economy at home than what was going on overseas. For the first time more Americans lived in cities than in rural areas. In 1920, 51 percent of Americans lived in urban areas. Kansas was becoming increasingly urban, with almost 35 percent of the population living in cities.

America was changing. Sometimes old-fashioned values clashed with new attitudes. Alcohol became illegal under the Eighteenth Amendment to the U.S. Constitution. Of course, Kansas had already adopted prohibition. Some people felt that restricting the use of alcohol was old fashioned. Secret nightclubs selling illegal liquor sprang up across America. Almost as soon as prohibition passed, some people began working to repeal it.

American women got the right to vote with the Nineteenth Amendment to the U.S. Constitution. Once again, Kansas was ahead of the nation, having already adopted equal suffrage in 1912. As America became more industrialized, there were more opportunities for women. In particular young single women gained more freedom, as they found jobs and earned income. Some people worried about the morals of society, as economic freedom gave women more choices.

There were increased ethnic and racial conflicts after the war. African American soldiers had fought and died for the United States during World War I. Many African Americans stationed overseas felt they had been treated well by the Europeans. It was tough for them to return home and face racial *discrimination*. Americans after the war also were less tolerant of new immigrants to this country.

Kansas Becomes More Industrial

The decade of the 1920s was one of great change in Kansas and the nation. Economically, the country saw great highs and lows. Agriculture remained central to the Kansas economy but industry began to grow. The Kansas economy had focused on food production during World War I, shipping products both within the United

By the 1920s, automobiles were becoming common in Kansas. Students were being bused to school in gasoline-powered school buses like this one in Rice County.

Before electricity reached rural America, lanterns allowed farmers to work in their barns after dark. A powerful lantern was made and sold by the Coleman Company of Wichita. By 1920, the factory was producing 50,000 lanterns a year.

States and overseas. Farmers had plowed new ground to keep up with production during the war. After the war, they continued to farm these new lands. This produced food surpluses—though at the same time there were fewer markets.

In Kansas, farming was becoming more mechanized. Farmers began to rely on tractors rather than horses. Combines, which cut, threshed, and cleaned grain all in one operation, had been invented much earlier, but they became increasingly popular among Kansas farmers. The use of these new machines allowed farmers to grow more grains by working more land. This, too, led to overproduction.

Extraction industries, such as coal mining, salt mining, and oil and gas production continued to be important to the state. During this decade, Wichita saw the rise of the airline industry. The first air passenger service in Kansas was established, making it possible to fly from Wichita to Kansas City in about three hours.

Kansas PORTRAIT

Minnie Johnson Grinstead
1869-1925

The 20th century brought new opportunities for women, including politics. Minnie Johnson Grinstead was the first woman elected to the Kansas Legislature. In 1924, Grinstead participated in nominating Republican Calvin Coolidge for president. This gave her national recognition.

Minnie Johnson was born in Crawford County. Her father was a Baptist preacher and a farmer. As with all farm children, she was expected to help around the farm. When she graduated from high school at the age of 14, she wanted to become a teacher. Kansas law required that all teachers be at least 16 years old. Until she was eligible to teach, she worked on her family's farm and hired herself out as a farm worker.

When Minnie Johnson was old enough, she taught school in Pittsburg, eventually becoming principal of an elementary school. It was during this time that she became interested in politics. Her first run for office was unsuccessful. After being defeated for the office of school superintendent, she left the field of education to become a lecturer for the Women's Christian Temperance Union. She also worked to pass women's suffrage.

She married Virgil Grinstead, a lawyer. Together they had four children, two of whom died before reaching adulthood. The family lived in Liberal, where Mr. Grinstead was a judge. Minnie Johnson Grinstead decided to try her hand at politics again. This time she ran for the Kansas House of Representatives. Upon winning, the family packed up and moved to Topeka.

In the legislature she became known as "The Lady from Seward." Grinstead was elected to two more terms in the House of Representatives. In her second term, three more women joined her. The four women became known as the "Kansas Legisladies," when an article about them was published throughout the country. During her time in the state legislature, Grinstead introduced legislation protecting women's financial rights, prohibiting the sale of cigarettes, and allowing small towns to fund local libraries. After her husband died, Grinstead was elected to his seat as judge in Seward County.

When Governor Henry Allen wanted to replace striking coal miners he looked to the universities. These students from Kansas State University volunteered to work the mines. Governor Allen is standing in front of the students.

Labor Strikes

Coal mining was a major industry in southeast Kansas. Removing coal from underground mines was hard and dangerous work. The United Mine Workers of America was the *union* that represented the coal workers. The union looked out for the well-being of the miners. In order to improve working conditions or increase wages, the union sometimes organized labor strikes.

During World War I, the union agreed not to strike. The nation was at war and needed coal for fuel. But after the war, the union called for a nation-wide work stoppage. President Woodrow Wilson declared the strike illegal, and the United Mine Workers of America called off the strike. Kansas miners, however, ignored the order to go back to work.

Alexander Howat was president of the southeast Kansas chapter of the United Mine Workers of America. Like many miners in southeast Kansas, Howat was an immigrant. Born in Scotland, he came to America at the age of three. By the age of 10, Howat was working in the coal mines. As president of the local chapter, Howat defied both the national union and President Wilson's order to go back to work. Ten thousand miners remained on strike and shut down the Kansas coal mines.

During the strike, Kansas was running out of fuel and facing a cold winter. The state wanted to end the strike. Negotiations between the workers and the mine owners failed. Governor Henry Allen asked the Kansas Supreme Court to allow the state to take over the mines. The miners still refused to return to work so the governor recruited volunteers to work in the coal mines. Men were recruited from college campuses—even at football games. More than 10,000 inexperienced men agreed to work the mines.

Within a few weeks, the strike was settled when the union and the owners of the coal fields agreed on a new pay plan. The miners went back to work, and the volunteers returned to their college campuses. The state ended its brief control of the coal mines.

Kansas Court of Industrial Relations

The coal mining strike made Governor Allen fearful of future labor strikes. He called a special session of the state legislature, and together they established the Kansas Court of Industrial Relations. The court was to *arbitrate* between workers and management. It would settle disputes and even take over companies if necessary. Workers were no longer allowed to strike, but they gained the right of *collective bargaining*.

The Kansas Court of Industrial Relations was a new idea. Once again, Kansas was in the national spotlight. Allowing workers the right to bargain for better working conditions and better wages was something new in most industries. But taking away the right to strike was very controversial among workers. Work stoppages had been a successful way for workers to call attention to their grievances.

Alexander Howat opposed the Court of Industrial Relations. He called for an immediate strike to protest the creation of the court. The United Mine Workers of America told Howat to call off the strike. He refused. For challenging the Court of Industrial Relations, Howat ended up in jail. When he still refused to call off the strike, he was kicked out of the United Mine Workers of America.

In time the U.S. Supreme Court overturned several of the Court of Industrial Relations' rulings. This led to the Kansas legislature abolishing the Court.

Amazon Women

When the miners of southeast Kansas went on strike, they wanted to shut down coal production so that people would listen to their demands. When a strike occurred, the company tried to recruit new workers, allowing coal production to continue. Workers who refused to strike or those who replaced striking workers were called "scabs."

During one strike in 1921, the families of the coal miners were very upset that scabs were being hired. A group of southeast Kansas wives, mothers, and sisters marched from coal camp to coal camp. Most were immigrant women who wanted to protest the hiring of scab labor. The women became known as the "Amazon Army."

The poem to the right by Gene DeGruson tells of his mother's experience in the "Amazon Army." How does DeGruson portray the emotions of the strike?

Alien Women

In '21, my mother still herself
at seventeen marched for Alexander
Howat to bust the scabs who worked
the mines in place of the fathers
and husbands of the thousand women
who marched with her carrying
their men's pit buckets filled
with red pepper to throw in the eyes
of the poor scabs who cursed back
in English to their Slovene, German,
French, and Italian over
the State Militia's rifle fire.
It's all dim in her mind now. She
remembers only that she was hungry
and frightened. She does not remember
Judge Curran, who said, "It is a fact
that there are bolsheviki, communists,
and anarchists among the alien women
of this community. It was the lawlessness
of these women which made necessary
the stationing of the State Militia
in our county for two months
to preserve law and order."
She does not remember they
were called an Army of Amazons.

This photograph of "Marching Women" was published in the Topeka Daily Capital *on December 20, 1921. Fannie Wimler, who was one of the women who marched in favor of the striking coal miners, wrote a letter to the Pittsburg Daily Headlight. It read, "What we want is our industrial freedom and liberty and we want our men to be good, true, loyal union men and 100 percent American citizens."*

Kansas and the Ku Klux Klan

The Invisible Empire, Knights of the Ku Klux Klan, was organized in the South during World War I. It took the name and the attitudes of an earlier organization. The earlier Klan was organized after the Civil War to keep African Americans from gaining political power in the South. The Klan of the 1920s spread its influence into the Midwest.

Membership in the Ku Klux Klan was open to American-born, white, Protestant males, 16 years of age or older. The Klan opposed anyone who was African American, an immigrant, Roman Catholic, or Jewish. The organization used tactics meant to intimidate. They burned crosses to frighten people. They wore masks and marched through towns. They kidnapped, beat, and even killed people they did not like.

In Kansas, the rise of the Ku Klux Klan happened at the same time as a railroad strike. Railroad workers in Kansas joined a national strike. But a large number of African Americans chose not to strike. The Klan wanted to move into Kansas. They saw an opportunity as racial tensions increased over the strike. The Ku Klux Klan gained members in Kansas when it sided with the union and the striking workers.

Members of the Ku Klux Klan wore white robes and hoods and burned crosses to scare people. In the 1920s, our state government took a stand against the Klan.

Governor Henry Allen Fights the Klan

The governor of Kansas felt it was important to take a stand against the Ku Klux Klan. As railroad workers went on strike, the Klan planned parades to recruit new members. Governor Allen issued a proclamation that made it illegal to wear a mask on Kansas streets. Although Governor Allen did not like the Klan interfering in a labor dispute, he also disliked the motives of the organization. He asked if the Klan stood for Christian values then why "do they have to be masked to stand for that?"

Governor Allen called the Klan "the greatest curse that can come to any civilized people." He was concerned that tolerating the Klan meant that Kansas could be seen as supporting racial and religious bigotry. He wrote of his fears about the Klan operating in Kansas.

> *We teach to our young men and women the dangerous doctrine that violence and hatred are justifiable, that mob law is consistent with freedom, that lawlessness is to be met by lawlessness, and that self appointed guardians of other people's rights may set themselves above the sacred duty of the constitutional authority.*

Governor Allen had an idea. He decided to fight the Klan through the court system. It was illegal for a foreign corporation to do business in Kansas without a charter. Because the Klan was chartered in Georgia and not Kansas, it was considered a foreign corporation. The state of Kansas filed a petition asking that the Ku Klux Klan be prevented from doing business in the state. The Kansas Supreme Court agreed.

The only way for the Klan to operate legally in Kansas was to get a charter. The board that granted charters in Kansas was made up of politicians who opposed the Klan. This meant that the Klan would have to influence future elections. If pro-Klan members got elected to the charter board, then the Klan would get its charter. In the meantime, the Ku Klux Klan appealed its case to the U.S. Supreme Court.

Defeating the Klan

During the election of 1924, William Allen White, the well-known journalist from

William Allen White traveled the state in this car while campaigning against the Ku Klux Klan.

Emporia, worried about the influence of the Ku Klux Klan in Kansas. He feared that neither the Republican nor the Democratic candidates for governor would fight against the Ku Klux Klan the way his friend Governor Allen had. White decided to run for governor as an independent. His purpose was to defeat the Ku Klux Klan.

According to White, someone needed to protect the citizens of Kansas who were the targets of the Klan.

Kansas with her high intelligence and pure American blood, of all states should be free of this taint of bigotry and terror. I was born in Kansas and have lived all my life in Kansas. I am proud of my state. And the thought that Kansas should have a government beholden to this hooded gang of masked fanatics, ignorant and tyrannical in their ruthless oppression, is what calls me out of the pleasant ways of my life into this distasteful, but necessary, task. I cannot sit idly by and see Kansas become a by-word among the states.

William Allen White never thought that he would win the election. He came in third behind the two major party candidates. But he got 150,000 of the 600,000 votes. He also got a great deal of publicity for his cause. He was such a well-known figure that many Americans watched as White fought the Klan.

More than two years after William Allen White ran for governor, the U.S. Supreme Court refused to hear the Ku Klux Klan's appeal. The Klan had appealed the state's judgment that denied them the right to do business in Kansas. This was the Klan's last chance in the state. The refusal of the Supreme Court to hear the appeal meant that the Klan could no longer operate legally in the state. Kansas became the first state in the union to outlaw the Ku Klux Klan.

Wichita–the Air Capital

After World War I, the aviation industry in Kansas grew rapidly. Money from the expanding oil industry in Kansas helped finance its expansion. Three aviation pioneers, Walter Beech, Clyde Cessna, and Lloyd Stearman, came together to form Travel Air Manufacturing Company. The company became the leader in manufacturing light commercial aircraft. The company was not only important to Kansas but made significant contributions worldwide. At this time, commercial aircraft manufacturing was just beginning.

Stearman and Beech

Lloyd Stearman became a well-known aircraft designer. Stearman was studying architecture in Kansas when World War I broke out. He left school to become a Navy pilot. After the war, he was hired as a mechanic by the Wichita company that had manufactured the first commercial airplane in the United States. At Swallow Airplane Manufacturing Company, Stearman worked hard and was promoted to chief engineer.

Stearman worked with Walter Beech at Swallow. Beech was a native of Tennessee. He left home to work as an automobile

mechanic in Minnesota. While living there, he bought his first airplane. The plane had been damaged, and Beech repaired it so it would fly again. He then taught himself to fly. When the United States entered World War I, Beech joined the Army. Stationed in Texas, his job was to repair airplane engines. After the war, Beech remained in the army, becoming a pilot. Beech eventually left the army and came to Kansas to fly airplanes.

Up until then, most planes were made out of wood and cloth. Stearman and Beech both believed that the future of aircraft manufacturing lay in metals. The men proposed the use of steel in designing the cabins of airplanes. Their boss disagreed. So strongly did Stearman and Beech believe in the steel *fuselage* that they left their jobs. They wanted to start their own manufacturing company, but they needed another partner.

Cessna Joins

Clyde Cessna had been successful as an automobile dealer in Oklahoma. He became more and more interested in aviation. He moved briefly to New York City to work for an airplane manufacturer. Cessna bought himself a plane and moved back to

Planes were built by Travel Air at their production plant in Wichita.

Oklahoma where he taught himself to fly. He soon took up exhibition flying. Moving to Wichita, Cessna opened up a shop to build airplanes and train new pilots.

Lloyd Stearman and Walter Beech knew that Clyde Cessna was an expert in aviation. They also knew he had the money and equipment to start an aircraft manufacturing business. Stearman and Beech talked Cessna into joining them as president of Travel Air Manufacturing Company. Under the leadership of Stearman, Beech, and Cessna, the company became one of the most successful aircraft manufacturers in the world.

The legacy of Travel Air Manufacturing made Wichita the air capital. Stearman eventually started his own aircraft company that became Boeing Military Airplane Company. Beech, along with his wife, founded Beech Aircraft Company, which specialized in planes for business travel. Clyde Cessna created the C.V. Cessna Aircraft Company that built small racing airplanes.

Clyde Cessna brought both capital and expertise as president of Travel Air.

Olive Ann Mellor Beech
1903-1993

Olive Ann Mellor Beech is considered the "First Lady of Aviation." She is not only a member of the national Aviation Hall of Fame, but she is the first Kansan to be inducted into the National Business Hall of Fame.

When Stearman, Beech, and Cessna started Travel Air Manufacturing, they hired a young woman to help in the office. Olive Ann Mellor had been interested in business and finance since she was a young girl. By age 11, she was in charge of her family's bank records. As a young woman she entered the business world as an office manager and bookkeeper. In 1930, she married Walter Beech.

Walter and Olive Ann Beech together founded the Beech Aircraft Corporation. During the Great Depression of the 1930s, times were tough, but the Beech Aircraft Corporation managed to stay in business. During World War II, the company did extremely well, making planes for the military. After the war, the company began serving the needs of business travelers.

Olive Ann Beech served as an officer of Beech Aircraft Corporation for 50 years. After the death of her husband, she ran the business alone for 20 years, nearly tripling sales. The company grew from a few employees to over 10,000. At one point sales exceeded $900 million. The Beech company even had a hand in the NASA space program. Many attribute the success of the company to Olive Ann Beech's strong business abilities.

Kansas PORTRAIT

The Consumer Economy

During the 1920s, the American lifestyle was based on a consumer economy. Industry and science produced many new things for families to buy. Instead of saving money, people in the 1920s spent it! Less of a family's income went to buying necessities and more to recreation and new products. Automobiles were becoming more affordable. The country doubled its number of roads and highways.

Electricity was becoming commonplace. Two-thirds of all American homes became electrified, creating a new industry of electronic appliances. Toasters, refrigerators, vacuum cleaners, and washing machines were sold to the American public as machines that would save time and improve family life. In reality, new appliances created new social pressures on families. Changing ideas about cleanliness meant that houses had to be vacuumed daily and bed sheets washed once a week.

Ready-to-wear clothing was popularized in the 1920s. Until then, many families made their own clothing. If you were wealthy, you often hired a seamstress or tailor. During World War I, the U.S. government needed to buy uniforms for a large number of soldiers, resulting in the creation of standard clothing sizes. Standard sizes made it easier to mass-produce clothing. As fashion became more important to consumers, so did cosmetics and hair products.

Most families had one income. In order to pay for all of these new things, people began to rely on credit. The first nationwide credit agencies were set up to assist people in buying cars. This allowed families to borrow money, for a fee, to make purchases. The loan could be paid back in *installments*.

Fast Foods

The consumer economy changed how Americans ate. Tradition was that families usually ate at home, preparing their meals themselves. During the 1920s, many Americans began to purchase prepared and processed foods. More meals were made from canned or frozen foods, purchased from a chain grocery store.

In Kansas, the Dillon family began building grocery stores throughout the state. Fifteen J. S. Dillon and Sons grocery stores could be found in 10 different towns. Before the chain grocery store, food was purchased from individual specialty shops. It also could be purchased on credit from an individual grocer, who delivered the food to your house. Dillon's introduced the concept of cash and carry in Kansas. Consumers could save money by paying cash and picking up their groceries themselves. Chain stores offered more variety at lower prices.

The fast food industry had its beginnings in Kansas. Walter Anderson of

White Castle hamburgers were born in Wichita and introduced the world to fast foods.

Wichita developed a new way to cook hamburgers. The original hamburger was more like a large meatball and took a long time to cook. Anderson began flattening a ball of ground meat and cooking it along with onions on a hot griddle. This new hamburger took very little time to prepare, and the modern hamburger was born.

Anderson and his partner opened White Castle in Wichita. The hamburger fast food business was so successful that the partners soon opened another White Castle in Kansas City. During the 1920s, the company expanded into 12 major cities in the eastern United States. As a chain restaurant, White Castle proved successful because the company had a set of standards for operations, food preparations, and employee appearance. This meant that the customer could count on every White Castle having the same product and giving the same service. This idea of uniformity built the fast food industry we know today.

The Censor

As movies became popular entertainment, some people worried about their content. Kansas, like other states, developed a system to review all movies. It was the job of the Kansas Board of Review to *censor* all films that were "cruel, obscene, indecent or immoral."

The Board of Review had three members. By the 1920s, these positions were held mostly by women. The members previewed all films before they could be shown in Kansas. The Board had the power to delete a scene or ban a film entirely. The film industry did not like the Board of Review, and they legally challenged some of its decisions. The movie industry also spent money lobbying state legislators and put money into Kansas elections, trying to defeat political candidates who believed in censorship.

One of the board's best-remembered rulings was banning the movie *The Birth of a Nation*. The critically acclaimed film favored the South in its depiction of the Civil War and included positive images of the Ku Klux Klan. The Kansas Board of Review banned the film from 1915-1923 because it promoted *racism* and was historically inaccurate.

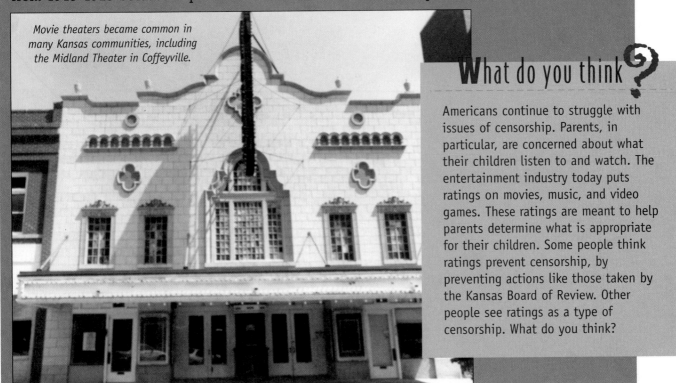

Movie theaters became common in many Kansas communities, including the Midland Theater in Coffeyville.

What do you think?

Americans continue to struggle with issues of censorship. Parents, in particular, are concerned about what their children listen to and watch. The entertainment industry today puts ratings on movies, music, and video games. These ratings are meant to help parents determine what is appropriate for their children. Some people think ratings prevent censorship, by preventing actions like those taken by the Kansas Board of Review. Other people see ratings as a type of censorship. What do you think?

The Age of Play

The 1920s is sometimes called the Age of Play. Many new games and fads spread across the nation. Americans played miniature golf and worked crossword puzzles. Young people stayed up all night, participating in dance marathons. The radio and phonograph brought entertainment into the home. Talking motion pictures were introduced.

Sports became extremely popular, and Kansas had its own sports hero in Walter "Big Train" Johnson. Born on an Allen County farm, Johnson was known for the speed of his pitch. It was said that his fastball traveled as fast as a locomotive. That is how he got the nickname "Big Train."

Johnson became a pitcher for the Washington Senators. The Senators were considered one of the worst teams in baseball. Through Johnson's talent and hard work, the Senators became a great team and won the World Series in 1924 and 1925. "Big Train" Johnson was such an outstanding pitcher that he became one of the first players inducted into the Baseball Hall of Fame.

Although the 1920s was a time of great social change, racial segregation continued to exist in many aspects of life, including baseball. Because African Americans were not allowed to play alongside white players, they formed their own teams. Black baseball, as it was called, was highly successful. The exciting games emphasized speed over power. African American players perfected the bunt and were known for their skill at stealing bases. This drew big crowds of both black and white fans.

Soon the owners of the best black baseball teams got together and formed the Negro National League. Perhaps the most famous team from that league was the Kansas City Monarchs. Both Jackie Robinson and Satchel Paige played for the Monarchs. This team introduced night baseball to the world by inventing a portable lighting system.

Walter "Big Train" Johnson became famous for helping the Washington Senators win two World Series.

The Kansas City Monarchs were one of the most successful teams in the Negro League. Here, Satchel Paige is warming up for a game at New York's Yankee Stadium.

Kansans and the Harlem Renaissance

During and after World War I, so many African Americans from the rural South moved into northern cities that it was called the Great Migration. Jobs were a primary motivation of the Great Migration. A growing black middle class developed in America. The idea of racial equality became the centerpiece of African American culture, even though there were different ideas about how to achieve equality. An increasing pride in being African American was often expressed through the arts.

The Harlem neighborhood in New York City became home for many African Americans migrating north. During the 1920s, it became the center of African American culture in the United States. This was called the Harlem Renaissance. Theaters, art galleries, and jazz clubs in Harlem drew both black and white audiences. Perhaps nothing characterized the Harlem Renaissance more than the number of books published by black writers.

Many Kansans contributed to the Harlem Renaissance. One of the most important writers of the period was Langston Hughes, from Lawrence. In his lifetime, Hughes produced more than 60 books. He had the ability to communicate life in black America to a diverse audience. Another Kansan, Aaron Douglas, used African designs in his paintings. Born in Topeka, Douglas became an important painter. Douglas' illustrations were published in major magazines and books. African art and American jazz influenced his paintings. They reflected his pride in his African American heritage.

Langston Hughes was a famous poet and writer.

18th and Vine: Kansas City Jazz District

The Great Migration of African Americans from the South to northern cities had its impact on neighborhoods other than Harlem. The neighborhood of 18th and Vine in Kansas City, Missouri, was a center of African American life. Blacks living in a segregated society created their own business district. Clothing stores, beauty shops, theaters, churches, doctors' and lawyers' offices could all be found there. Restaurants offered fine dinning, and nightclubs produced a new kind of jazz.

Kansas City jazz was upbeat and based on *improvisation.* This meant that much of the music was not written down-but made up by the musician as he played. The saxophone was one of the most important instruments in this type of jazz. Coleman Hawkins received a tenor saxophone for his ninth birthday and began playing at school dances by the time he was 12. As a young man, Hawkins studied music at Topeka High School before he became a well-known Kansas City jazz artist.

Charlie "Bird" Parker was another Kansan who made it big in the jazz world. Parker became interested in music after joining his high school marching band in the ninth grade. He developed his interest in jazz when he listened to music in alleys behind Kansas City jazz clubs. Parker helped invent a type of jazz improvisation called bebop. This sound led to the modern era of jazz.

Charlie Parker was born in Kansas City, Kansas. He helped invent bebop

The Great Depression

The 1920s were good economic times for many Americans. When Herbert Hoover was elected president, he said, "We in America today are nearer to the final triumph over poverty than ever before in the history of any land." Yet three years earlier he warned there was too much *speculation* in the stock market.

For several years, rising *stock* prices signaled a "bull market." Investors in the market were able to make a great deal of money speculating on stocks. This speculation, or gambling, drove the price of stocks up, at least on paper. Investors would speculate on stocks using credit. Expecting the stocks to rise in price quickly, investors would then be able to pay off their debt. By 1929, the prices of company stocks were greater than the actual profits of the companies. Stock prices rose, while the sales of goods and services fell.

In October of 1929, the stock market crashed. Falling prices signaled a "bear market." People began to sell their stocks for whatever amount of money they could get. Eventually, stock prices fell so low that $30 billion was lost. This is the same amount of money the U.S. government spent fighting in World War I. The American public lost confidence in the economy.

There had been bad economic times before. President Hoover chose his words carefully when he spoke to the nation. He called the country's economic problems a "depression." What became known as the Great Depression lasted throughout the 1930s. Eventually, one-fourth of all American workers were out of work. As unemployment rose, most people stopped buying goods and services. This made the economy worse.

◄ *Clifford R. Hope, Sr., from Garden City, served in the U.S. House of Representatives during the Great Depression. He wrote of those days, "The great depression which began in the fall of 1929 affected Kansas just as it did every other part of the country, but on top of it there was superimposed almost a decade of drought and duststorms. In other words, Kansas . . . got a double dose of misery and calamity." The photograph to the left is of an abandoned farm in Haskell County.*

Charles Curtis
1860-1936

By the end of the 1920s, a Kansan was serving as U.S. Vice President. Charles Curtis was also the first American Indian to hold the office. His father was a white abolitionist who fought in the Civil War. His mother was part French and part Kansa.

After his mother's death, Curtis grew up in the homes of his white and Indian grandparents. At age six, Curtis found himself living on the Kansa Reservation near Council Grove. There he attended a mission school. When the Kansa were removed to Indian Territory, Curtis remained in Topeka with his white grandparents. He later remembered, "as the wagons pulled out for the south, bound for Indian Territory, I mounted my pony and with my belongings in a flour sack, returned to Topeka and school."

By the age of 21, Charles Curtis was a lawyer. He began in politics by serving as the attorney for Shawnee County. Curtis made a name for himself by closing down illegal drinking establishments. Soon he was elected to the U.S. House of Representatives. In Washington, he became involved with issues surrounding American Indians, though he seemed to believe that Indians should assimilate into the American way of life.

Curtis became a U.S. senator from Kansas and supported women's suffrage and a bill to make American Indians citizens of the United States. In 1928, Curtis ran for the Republican nomination for president. Herbert Hoover won the nomination, but Curtis accepted the vice presidential nomination. The ticket of Hoover and Curtis won the general election.

Many Americans blamed Hoover for the Great Depression. When Hoover and Curtis ran for re-election in 1932, they were defeated. Charles Curtis decided to stay in Washington, D.C., and work as an attorney. Four years later, he died.

Hard Economic Times in Kansas

In Kansas, the Great Depression hit hard. It did not matter if you lived in the city or on the farm. Many people lost their incomes.

The aviation industry in Wichita, which was going strong just a few years earlier, was almost wiped out. Sales of new aircraft had begun to decline before the stock market crash. Believing this was a temporary problem, the airplane manufacturers continued to produce as if their businesses would grow. After the crash, buying new airplanes was not a high priority for anyone. Only a few of the 29 aircraft manufacturing companies in Wichita survived the Depression. Many workers who lost their aircraft manufacturing jobs left Wichita. Others stayed because they had no money to leave.

People without jobs also had no money to spend. This caused local businesses to suffer or go out of business. Many storeowners, who had once offered credit, began requiring cash for purchases. Even when grocery prices dropped, many people could not afford them. Families survived by buying just the basics, such as beans, flour, and milk. These basic products were supplemented with food grown in their gardens. Many families could not afford meat. Some people in cities began raising chickens to help feed their families.

The Great Depression also was hard on farmers. Modern machinery made farming more efficient, but many farmers went into debt to buy the machinery. Because people did not have money to spend, even on food, prices paid for crops were low. This meant that the farmers could not pay their debts. To add to the economic problems, a severe drought came to Kansas and raising crops was nearly impossible in some parts of the state.

How Do We Know This?

Recording the Past Through Oral History

History is about the stories of families and individuals who came before us. To learn more about events and people in the past, we can interview people about their experiences. These interviews are called oral histories. Oral histories can tell us a lot about how people lived and their everyday life. They can also tell us how people felt about a specific place or event.

Lorenzo Mattwaoshshe, a member of the Prairie Band Potawatomi, was a teenager during the Great Depression when many people had little or no money to buy food. Years after the Depression, Mattwaoshshe was interviewed about his experiences. In 1931, he was 15 years old and working with his family to survive the drought and harsh economic conditions in Jackson County.

Interviewer: The Depression really hit you?

Mattwaoshshe: You better know it! There were many times when I didn't have [anything] to eat. Now when you can't eat, you have to do something. We hunted. We were so down and out. There were four fields that I used to walk through around us. They were full of milkweeds. There's a good vitamin in that milkweed. That's what we'd eat. One field, I'd clean it out. We'd eat that milkweed, and I'd just circle around and go to the next field and the next. About every fourth day, the milkweed would come up again and I'd get them.

Interviewer: What part of the plant were you eating?

Mattwaoshshe: The whole, the leaves, the tender part. The Indian women knew how to fix it. What would you call that? Like a cabbage.

Lorenzo Mattwaoshshe used ingenuity to survive. He also used tradition. Milkweed is a common native plant that American Indians once ate. According to Mattwaoshshe's oral history, the Potawatomi women knew how to prepare the plant. Many people survived the Great Depression using ingenuity and tradition. If we found ourselves in a similar economic depression today, what would you do to survive?

Interview from "Model Ts, Pep Chapels, and a Wolf at the Door: Kansas Teenagers 1900-1941". Printed with permission from James Wabaunsee and Lorenzo (L.D.) Mattwaoshshe

Families faced difficult times during the Great Depression. Many were forced to move from their homes and struggled to make ends meet.

In 1935, a dust storm overtook Morton County. This was the worst year for dust storms, sometimes referred to as "Black Blizzards."

The Dust Bowl

The 1930s in the Great Plains is often referred to as the "dirty thirties" or the "Dust Bowl." These names came from blowing dust that was the result of a series of severe droughts. Little rain, hot days, high winds, and soil-eroding farming practices literally created storms of black dust. These dust storms could turn the daytime sky black, make cattle go blind, and bury cars and farm equipment.

Erich Fruehauf, a farmer in Stafford County, described a dust storm.

> Once I was on the road in my car to help a friend in an emergency situation with a cow, when a fast moving dust cloud surprised me. It became so dense that it swallowed the headlight beams. Visibility became less than the distance from the driver's seat to the radiator. The road was invisible. When I could tell no more whether I was headed down the road or toward the ditch there was nothing I could do but stop and wait. An hour later it got light enough so that I could carefully proceed to my destination.

Sometimes, dust storms would last for several days. High winds would blow around the dry topsoil. Dust clouds could be up to 8,000 feet high. Storms sometimes included thunder and lightning but very little rain. Dust was everywhere. It would creep into houses through keyholes and the frames around windows and doors. To try and keep the dust out, people hung wet sheets and towels around doors and windows. When people got caught outside in a dust storm, they inhaled dirt. In extreme cases, this led to death through suffocation.

Farming Practices Eroded the Soil

What caused the Dust Bowl? For most of the 1930s, the Great Plains experienced severe drought. It just would not rain. It was also hot and windy. Grasshoppers and jackrabbits damaged many of the crops. Nature seemed to be fighting farmers, refusing to give them a break.

But it was not all nature's fault. Humans contributed to the tragedy. Originally the soil on the plains was kept in place by native grasses. Once the prairie was plowed, the topsoil was no longer held in place. To meet the high demand for wheat during World War I, farmers had over-plowed their lands. Cattle and sheep overgrazed the land that was not plowed.

Dust Storm Damage

Legend

- Dust Bowl States
- Severe Dust Storm Damage
- Other Areas Damaged by Dust Storms

The Kansas Journey

Farming practices contributed to the problem of soil erosion. When the rain stopped, there was simply nothing to hold the topsoil in place, and it blew away.

Lessons Learned From the Dust Bowl

Some Kansans did not survive the dust storms of the 1930s. Unable to make a successful living and deeply in debt, they packed up their belongings and migrated west. Most Kansans stayed on their farms and learned valuable lessons from the Dust Bowl. People did not like their farming practices criticized. In order to encourage changes in agriculture the U.S. government offered education and financial incentives. These incentives came through a variety of government programs designed to help reduce farm surpluses, stop soil erosion, and return some prairie land to native grasses.

Soil erosion was a major cause of the Dust Bowl. Many Kansas soils erode easily. Erosion can be caused by water or wind. The topsoil is valuable because it contains the nutrients that plants need to grow. If the topsoil is washed or blown away, then only the poorer soil remains.

To prevent soil erosion, the government encouraged the use of terracing and contour farming techniques. Contour farming means plowing and planting crops around hills. If farmers plow up and down hills, they create small ditches that lead to soil erosion. Terracing means creating ditches that go with the contour of the land. This allows water to be collected and carried away from the field in a more natural manner. Both terracing and contour farming are techniques that follow the land's natural patterns.

When soil is eroded by wind there is not enough moisture in the ground. Techniques to retain moisture in the soil were encouraged to prevent another Dust Bowl. Conservation of water is critical in an environment that receives little rainfall in good years and even less during a severe drought. Most water from rain and snow runs off the surface of the land before it can be stored. Terracing helps reduce unnecessary runoff. Soil covered with crop stubble also reduces water runoff. Stubble mulching was encouraged. This is the

Contour farming helps reduce soil erosion. It also helps hold moisture in the soil.

practice of leaving some straw or stalks on the surface after the field is lightly tilled to prevent the soil from eroding.

Irrigation is another way to keep the soil moist and prevent erosion. Using man-made methods to bring water to the crops allows farmers to improve production during normal years and survive periods of drought.

The government also financed the planting of millions of trees to help prevent soil erosion and future dust storms. Trees were usually planted in rows. When the trees began to grow, they created shelterbelts or windbreaks, and reduced blowing.

Farmers were encouraged to practice crop rotation. Many farmers would plant the same crop on the same field, year after year. Eventually, this robbed the soil of important nutrients and caused it to become unproductive. The farmers then simply moved on to another field. This left the original field subject to soil erosion. If crops are rotated, it helps maintain the health of the soil and controls weeds, diseases, and insects, making the field more productive.

What do you think?

Land use on the Great Plains continues to be a controversial subject. Some people worry that farming practices today continue to deplete, rather than conserve water on the plains. Could this lead to damaging dust storms? Others believe that farming practices today are helping to prevent another environmental disaster by using modern high-yield seeds and chemical fertilizers. Through fertilizers, farmers are putting more nutrients back into the soil. Does this make another dust bowl unlikely? Still others feel that the Great Plains is not a suitable place to live or farm. It is argued that the land should be turned back to the wildlife that once lived here. What do you think?

Activity

Understanding Art: *Kansas Pastoral* by John Steuart Curry

John Steuart Curry was one of the most important American artists of the 1930s. His work helped define a style of painting called "regionalism." Curry loved to paint scenes of his home state, Kansas. He painted scenes of everyday rural life.

Curry began drawing and painting as he grew up on a Jefferson County farm. At age 18 he left Kansas to study art in Kansas City, Chicago, and Paris, France. He eventually settled in Connecticut where he made his living as an artist. Many of the people in the eastern United States liked his paintings of Kansas, but Curry wanted to paint for the people of his home state.

During the Great Depression, Curry got his chance to bring his art home. A group of newspaper editors convinced the legislature to commission John Steuart Curry to paint murals in the state Capitol. Curry was thrilled to be home, and many Kansans were happy to see such a well-known artist at work on the Capitol. But soon, some began to criticize Curry's depiction of Kansas history.

Some Kansans did not like the subjects Curry chose for his murals. Others expected Curry to paint in a realistic manner, like a photograph. They complained the pig's tail curled the wrong way and the farmer's wife was wearing too short a skirt. The relationship between Curry and the legislature became strained,

You can see the entire mural, Kansas Pastoral *by John Steuart Curry, on the second floor of the state Capitol.*

and Curry never finished the statehouse murals.

Curry left Kansas and in an angry statement said, "Because the project is uncompleted and does not represent my true idea, I am not signing these works." Curry's heart was broken. The artist was convinced that the completed murals were his best work, and he was hurt by the criticism. Unfortunately, Curry died shortly after he left Kansas. Today the Curry murals in the Capitol are thought to be a Kansas treasure.

Paintings are an artist's expressions and impressions of a subject. Art is meant to evoke emotions. John Steuart Curry painted the murals in the Capitol during a time when his own father was struggling to survive on the family farm. His father wrote, "the toll of the elements—five years of dreadful acts of God; no corn, no cattle;...the money from my wheat crop eaten up by taxes and interest on borrowed money."

Study these sections from the mural *Kansas Pastoral*. Is Curry portraying the farms of the Great Depression? Is he portraying the future, the present, or the past? Does the painting evoke hope or fear? Imagine you are a newspaper editor in 1930s Kansas and have just seen the sketches for Kansas Pastoral. Write an editorial commenting on Curry's mural, making reference to the problems of the Great Depression.

The most famous mural in the Capitol is John Steuart Curry's painting of John Brown.

The New Deal

By the early 1930s, Kansas and the country were experiencing horrible economic times. Twenty-five percent of the population was unemployed. Franklin Delano Roosevelt was running for president on the promise of a New Deal for America. Roosevelt felt that it was the government's responsibility to help the public.

Kansas, like other states, was suffering. The people of Kansas liked what they heard from Roosevelt, especially when he supported the farmers. In a radio address on April 7, 1932, Roosevelt spoke the following words:

...approximately one-half of our whole population, fifty or sixty million people, earn their living by farming or in small towns

During the 1932, campaign Franklin D. Roosevelt came to Kansas to ask Kansans for their votes. Here he is on a train after speaking in Topeka.

whose existence immediately depends on farms. They have today lost their purchasing power. Why? They are receiving for farm products less than the cost to them of growing these farm products. The result of this loss of purchasing power is that many other millions of people engaged in industry in the cities cannot sell industrial products to the farming half of the Nation. This brings home to every city worker that his own employment is directly tied up with the farmer's dollar. No Nation can long endure half bankrupt. Main Street, Broadway, the mills, the mines will close if half the buyers are broke.

I cannot escape the conclusion that one of the essential parts of a national program of restoration must be to restore purchasing power to the farming half of the country. Without this the wheels of railroads and of factories will not turn.

Kansans and the rest of the nation voted overwhelmingly to elect Roosevelt president. Many people and businesses were **bankrupt**, and they responded to Roosevelt's call to meet the challenge of this emergency.

President Roosevelt offered the American people a series of new programs that together were known as the New Deal.

This painting by Alden Krider shows the activities of the National Youth Administration. The NYA provided jobs for young adults. Krider was a member of the Kansas NYA and painted this canvas for the Kansas State Fair. In the background of the painting, Krider depicted the problems facing America's youth. The front of the painting shows the jobs provided by this New Deal program. Can you describe the problems and the solutions presented here?

The President's first act was to close down the nation's banks for four days. As economic conditions became worse, people panicked. People and businesses begin removing their money from banks for fear of losing it. If enough people removed their savings, then the bank would shut down. Roosevelt and Congress came up with a plan for the U.S. government to guarantee the safety of bank deposits. When the banks reopened after the four-day shut down the public regained trust, knowing that their money was safe.

The New Deal included programs that helped people who were unemployed. People who could not find work were given government jobs. Workers planted forests, made public art, and built reservoirs, bridges, public buildings, and parks. Farmers received money to reduce the amount of crops they produced to prevent food surpluses. Farmers facing bankruptcy got loans, so they would not lose their farms. Other programs helped people who could not pay their mortgages, so they could keep their homes. The New Deal programs gave people hope and a chance to survive the hard economic times.

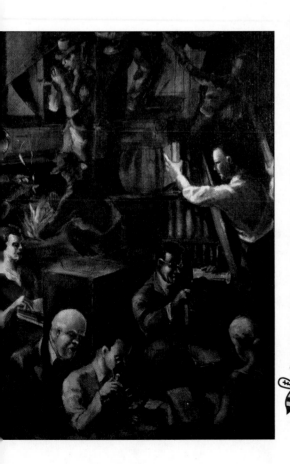

Kansas PORTRAIT

Birger Sandzen
1871-1954

Birger Sandzen was a professional artist and language teacher. Born in Sweden, Sandzen immigrated to Kansas when he was 23 years old. He arrived in Lindsborg to teach French, Swedish, German, and Spanish at Bethany College. Within five years, Sandzen became the art teacher at the college.

As an artist, Sandzen was well-known for his work in oils, watercolors, and prints. During the 1920s and 1930s, Sandzen exhibited his work in New York City but he continued to live in Kansas. He painted landscapes in an expressionist style. This means that he interpreted the land, rather than painting in a realistic manner. An art critic once wrote that Sandzen "surpasses all expectations."

Birger Sandzen was a founding member of the Prairie Print Makers. The goal of this group of artists was to increase the public's interest in printmaking. One of the founding members said, "I have dreams of providing original prints and good paintings for the walls of every schoolhouse in Kansas." The Prairie Print Makers wanted to make their art accessible to all people, no matter how much money they had.

New Deal programs gave many people jobs, including artists. Artists were paid to make art for public places. Murals and paintings were placed in public building such as post offices. Birger Sandzen and other Kansas artists participated in these programs. Sandzen created oil paintings for the post offices in Belleville, Halstead, and Lindsborg.

Kansas PORTRAIT

Arthur Capper
1865-1951

During the period of the New Deal, Arthur Capper was one of the U.S. Senators from Kansas. Born in Garnett, he became the first native-born governor of the state of Kansas in 1914. As a politician, Capper was known for his work on behalf of farmers. He once said, "My idea of representing people is to find what they want me to do and then do it." Capper was not only a distinguished politician, but he was also a well-known newspaperman and the founder of the Capper Foundation that assists children with disabilities.

At age 14, Capper started his career in newspapers by serving as an apprentice at the *Garnett Journal*. Rolling ink onto the rollers of the press was his first job. In order to reach the rollers, he had to stand on a box. For his work, he was paid $1 a week. Capper went on to become quite wealthy as the owner of the *Topeka Daily Capital* and several farm publications. He also owned radio stations.

Arthur Capper always had an interest in children. At Christmas, he sent his car filled with candy and toys out to the poorer neighborhoods of Topeka. One day a young boy wrote to him, asking for money to buy a pig. Capper gave him the money. This gave Capper an idea, and he started a program to provide loans to children to buy pigs and chickens. The children could then learn to raise livestock for market. Each child who received a loan had to promise to pay it back.

In Topeka, Capper hosted an annual birthday party around the fourth of July. Crowds of up to 20,000 attended these picnics and enjoyed free ice cream and a variety of fun activities. Capper was greatly admired for his generosity and his dedication to Kansas. He lived his life believing, "If you trust in people, they will trust you."

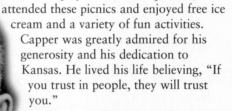

Kansas' Own New Deal

Governor Alf Landon and the Kansas legislature were also worried about the economy. They noticed that out-of-state banks were withdrawing funds from Kansas banks. They passed a law that limited the amount that could be withdrawn from an account. The law also placed banks under the control of the state government for two years. This took place before President Roosevelt closed down the nation's banks for four days. Most Kansas banks remained stable and were able to continue in business.

The Kansas legislature worked with Governor Landon to find new ways to help the Kansas economy. New laws were passed. Some used economic *disincentives*. One law added taxes to products that used foreign agricultural products. This gave domestic agricultural products an advantage. Another bill prevented banks and lending institutions from foreclosing on homes and businesses.

Rural electrification changed Kansas. This photograph is of the first project that brought electricity to rural Brown and Atchison Counties.

Rural Electrification

In the 1930s, residents of Kansas towns and cities enjoyed the use of electricity. But farmers did without, using kerosene lamps for lights and burning coal and wood for heat. If you wanted to take a warm bath, you had to start a fire to heat the water first. Can you imagine what it was like to wash, dry, and iron cloths without electricity?

One of the New Deal programs that had a major effect in Kansas was Rural Electrification. This program provided loans to farmers who wanted to bring electricity to their farms. Most farmers could not afford another loan, so they formed *cooperatives*. By cooperating, groups of farmers could share the expenses. The Brown-Atchison Electric Cooperative developed the first rural electrification project in Kansas. The power was turned on March 31, 1938. World War II delayed many rural electrification projects in Kansas. It took until the 1950s to bring electricity to all Kansans.

Lorena Hickok Reports on the Great Depression

Lorena Hickok was a newspaper reporter and a close friend of Eleanor Roosevelt, the wife of Franklin D. Roosevelt. For three years, during the 1930s, Hickok visited 32 states on behalf of the Federal Emergency Relief Administration. She reported on the living conditions of Americans coping with the Great Depression, along with their reactions to the New Deal programs. In 1934, Lorena Hickok traveled through Kansas, reporting on what she saw. In Graham County she reported, "out of 1,800 families, 1,036 are on relief, and applications are piling up. Nothing grows there at all save a few fields of badly stunted cane." Being "on relief" meant that you were receiving financial help from the government. Hickok continued her report writing, "in Graham county . . . more than 50 percent of [the] people were in need of clothing and bedding right now."

Life Goes On

Even though people faced hard times during the Great Depression, life went on. People may have done without some things, but they were still interested in having fun. In some communities, neighborhood musicians gathered in someone's home. They removed all the furniture from the main room and held dances into the late hours of the night. Other nights, neighbors and friends would gather for a potluck supper in which everyone brought a part of the meal. In church basements, women gathered for weekly quilting bees, making quilts and sharing time together.

Sports

Sports remained of great interest to most Kansans. Kansas and the nation had a sports hero in the "Kansas Flyer," Glenn Cunningham. Cunningham was a world-class runner and a great role model. As a child, his legs had been burned in a fire at his Elkhart school. At the time, the doctors did not know if he would ever walk again. But Cunningham never gave up and remained positive, personality traits he would carry into adulthood.

In high school, Glenn Cunningham set a new state record for running the mile and went on to set a national record for high school runners. As an adult, Cunningham held many world records for track and earned an Olympic silver medal. Cunningham always demonstrated good sportsmanship and never smoked or drank alcohol. He was so respected by the fans that crowds at track events would stop smoking when Cunningham entered the arena.

One sports writer said about Glenn Cunningham, "he was a great runner who didn't go around telling everyone that he was."

A Famous Journey

Another Kansan to make news during the 1930s was Amelia Earhart— the first women to fly solo across the Atlantic. Earhart spent much of her youth in Atchison, in the home of her grandparents. As an adult, she moved to California, where she experienced her first airplane ride in an open biplane. After flying as a passenger for 10 minutes over Los Angeles, Earhart recalled, "As soon as we left the ground I knew I myself had to fly."

Amelia Earhart went on to be the most famous woman aviator of all times. Although she had great determination, she was living in a time when there was little support for women who wanted to find success in fields dominated by men. Earhart's 14 hour and 56 minute solo flight across the Atlantic was the first by a women pilot. It earned her the Distinguished Flying Cross, the first one that Congress ever awarded to a woman.

Before Amelia Earhart flew solo across the Atlantic, she set many other world records.

236

That same year she became the first woman to fly non-stop across the United States from coast to coast. Earhart disappeared attempting to fly around the world. Throughout her life, she always looked for new opportunities. Her belief was, "Adventure is worthwhile in itself."

Images from Afar

Two other Kansas adventurers entertained and educated the public during this decade. Martin and Osa Johnson from Chanute brought photographs and movies from faraway exotic places to people across the country. The Johnsons studied the wildlife and peoples of east and central Africa and the South Pacific Islands. They used some of the most advanced motion picture equipment of the day, some of it designed by Martin Johnson. The couple produced eight feature movies, published nine books, and lectured throughout the country.

Martin and Osa Johnson popularized the idea of going on safaris and helped to increase the world's interest in African wildlife.

A Kansan Runs for President

As the American economy slowly improved, Franklin D. Roosevelt became an increasingly popular president. The Republican Party wanted to find a presidential candidate who was up to the challenge of running against the well-liked president. They found a good opponent in Alf Landon, the governor of Kansas.

How did Alf Landon find himself running for president? Landon's father was in the oil business. When Landon was 17, the family moved from the eastern United States to Independence, Kansas, in search of oil. Although he went to law school at the University of Kansas, Landon preferred to work in business. As a bookkeeper for a bank in Independence, Landon was able to save enough money to invest in oil. Within four years, he was able to start his own independent oil company.

Landon entered politics by supporting Theodore Roosevelt and the Progressive Party. He became acquainted with William Allen White through his interest in progressive politics. When White ran for governor as an Independent, Landon was a supporter. But for most of Landon's political life, he was a Republican. He would later characterize his beliefs as a "practical progressive."

In the same year Franklin D. Roosevelt was elected president, Alf Landon was elected governor of Kansas. Landon supported much of Roosevelt's New Deal, but he felt that many of the programs wasted the public's money. Landon was socially progressive but fiscally conservative. As governor, he reduced state spending and balanced the budget. He complained that the New Deal was unfriendly to businesses. Landon was, after all, a businessman. He also criticized Roosevelt for ignoring the U.S. Constitution. Landon felt that Roosevelt took on too much power himself and ignored the role of state governments.

Two years after Roosevelt became president, the Democrats dominated the elections. Alf Landon was the only Republican incumbent governor in the entire United States to win reelection. This made the national Republican Party look to him to be the next presidential candidate in 1936. Landon did not seek out the Republican nomination, but he accepted it when he was chosen. Perhaps he never expected to win, running against such a popular president. Landon lost the election, carrying only the states of Maine and Vermont. Even Kansas voted for Roosevelt. Landon took his defeat well and remained active in the Republican Party.

Alf Landon used this podium in his campaign for president. He later said that, "My entire security consisted of a bulletproof-steel speaker's podium that reached up to my chin - all you could see was my head...That podium went everywhere with me on the train. It took four big men to load and unload it."

Alf Landon was home in Topeka when he won the Republican presidential nomination. The delegates at the Republican Convention elected him on the first ballot.

The Kansas Journey

Chapter 10 Review

What Do You Remember?

1. Who were the "Kansas Legisladies?"
2. What impact did mechanized farm equipment, such as the tractor, have on Kansas farmers?
3. Why did state government take over the coal mines for a few weeks?
4. Explain the purpose of the Court of Industrial Relations.
5. How did Governor Henry Allen outlaw the Ku Klux Klan in Kansas?
6. Why did William Allen White run for governor as an independent?
7. Why did Stearman and Beech want to start their own airline manufacturing company?
8. Describe what is meant by the "consumer economy" of the 1920s.
9. How did the eating habits of Americans change during the 1920s?
10. How did racial segregation affect baseball?
11. What was the Harlem Renaissance?
12. What was one cause of the stock market crash of 1929?
13. What caused the Dust Bowl?
14. Name at least two ways in which farmers changed the way they work the land after the Dust Bowl.
15. Why did John Steuart Curry refuse to sign his murals in the Capitol?
16. How did President Franklin Roosevelt propose to get the country out of the Great Depression?
17. Why was rural electrification important to Kansas?
18. Name at least one way life went on during the Great Depression.
19. Why was Alf Landon picked by the Republican Party to run for president?

Think About It!

1. In the 1920s, many families began to buy goods and services on credit. Credit gave many families quicker access to new products. This made their lives easier. But using credit also means that consumers end up paying more for items, once interest on the loan is paid. Also debts can be difficult to pay off when the economy is not good. How can you as a consumer learn to use credit wisely and not find yourself in trouble with debt?
2. The Great Depression affected everyone's life. A large number of Americans were out of work, and they even found it hard to feed their families. Do you think we can keep this from happening again? Defend your answers.

Activities

1. Research the airline manufacturing companies in Kansas today. Explore why they are so important to the Kansas economy. Pretend you are running for a seat in the Kansas legislature. Write a speech that outlines your concerns about and solutions for keeping the airline industry in Kansas.
2. There were many famous Kansans during the 1920s and 1930s. As a class, create a series of famous Kansans trading cards. Place a picture or drawing of the Kansan on one side of the card and a short biography on the other.

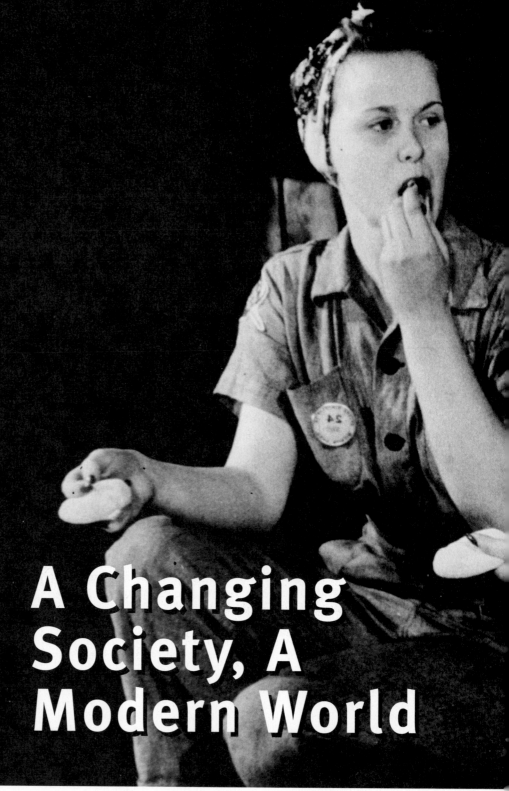

THE TIME
1939–1973

PEOPLE TO KNOW
Jesus Alvarado
Luz Alvarado
Oliver L. Brown
Dan Carney
Frank Carney
Harry W. Colmery
Marcos De Leon
Dwight D. Eisenhower
Georgia Neese Clark Gray
J. C. Nichols
Gordon Parks
Victorina Perez
William Stafford

PLACES TO LOCATE
Abilene
Johnson County
Korea
Mission Hills
Normandy, France
Pearl Harbor, Hawaii
Prairie Village
Richland
Topeka
Tuttle Creek
Vietnam
Wichita

World War II created opportunities for women to enter the work force. At the Cessna Aircraft Company's plant in Wichita, Miss Mina Weber is taking a quick time out for facial repair, using a gleaming sheet of aluminum in the stock room as a mirror.

A Changing Society, A Modern World

Timeline of Events

240

1939-1945
World War II

1941
Japan attacks Pearl Harbor. The United States enters World War II.

1943
Planeview begins as a community to house aircraft workers building planes for defense.

1940

1944
Eisenhower leads the Allied forces onto the beaches of Normandy. President Franklin D. Roosevelt signs the G.I. Bill of Rights.

1945

1948
Kansans vote to repeal prohibition.

1950-1953
The Korean War

1950

1951
Kansas experiences the worst flooding in its history.

WORDS TO UNDERSTAND
capitalism
catalyst
civilian
civil disobedience
civil rights
class action
communist
conformity
conscientious
conscription
franchise
grassroots
incorporated
integrated
isolationist
liberate
middle class
nuclear
per capita
plaintiff
propaganda
radioactive
reservoir
suburban

1954
In *Brown v. Topeka Board of Education*, the U.S. Supreme Court strikes down segregation in public schools.

1962
Tuttle Creek dam is completed.

1963
Gordon Parks publishes *The Learning Tree*.

1973
An agreement is signed to end the Vietnam War.

1955

1960

1965

1970

1952
Dwight D. Eisenhower is elected U.S. president.

1957
The Soviet Union launches the first satellite into space.

1958
Frank and Dan Carney open the first Pizza Hut in Wichita. The NAACP youth group in Wichita stages the first lunch counter sit-in for civil rights.

1965
The first U.S. troops are sent to the Vietnam War.

1969
The United States puts a man on the moon.

Japanese airplanes dropped bombs on Americans navel ships in Pearl Harbor. The day after the attack, the United States congress declared war on Japan.

The Attack on Pearl Harbor

December 7, 1941 began as a quiet Sunday. In the afternoon, many Kansans were listening to the radio. At about 1:30, Kansas-time, the networks broke into their programs with terrible news. American naval ships stationed in Pearl Harbor were under attack by the Japanese. If you were listening to the National Broadcast Company (NBC) you heard a reporter giving an eyewitness account. Standing on the roof of a downtown building in Honolulu, Hawaii, the reporter addressed the nation with the words, "It is no joke, it's a real war."

For the rest of the day, Kansans, like other Americans, gathered around their radios waiting for news on the attack. Unlike other wars, Americans heard about this one with record speed. News bulletins gave radio listeners information while the events were still unfolding. On December 7, the news was grim. Most of the battleships in the harbor were sunk or severely damaged. American combat planes at rest on the airfields were destroyed. Tragically,

more than 2,400 Americans were dead. The Japanese also attacked the American air force stationed in the Philippines.

The next day President Franklin D. Roosevelt spoke to the American people through a speech given to Congress.

Yesterday, December 7, 1941—a date which will live in infamy—the United States of America was suddenly and deliberately attacked by naval and air forces of the Empire of Japan...

Japan has, therefore, undertaken a surprise offensive extending throughout the Pacific area. The facts of yesterday speak for themselves. The people of the United States have already formed their opinions and well understand the implications to the very life and safety of our nation...

I believe I interpret the will of the Congress and of the people when I assert that we will not only defend ourselves to the uttermost but will make very certain that this form of treachery shall never endanger us again...

I ask that the Congress declare that since the unprovoked and dastardly attack by Japan on Sunday, December seventh, a state of war has existed between the United States and the Japanese Empire.

World War II

The attack at Pearl Harbor caused the United States to enter World War II. We joined the Allies (Great Britain, France and Russia). They had been involved in a war that had been going on for two years already. While Kansas was suffering through the Great Depression and the Dust Bowl, conflicts were brewing in the rest of the world. Adolph Hitler and the German Nazi Party aggressively moved through Europe. Japan was determined to control the Pacific, beginning with China. Many Kansans were *isolationists* before the attack on Pearl Harbor. They did not want the United States getting involved with international affairs.

Like most Americans, Kansans supported the Allies in their fight against Germany. They just did not want to see the United States enter the war. William Allen White, the editor of the *Emporia Gazette*, was one of the founders of the national Committee to Defend America by Aiding the Allies. White's Committee actively worked to convince the public that the United States should provide supplies and money to the Allies. By helping Great Britain, France, and Russia, the Committee believed that the Allies would be strong enough to defend themselves. It was believed that this would keep the United States out of the war. William Allen White wrote in July of 1940, "I have no great love for the British but so long as they fight they are saving our skins and if they are licked, we will have to go on with the battle or let Hitler control our commerce which is unthinkable."

When Pearl Harbor was attacked, change came quickly. Isolationists, like Kansas Senator Arthur Capper, showed their support for the war. "Japan's attack means war and we will see it thru," said Capper. In Kansas, the governor ordered that bridges, telephone lines, and any other potential targets be guarded against enemy attacks. Things not only changed at home. Many Kansans participated in military operations throughout the world. More than 215,000 Kansas men and women served in the military during World War II.

Victory banners were hung in homes to show that families had sons or daughters fighting overseas. Made by his mother, this one honors Otis Hughes Darrow. Darrow served in the Army Medical Corps. His mother was blind, but skilled at needlework.

Building the American Armed Forces

The U.S. Constitution gives Congress the power to raise and support armies. However, the Constitution says nothing about how the country should build such armies. At times, the United States has used *conscription*, commonly known as the draft. Under the draft, citizens are required by law to serve in the military.

The first national draft occurred during the Civil War. Both the Union and the Confederacy drafted men into their armies. In the South, men of a certain class, such as those who owned large plantations, were exempt. In the North, a man could escape his military duties by paying a fee or hiring someone to take his place. This, too, favored the upper classes. Many people protested the draft because it put a burden on lower class families.

The United States again used a national draft during World War I. This was the first time the majority of the soldiers were draftees. By law you could no longer buy your way out of service.

Before the country entered the war, President Roosevelt and Congress began preparations in case the country was pulled into the war. They provided military equipment to Great Britain. They also appropriated money for airplanes and ships to aid in the defense of this country. As part of this preparedness, President Roosevelt signed into law the first peacetime draft. On October 16, 1940, all men between the ages of 21 and 36 were asked to register for the draft. Each man was given a random draft number. At the University of Kansas 1,083 men registered that day.

Within two weeks, the draft began. The Secretary of War picked a number out of a goldfish bowl. The number selected was 158. In Douglas County, Kansas, that number belonged to a University of Kansas graduate student. Elmo Hardy was studying entomology (the study of insects) when he became a member of the first class eligible for the draft. Hardy served during World War II, using his knowledge of insects in the medical corps.

After the attack on Pearl Harbor, most of the opposition to the draft fell silent. Many American men and women volunteered for military service. Congress changed the draft to include men ages 18 to 38. About 10 million American men were drafted to fight in World War II. Another 6 million volunteered.

Many soldiers in World War II trained in Kansas. In 1944 this group of Navy men attended Washburn University as part of their training.

William Stafford
1914-1993

William Stafford was born in Hutchinson. While he was growing up, his family moved around Kansas. Stafford graduated from high school in Liberal and attended college at the University of Kansas. William Stafford became one of the best-known U.S. poets. He wrote 67 books and received many honors for his work.

World War II was a defining moment in Stafford's life. He was a pacifist and did not believe in carrying arms. During the war he was a *conscientious* objector. Stafford served his country during the war, just not in the armed forces. Stafford spent the war years in Civilian Public Service camps. He fought forest fires, built roads, and worked the land to prevent soil erosion. This work was done in the name of peace.

In his book *Down in My Heart: Peace Witness in War Times,* William Stafford writes about his experiences as a conscientious objector. Although he and his fellow pacifists were also serving their country, many people looked down on them. Stafford wrote, "At first some of the Forest Service men had talked largely, among themselves when some of our men had happened to overhear, about their enmity for CO's; and I myself had overheard one man, later our friend, say in the ranger station, 'I wish I was superintendent of that camp; I'd line 'em up and uh-uh-uh-uh'–he made the sound of a machine gun."

About 12,000 American men of draft age served in the Civilian Public Service. They did so without government pay. They were motivated by their religious and moral beliefs.

General Eisenhower is seen here with American troops in England.

General Eisenhower and the Defeat of Nazi Germany

During the war, Nazi Germany invaded and occupied much of Europe, including France. The leaders of both the United States and Great Britain wanted to *liberate* France. A commander was needed to lead the Allied Forces and Dwight D. Eisenhower was appointed to that position.

Dwight D. Eisenhower grew up in Abilene, Kansas. After high school he attended the Military Academy at West Point, becoming a professional soldier. Eisenhower was a strong leader. He brought people of different backgrounds together to work toward a common goal. His objective was to take back France and defeat Nazi Germany. A surprise attack was planned to cross the English Channel and land on the beaches of Normandy, France.

As commander, Eisenhower was in charge of men from different nations. Nearly three million men were gathered in southern England. About 4,000 American, British, and Canadian ships waited in the English Channel. More than 1,200 airplanes were readied. When Eisenhower gave the word, the invasion began. D-Day, as it was called, was one of the most significant moments of World War II. General Dwight D. Eisenhower led the single biggest invasion in history. After months of fighting, Germany finally surrendered.

Although D-Day was highly successful, the Allied troops suffered many casualties. Of the Americans who invaded France that day, 1,465 died, 3,184 were wounded, 1,928 were reported missing, and the enemy captured 36.

Eisenhower's Order of the Day, June 6, 1944

General Dwight D. Eisenhower wrote the following "Order of the Day" to the 175,000 men who were to arrive on the beaches of Normandy that first day. If you were a soldier waiting on the coast of England to invade France, how do you think Eisenhower's order would make you feel? What words does Eisenhower use to inspire the troops? Do you think Eisenhower knew the importance of what they were about to do? What type of inspirational message would you have given to the troops if you had been in Eisenhower's position?

SUPREME HEADQUARTERS
ALLIED EXPEDITIONARY FORCE

Soldiers, Sailors, and Airmen of the Allied Expeditionary Force!

You are about to embark upon the Great Crusade, toward which we have striven these many months. The eyes of the world are upon you. The hope and prayers of liberty-loving people everywhere march with you. In company with our brave Allies and brothers-in-arms on other Fronts, you will bring about the destruction of the German war machine, the elimination of Nazi tyranny over the oppressed peoples of Europe, and security for ourselves in a free world.

Your task will not be an easy one. Your enemy is well trained, well equipped and battle-hardened. He will fight savagely.

But this is the year 1944! Much has happened since the Nazi triumphs of 1940-41. The United Nations have inflicted upon the Germans great defeats, in open battle, man-to-man. Our air offensive has seriously reduced their strength in the air and their capacity to wage war on the ground. Our Home Fronts have given us an overwhelming superiority in weapons and munitions of war, and placed at our disposal great reserves of trained fighting men. The tide has turned! The free men of the world are marching together to Victory!

I have full confidence in your courage, devotion to duty and skill in battle. We will accept nothing less than full Victory!

Good luck! And let us beseech the blessing of Almighty God upon this great and noble undertaking.

A Changing Society, A Modern World

In Wichita, Boeing started producing the B-29 bombers. The Boeing plant was active day and night, with workers completing 10-hour shifts each day. The difficult job of producing the B-29s quickly became known as the "Battle of Kansas."

The War Economy

World War II helped end the Great Depression at home. The war also created new economic opportunities in Kansas. The U.S. government built several military air bases in the state. Many of the soldiers who fought in World War II were trained in Kansas. The military bases brought soldiers from all over the country. They also brought jobs for *civilian* workers.

During the war, new industries developed and old ones expanded. The federal government gave out defense contracts to industries that could support the war effort. Kansas was a good place to build the country's defense because of its geographic location. People thought there would be less threat of a foreign attack since Kansas is located so far from the coasts. Kansas received nearly three billion dollars in war contracts.

The Coleman Company that had specialized in lanterns before the war, made portable stoves for soldiers overseas. They also produced ammunition chests and shell casings. Gunpowder and artillery shells were produced at munitions plants across the state. The airline industry was largely transformed by the war. The Wichita aircraft manufacturers almost overnight began making planes for war.

Wichita gained the distinction of the American city with the highest number of war contracts *per capita*. By 1943, half of all workers in Wichita were employed by the aircraft manufacturers. The majority of industrial workers in Kansas during the war were employed in Wichita or Kansas City.

Planeview: A Planned Community

The aircraft industry of Kansas received more than two billion dollars in defense contracts during World War II. New jobs with good wages attracted people from all over the country. Nearly 67,000 new residents came to Sedgwick County during the war years, most worked in the aircraft industry.

The aircraft manufacturers in Wichita ran their plants 24 hours a day in order to meet the military's needs. Many of the shops, theaters, and restaurants stayed open 24 hours a day to accommodate three shifts of workers. But there were not enough houses for the workers. To solve the housing shortage, the federal government stepped in and helped pay for new construction. Planeview was the biggest of the planned communities. By the end of World War II, Planeview was the seventh largest city in Kansas.

Planeview, which was located next to the Boeing plant, consisted of 4,328 new houses. In less than a year, the community was filled with people from 42 different states. Planeview had its own police and fire departments, shopping centers, and grocery stores.

On the first day of school at the combined junior high and high school in Planeview, 1,900 students met each other for the very first time. Everyone was new! There were so many students that the school operated in shifts, just like the aircraft manufacturers. The school was open eight hours a day, with each individual student attending for six hours.

The aircraft industry attracted workers from all over the country to Wichita. Men and women worked side-by-side at the Boeing Plant.

"Rosie the Riveter" and the Changing Workforce

World War II changed the workforce in Kansas and the nation. As the country geared up for war, many new jobs were created. At the same time, the men who traditionally filled those jobs went off to fight the war. At the urging of the federal government, more industries began to hire women, African Americans, and others who had been discriminated against in the workplace.

Throughout much of history, American women were encouraged by society to take on the primary roles of wife and mother.

Women had worked outside the home before, but only certain types of jobs were available to them. With the shortage of male workers, many women had the opportunity to step into jobs that were traditionally held by men. In fact, the government encouraged women to do their patriotic duty and go to work in America's factories.

Many women in Kansas went to work for the aircraft industry. Women made up half of the workers at Boeing and 40 percent at Beech. In particular, more than 80 percent of the riveters at Beech were women. A riveter was traditionally a man's job.

To rivet means to fasten together two or more pieces of metal. It requires strength and patience. Riveters were very important to the aircraft industry.

The federal government used posters and other *propaganda* to encourage women to help with the war effort. Rosie the Riveter first appeared in posters. A song called "Rosie the Riveter" further popularized the image.

> *All the day long,*
> *Whether rain or shine,*
> *She's a part of the assembly line.*
> *She's making history,*
> *Working for victory,*
> *Rosie the Riveter.*
> *Keeps a sharp lookout for sabotage,*
> *Sitting up there on the fuselage.*
> *That little girl will do more than*
>   *a male will do.*

Propaganda used the image of a woman who was feminine and beautiful, sending a message that it was acceptable for women to become industrial workers.

Farm Production During the War

The availability of good jobs in the cities changed the Kansas population. By 1942, more than half of the people in Kansas were living in cities. However, agriculture remained an important part of the Kansas economy.

The droughts that had helped create the Dust Bowl were over. Nature was no longer fighting the Kansas farmer. World War II helped speed up changes in agriculture. Agricultural machinery was a continued need. Even though production of farm machinery was slowed down during the war so that efforts and materials could be used for the nation's defense, more and more Kansas farmers used tractors and combines.

The war created labor shortages on farms. The young men who once worked as hired hands went off to war or found higher paying jobs in the cities. High school students and urban women were asked to volunteer to help with harvest. Schools also helped by creating special classes on farm equipment repair. Women joined together and created a national organization called The Women's Land Army of America.

During the war, the production of crops in Kansas increased steadily. In addition to wheat and corn, Kansas farmers grew soybeans, flax, potatoes, peas, beans, and peanuts to help with the war effort.

Winning the War at Home

As it had during World War I, the U.S. government encouraged the sale of war bonds. In this way, the government asked Americans to help finance the war effort. Even school children were encouraged to sell bonds by going door to door in their neighborhoods.

Kansans, like all Americans, were asked to sacrifice at home during World War II. Steel, aluminum, coal, rubber, and gasoline were needed by the military. That meant they were in short supply for civilians. Scrap drives were conducted. All types of materials were saved and donated to the war effort. Kansas donated more scrap materials per capita than any other state in the country.

Americans were asked to make do with less in other ways. Fashion changed during the war, so that less fabric was needed to clothe Americans. Men, who traditionally wore three-piece suits, gave up their vests. Cuffed pants went out of fashion so that men's pants could be made with less fabric. To conserve fabric, women's skirts became shorter and tighter.

The eating habits of Americans also changed. Foods like coffee, sugar, canned goods and meat were rationed. That meant that families were allowed limited quantities of such products. To compensate, the federal government encouraged families to grow "Victory Gardens." Americans were asked to "Dig for Victory, Plant for Peace." Almost half of the nation's vegetables were grown in such gardens. Families were also encouraged to preserve their own homegrown food through canning.

Ration books were issued to every family member. There were strong punishments, including prison, for anyone caught violating the rationing rules. Children were taught about rationing so they could help their mothers and fathers who were at work on America's war effort.

Baking Without Sugar

During World War II many women's magazines printed recipes that helped home cooks to deal with food rationing. Recipes were given patriotic names such as "Victory Cake." The following recipe appeared in *Good Housekeeping* magazine in May 1942. Since sugar was in short supply during the war, each family had to limit the amount of sweets they ate. Recipes like these used substitutes for sugar. Can you figure out what is replacing sugar in this recipe?

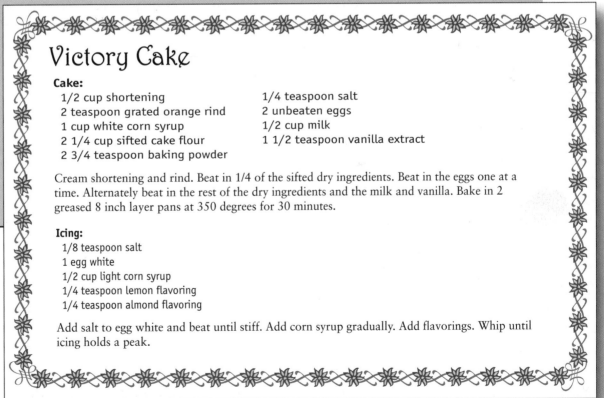

Victory Cake

Cake:
1/2 cup shortening
2 teaspoon grated orange rind
1 cup white corn syrup
2 1/4 cup sifted cake flour
2 3/4 teaspoon baking powder
1/4 teaspoon salt
2 unbeaten eggs
1/2 cup milk
1 1/2 teaspoon vanilla extract

Cream shortening and rind. Beat in 1/4 of the sifted dry ingredients. Beat in the eggs one at a time. Alternately beat in the rest of the dry ingredients and the milk and vanilla. Bake in 2 greased 8 inch layer pans at 350 degrees for 30 minutes.

Icing:
1/8 teaspoon salt
1 egg white
1/2 cup light corn syrup
1/4 teaspoon lemon flavoring
1/4 teaspoon almond flavoring

Add salt to egg white and beat until stiff. Add corn syrup gradually. Add flavorings. Whip until icing holds a peak.

General Eisenhower gives the sign for victory in a parade in Kansas City.

The GI Bill of Rights and a Changing America

World War II produced social and cultural changes in this country. During the war, the federal government mixed together soldiers of different backgrounds and from different regions of the country. Before going overseas, most soldiers trained at bases far from home. Until the war, many young men and women had no experience with life beyond their own hometowns. Their experiences as soldiers acted as a *catalyst* for changes in America. Men and women returning from the war saw a greater world in which they could live. In many ways this created a more mobile society.

Fifteen million servicemen and women returned home after the war. Veterans of earlier wars knew it would be difficult for the returning soldiers. After World War I, many servicemen faced unemployment and difficult financial times. One Kansas World War I veteran wanted to help World War II veterans. Harry W. Colmery was national commander of the American Legion, a veteran's organization. Colmery wrote what became known as the GI Bill of Rights. His vision was signed into law as the Servicemen's Readjustment Act before the war was even over. The bill provided benefits for returning soldiers, including:

- a free education
- a guaranteed loan for buying a home, farm, or business
- unemployment pay for a year
- assistance in finding a job.

The GI Bill of Rights transformed America. By 1947, almost half of the students enrolled in colleges were World War II veterans. This dramatically increased the number of college graduates in this country. The bill also contributed to a stronger national economy, allowing many veterans to buy businesses. As more and more houses were built to accommodate returning soldiers and their families, the United States saw a rise in *suburban* growth. All of these things led to a growing American *middle class*.

The War Ends

World War II ended in 1945, first in Europe and then in the Pacific. General Dwight D. Eisenhower returned home to Kansas to one of the biggest celebrations the state had ever seen. His hometown newspaper, the Abilene *Reflector-Chronicle*, reported the home coming on June 22, 1945.

> *General Dwight D. Eisenhower, back home at last among the people he grew up with, today expressed great emotion as he accepted their acclaim…*
>
> *Paying tribute to the parade that preceded his brief speech in the park where he played as a boy, Eisenhower said:*
>
> *'Every boy dreams of the day when he comes back home after making good. I too so dreamed but my dream of 45 or more years ago has been exceeded beyond the wildest stretch of the imagination. The proudest thing I can say today is that I'm from Abilene.'*

The End to Prohibition in Kansas

In 1933, the 21st Amendment to the U.S. Constitution repealed prohibition. But in Kansas the prohibition against alcohol continued. During World War II, liquor flowed into the state illegally. After the war, many returning Kansas soldiers wanted to make the drinking of alcohol legal again. Church groups and others wanted to keep Kansas dry.

The Kansas legislature sent the issue of prohibition to a vote of the Kansas population. Groups campaigned both for and against the repeal. The Temperance Tornado was a group that traveled 1,500 miles in 12 days working against the repeal of prohibition. It recruited teenagers to speak against the drinking of alcohol and used the celebrity of track star Glenn Cunningham for its cause. Despite the publicity surrounding the Temperance Tornado, prohibition was voted down. Fifteen years after the United States repealed prohibition, the Kansas voters agreed.

Kansas PORTRAIT

Georgia Neese Clark Gray
1900-1995

Georgia Neese Clark Gray was born in Richland, Kansas. She attended school in Topeka and graduated from Washburn University in the 1920s. After college, she left Kansas to become an actress. She worked first in the theaters of New York then she moved to Hollywood where she appeared in a few movies.

By the 1930s, she had returned to Kansas. She became an assistant cashier at her father's bank. Upon his death, she became the president of the Richland State Bank. At the same time she became active in the Democratic Party in Kansas. She was eventually elected National Committee Woman in Kansas.

In 1949, the position of Treasurer of the United States became open. President Harry S. Truman had promised to appoint a woman to the position if he had the opportunity. Georgia Neese Clark's name was submitted to President Truman as a possible candidate. When Truman approached her about the position he told her the job did not pay much. He asked her if she could afford to take the job. She replied, "Can I afford not to?"

Georgia Neese Clark became the first woman treasurer of the United States. Her name appeared on U.S. currency from 1949 to 1953.

We Like Ike!: A Kansan in the White House

Dwight D. Eisenhower's accomplishments during World War II made him very popular with the American public. One of Eisenhower's strengths was his ability to get along with both political parties. For this reason, both the Republicans and the Democrats wanted him to be their candidate for president of the United States.

Eisenhower chose to be a Republican for a variety of reasons. His belief that many issues could be solved at the state or local level was consistent with the Republicans. The party nominated Eisenhower as its presidential candidate. He campaigned for a well-run federal government. As a war hero, he appealed to America's patriotism. The phrase "I Like Ike" became a campaign slogan.

Eisenhower was one of the first politicians to effectively use television in his campaign, including the use of television advertising. On election night, Eisenhower and his family watched the election returns on television. Eisenhower was elected with 55 percent of the popular vote. America had a new president, and he was a Kansan.

The Interstate System

President Eisenhower is credited with creating the national interstate system of highways. The idea of a connected system of roads was talked about for a long time. Eisenhower had the experience of traveling across the country as a young Army officer. He traveled from Washington, D.C., to San Francisco on a series of dirt roads. His experience was typical and it took him two months to complete the journey.

A national interstate defense system was needed in case the United States mainland was ever attacked. An uninterrupted system of roads would allow the military to move troops and equipment quickly if needed.

After Eisenhower became president, he convinced Congress to authorize funding for the interstate system. The federal government paid for most of the construction. Interstates had to be a minimum of two lanes in each direction. The roads had to be designed for speeds of 50 to 70 miles an hour. The national system of roads that Eisenhower and others imagined is officially called the Dwight D. Eisenhower National System of Interstate and Defense Highways.

Interstate 70 can be seen here in this 1969 aerial photograph of Topeka.

Television: A Popular New Medium

In the 1950s, the popularity of television spread across the nation. The technology behind television was invented much earlier. In the 1930s, it is estimated that there were 200 television sets worldwide. But to make television happen, there needed to be more than the technology. Someone needed to broadcast programming so there would be something to see on the televisions.

On October 16, 1949, WDAF-TV became the first television station in the Kansas City area. At that time there were 78 commercial stations in 47 cities across the United States. WDAF-TV broadcast three to four hours of television programming each day. When programs were not available the station ran a static test pattern. Early programs included children's shows and local news broadcasts.

The first licensed commercial station in Kansas was KTVH in Hutchinson. It went on the air in 1953 as a CBS affiliate. The same year WIBW in Topeka began carrying CBS and ABC programming. About the same time, cable television was born. Although not wide-spread, cable allowed rural communities access to network programming. By the mid-1950s, two-thirds of American homes had at least one television set.

In the beginning, television programming was broadcast in black and white. It was not until 1967 that most programs were produced in color. Five years later about half the television sets in American homes could receive color.

Dwight and Mamie Eisenhower watch television while attending the Republican National Convention in Chicago in 1952.

Eisenhower's America

In many ways Eisenhower was the perfect president for the post-war years. Americans wanted peace and prosperity, and Eisenhower brought them both. During the 1950s, wages rose. There was a growing middle class. More people owned their own homes and filled them with new gadgets and conveniences. America entered another period of consumerism.

The 1950s are also characterized as a time of *conformity*. During the war, women had successfully gone to work. After the war, women were encouraged to go back to their traditional roles as wife and mother. In fact, it was considered patriotic for women to leave the workplace so that returning soldiers could have their jobs.

Suburban neighborhoods attracted traditional families. Neighborhoods consisted of rows and rows of houses that looked alike, but were affordable. Streets were clean and the schools were good.

Television contributed to the conformity of the era. All across the nation, people were viewing the same television programming. Before the war, regions of the country had their own culture including music and food specialties. Communities looked to local and regional talent to provide entertainment. After the war, America was a more mobile society. Families moved from place to place. Regional culture took a backseat to national trends.

Pizza Hut: Growing a Chain Restaurant

After World War II, chain restaurants became more common as people had more money and time to eat out. One of the best-known chain restaurants had its beginnings in Kansas.

Frank and Dan Carney were students at Wichita State University. Their parents owned a Wichita grocery store. A family friend suggested that the two college students open a restaurant in the building next door to the family grocery store. The Carney brothers borrowed $600 from their mother, bought a used oven, and started the first Pizza Hut.

Did you ever wonder how Pizza Hut got its name? Pizza was a food gaining popularity in the 1950s. The Carney brothers knew they wanted to serve pizza in their new restaurant. They were on a limited budget and wanted to reuse the sign that was already on the building. The sign only had room for about ten letters. Since the word "pizza" was a natural for the name, they were only left with a few letters to play with. "Pizza Hut" fit perfectly on the sign.

A year after Pizza Hut opened in Wichita, the business *incorporated* in Kansas and the first *franchise* opened in Topeka. Today, Pizza Hut is the largest pizza chain restaurant in the world.

"Pizza Hut Pete" was an early advertising campaign for the chain restaurant. This bank was a promotional giveaway.

Teenagers

More teenagers were graduating from high school in the 1950s. For the first time, teenagers became a major part of the American economy. Some businesses began advertising directly to young people. Rock and roll became a major force in the music industry, appealing to teenagers. By the end of the 1950s, teenagers were spending $22 million annually.

The Good Life: Suburban Kansas

In the 1950s, more and more people were moving to the suburbs. These are residential neighborhoods that surround cities. Kansas was no exception. In Johnson County, the population quadrupled as residents of Kansas City moved into the suburbs.

Good roads and the interstate system made living in the suburbs possible for many people who worked in the cities. Rather than living near their place of work, people began commuting to work. Suburbs offered nice, affordable housing with enough land for gardens and expansive

In the 1950s, Kansas City Power and Light built an all-electric house in Prairie Village. The house was a model for those seeking the good life in the suburbs. It featured the latest in technology including a hidden television set and electric curtain openers. Today, the home is part of the Johnson County Museums.

yards. On the other hand, the suburbs made people dependent on their cars.

The development of suburbs started in Kansas City long before the 1950s. J.C. Nichols is credited with starting the suburban movement in the area. Born and raised in Johnson County, Nichols started a real estate business in Kansas City. As early as 1905, Nichols began developing residential neighborhoods hoping to attract families who wanted "a better way of life." The first Nichols' development in Kansas was in Mission Hills. The homes were located on large pieces of land. The neighborhood streets curved through the hills.

Eventually, the J.C. Nichols Company created 56 residential neighborhoods surrounding Kansas City. They also built a variety of shopping centers, including the well-known Plaza in Kansas City, Missouri. Nichols believed that goods and services should be located near neighborhoods. Shopping centers were convenient for people who lived in the suburbs. They no longer had to go downtown to shop.

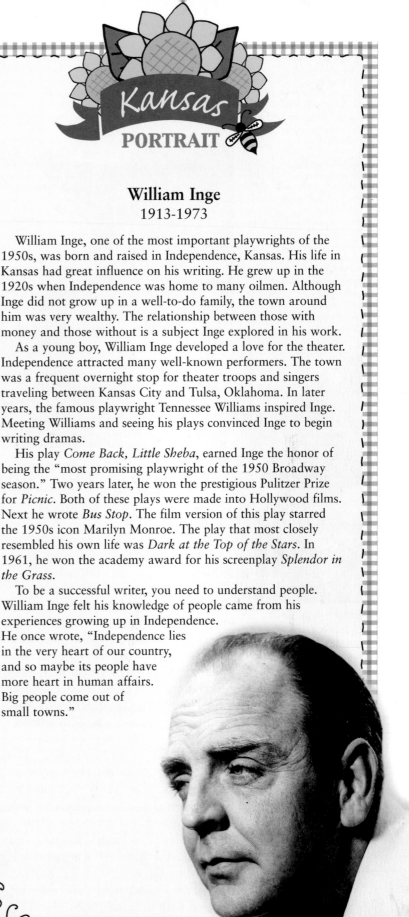

Kansas PORTRAIT

William Inge
1913-1973

William Inge, one of the most important playwrights of the 1950s, was born and raised in Independence, Kansas. His life in Kansas had great influence on his writing. He grew up in the 1920s when Independence was home to many oilmen. Although Inge did not grow up in a well-to-do family, the town around him was very wealthy. The relationship between those with money and those without is a subject Inge explored in his work.

As a young boy, William Inge developed a love for the theater. Independence attracted many well-known performers. The town was a frequent overnight stop for theater troops and singers traveling between Kansas City and Tulsa, Oklahoma. In later years, the famous playwright Tennessee Williams inspired Inge. Meeting Williams and seeing his plays convinced Inge to begin writing dramas.

His play *Come Back, Little Sheba*, earned Inge the honor of being the "most promising playwright of the 1950 Broadway season." Two years later, he won the prestigious Pulitzer Prize for *Picnic*. Both of these plays were made into Hollywood films. Next he wrote *Bus Stop*. The film version of this play starred the 1950s icon Marilyn Monroe. The play that most closely resembled his own life was *Dark at the Top of the Stars*. In 1961, he won the academy award for his screenplay *Splendor in the Grass*.

To be a successful writer, you need to understand people. William Inge felt his knowledge of people came from his experiences growing up in Independence. He once wrote, "Independence lies in the very heart of our country, and so maybe its people have more heart in human affairs. Big people come out of small towns."

The floods caused buildings to be knocked off their foundations or split into two pieces.

Volunteers built a wall with sandbags. Each bag weighed about 30 pounds and had to be passed from person to person through a human chain.

The 1951 Flood

Kansas weather is always unpredictable. The heavy rains of 1951 were extreme and dangerous. Strong storms caused the worst floods Kansas has seen since becoming a state. The most destructive floods occurred along the Kansas River near the cities of Manhattan, Topeka, Lawrence, and Kansas City. The Neosho, Marais Des Cygnes, and Verdigris Rivers also overflowed their banks.

The floods killed 19 people and left hundreds more injured. The property damage was great. Many roads and railroad tracks were closed for weeks. City water supplies and sewage-treatment plants were closed down. The homes, schools, and businesses that survived were covered in slime when the water receded. Many farms were covered with water, and were later covered with heavy deposits of soil and sand. The floods were dangerous, damaging, and left a real mess.

Topeka Unites to Save Drinking Water

As the waters of the Kansas River rose, the Topeka water treatment plant was threatened. If the plant failed then Topeka would loose its drinking water. The city would also be without water if fires broke out. The situation was critical.

A call for help went out into the community. About 4,500 people showed up to try to save the water treatment plant. The plant was surrounded by water on three sides and the volunteers had to be driven to the site in military trucks. The floodwaters were contaminated with dead animals, oil and gas, and parts of buildings that had been damaged by the raging waters. The dikes holding the water back were beginning to leak and the water was only 9 inches from the top, threatening to spill over.

The volunteers filled more than 50,000 sandbags. The sandbags were placed side-by-side and on top of each other in an attempt to form a wall to hold the water back. It worked! Friends, neighbors, and strangers stood side-by-side working for days to save Topeka's water.

Activity

Coping with the Flood: Report to the Board of Education, July 23, 1951

The 1951 floods happened in July, when school was out of session. In Kansas City, Kansas, the school district played a critical role in saving the community. School buildings were opened as temporary shelters for residents that were forced to evacuate. This is common in many communities when disasters occur.

The business manager of the Kansas City, Kansas schools gave a report to the Board of Education on July 23, 1951. This was about 10 days after the rain had stopped. The report is a valuable primary source because it gives us a glimpse into how disruptive the floods were to the community. The report refers to Armourdale, which is a low-lying neighborhood that was hit hard by the floods. The P.T.A. referred to is the Parent Teachers Association.

Read the excerpt from the report and make a list of all of the problems facing the school district. Pretend you are on the Board of Education. Have a discussion about how you might address each problem. As a class, develop a plan of action.

It is too early to estimate the damage to our buildings and equipment. We removed the furniture from the Clara Barton School before the flood and we have not seen the building since that time. We have been informed that it has been moved from its foundation and broken in two. We have also been advised that virtually the entire area served by the Clara Barton School is a total loss. These reports have not been verified....We have reentered the Emerson School and have started cleaning operations. The water did not reach the ceiling of the first floor and our furniture which had been moved upstairs is apparently in good condition. As a minimum we will have replacement of plastering, flooring, electrical circuits below the second floor and it is possible that moisture in the building will cause warping of the flooring on the second floor....

It is impossible to open school buildings in an emergency as we did without accepting the possibility that they will suffer considerably from the unusual occupancy....We have commandeered P.T.A. cooking equipment without having time to contact P.T.A. officers....The emergency was too great to lose time and we feel sure all will agree that immediate action was necessary....

Could it Happen Again? Flood Control Projects

The flood of 1951 changed the Kansas landscape. The waters eroded river and creek banks. The floods also widened river channels and changed the flow of the streams and rivers. In some places the receding waters left four feet of sand and silt. Could disastrous flooding happen in Kansas again? The answer is yes, but it is less likely than in the 1950s. Before the 1951 flood, a series of dams and **reservoirs** had been discussed. After the flooding, the construction of such flood control projects moved ahead. Perhaps the most controversial was Tuttle Creek, near Manhattan.

The Tuttle Creek project was designed to control the water in the Big Blue River. Some of the people who lived in the area were opposed to the project. In order for the project to proceed, the U.S. government had to buy the land from the residents. Many people did not want to lose their community, so at first they refused to sell. This was land on which their ancestors had lived. They also feared that they would face an economic loss. Eventually, Tuttle Creek was built as planned. The U.S. government negotiated with 1,713 different landowners to complete the project. It took 13 years. The Tuttle Creek Reservoir is "considered the most effective single unit in the flood control reservoir system," according to the U.S. Army Corps of Engineers. Many other flood control projects were also carried out in Kansas.

In 1993, the state again saw an unusual amount of rain. The dams and reservoirs built after the 1951 flood prevented another widespread disaster. However, damage did occur. At that time, people began to reexamine the issue of flood control. The current dams and reservoirs can control the flow of the water in rivers and streams, but they cannot prevent flooding from direct rainfall.

The Struggle for Civil Rights

Kansas entered the union as a free state in 1861, rejecting the idea of slavery. During the 1870s, Exodusters came to Kansas as the land of freedom and opportunity. In 1874, legislation in Kansas prohibited segregation in public places and on public transportation. By 1883, Kansas had elected Edward McCabe, an African American, to the position of state auditor.

But in 1883, the U.S. Supreme Court ruled that the federal Civil Rights Act of 1875 was unconstitutional. This meant that the federal government could not prevent people or private organizations from acting in a discriminatory way. By 1896, the U.S. Supreme Court ruled in favor of state segregation laws in *Plessy v. Ferguson*. The ruling allowed states to provide separate but equal facilities based on race.

No matter what the legal history, Kansas, like other states, practiced discrimination based on race and ethnicity.

Although Kansas had very few laws that mandated segregation, communities in the state practiced segregation. Neighborhoods were often segregated by race or ethnicity. Both public and private facilities, including swimming pools, theaters, and drug stores, practiced segregation.

During the years of practiced segregation in Kansas, many African American communities developed their own successful businesses and organizations. They also developed *grassroots* movements to fight against racism and discrimination. The NAACP (National Association for the Advancement of Colored People) became an important organization with local chapters throughout Kansas.

The modern struggle for *civil rights* had one of its most important victories in Kansas with the U.S. Supreme Court case *Brown v. Topeka Board of Education*. The ruling that held that "separate but equal is inherently unequal" struck down segregation in public schools and changed our lives forever.

Washington School was one of Topeka's African American schools. Here Miss Ray's first-grade class practices reading.

Segregation in Kansas Schools

One of the early state superintendents of public instruction in Kansas believed in *integrated* schools. In an 1869 report he wrote,

Separate schools in nearly every case are bad economy, as well as a disgrace to republican institutions. If colored persons are human, treat them as humanity deserves. Why close the school room against a child because he is of darker hue than his fellows? Why waste funds in supporting a separate school for a handful of colored children? The time will soon come when such a course will be looked upon as both foolishness and barbaric injustice combined.

In the state's early history it seemed as if integrated schools would be the norm. As early as 1879 things began to change in Kansas. A law was passed that allowed school districts in cities of more than 15,000 people to segregate their schools in the lower elementary grades. Segregation was not permitted in high schools in the state, with one exception. Because of a racial incident that resulted in a student's death in Kansas City, Kansas, an exception was made for that city only. At the time, some people felt the state was taking a step backward. Kansas never required school districts to have segregated schools. Instead, the state permitted it in larger cities.

Activity

Letter to Henry Allen from N. Sawyer, Topeka, Kansas, 1919

During the 1919 Kansas legislative session, a bill was introduced that would allow segregated schools in smaller cities in the state. Many people were against this bill. The national office of the NAACP wrote against it. Citizens of Kansas protested the bill by writing to Governor Henry Allen. The following is an excerpt from a letter written by N. Sawyer of Topeka to Governor Allen. After reading it, answer these questions:

1. What arguments does Mr. Sawyer use against the bill?
2. Were his arguments still valid in the 1950s when *Brown v. Board of Education* was argued?

Dear Sir:

I am writing you this letter to call your attention to a bill to be introduced in the next legislature the object of which is to separate the schools in the primary and grammar grades in cities of the second & third class.

We, the colored people of this state are opposed to further segregation in the schools of the state for the following reasons; such action is undemocratic, it is a backward step and inconsistent with Kansas history, it will finally result in the practical destruction of school facilities for colored children in the villages and rural communities....

Democracy if accorded to darker people increases its own self respect and besides raises it in the estimation of others. Separation & segregation tends to lower the segregated class both in its own estimation & in that of its fellows. The American colored man is being robbed of his self respect by a treatment in schools and public places which accentuates complexion differences and masses all into a single body without regard to personal worth or character....

But you may say equality of opportunity does not involve the idea of sameness of opportunity. It does if separation implies a stigma upon persons separated. It does if the people so separated are so few in a locality as to preclude the possibility of equality in buildings, teachers and other instrumentalities which go to make an efficient, adequate institution....

Thanking you in advance for what I believe will be a favorable consideration. I am

Respectfully yours,
N. Sawyer

A mural in Kansas City, Kansas tells the history of Argentine. Many workers from Mexico settled here to work on the railroad.

The Fight to Integrate Argentine High School

Issues of segregation and discrimination in Kansas were not exclusive to the African American communities. They touched other groups as well. In the 1920s, Mexican students fought to attend the all-white Argentine High School in Kansas City, Kansas.

Jesus and Luz Alvarado, Marcos De Leon, and Victorina Perez graduated from the eighth grade in Kansas City and enrolled in Argentine High School. After one week of classes, a group of white parents presented a petition to the local Board of Education. They wanted the four Mexican students removed from the school. The board refused to take any action. In anger, the white parents made threats against the Mexican community. This prompted the four students to withdraw from school because they were concerned about their safety. However, they continued to fight for their rights to attend high school.

Kansas City, Kansas was the only school district in the state legally allowed to have segregated high schools. This gave the African American students their own high school. Four Mexican students were not a large enough group to create a separate school. Instead, the Board of Education offered them a separate classroom, with their own teacher. The four students refused. The school board offered to pay tuition and transportation for the students to cross the border and attend a Kansas City, Missouri high school. Again, the students refused.

The Board of Education told the parents of the Mexican students to send the students to school "if they thought it safe to do so." But the board did not offer the students any security. Since the Mexican students were considered "friendly aliens" under the law, the parents filed a complaint with the Mexican consul. The governor of Kansas questioned the superintendent of schools asking him to justify the segregation. The Wyandotte county attorney said the white parents "violated the constitution, international treaty rights . . . and the promise between Mexico and the United States."

The students lost a year of school, and the case never resulted in a lawsuit, but the Mexican students eventually won the right to attend Argentine High School. The Board of Education was not able to provide separate but equal facilities to the four students. Pressure from state and local forces, as well as the Mexican consul, eventually ended the dispute.

Brown v. Topeka Board of Education

The landmark U.S. Supreme Court case *Brown v. Board of Education of Topeka* was not the first legal challenge to school segregation in this country. Cases had been going before the courts for a long time, even in Kansas. *Brown v. Board of Education of Topeka* started out as a local case.

The Topeka school district segregated its elementary schools. In the 1950s, the city had 18 elementary schools for white children and four for African American students. The Topeka NAACP, wanted to legally challenge the state law that allowed elementary schools in larger cities to be segregated.

Thirteen parents in Topeka agreed to become plaintiffs. They represented 20 African American students. The NAACP asked the parents to try to enroll their children in the neighborhood schools that were designated for white students. The black students were not allowed to enroll. The plaintiffs then came together in a *class action* lawsuit. The case was named for Oliver L. Brown because he was a local minister and the only man.

When the Topeka case was heard in the U.S. District Court for Kansas the NAACP argued that segregated schools sent the message to African American students that they were inferior. For that reason, separate schools were inherently unequal. The NAACP lost the case because the U.S. Supreme Court in *Plessy v. Ferguson* allowed the idea of separate but equal.

The case was appealed to the U.S. Supreme Court. There the local case was combined with four other cases. Oliver L. Brown, the Kansan for whom the case was named, was one of nearly 200 *plaintiffs*. The plaintiffs came from five states including Delaware, Kansas, South Carolina, Virginia, and Washington, D.C.

On May 17, 1954 the U.S. Supreme Court unanimously overturned *Plessy v. Ferguson*, ruling in favor of the plaintiffs. *Brown v. Board of Education of Topeka* meant the desegregation of all public schools in America. However, the Supreme Court did not give a timetable by which the school districts had to end segregation. There were still battles ahead.

In Kansas, the Topeka School District had begun to end segregation in the public schools before Brown v. Board of Education of Topeka reached the U.S. Supreme Court.

STATE THE TOPEKA **JOURNAL**

AN INDEPENDENT NEWSPAPER

By Stauffer Publications, Inc.

Topeka, Kansas, Monday, May 17, 1954—Twenty-four Pages

Official City Paper

Home Edition

FIVE CENTS

SCHOOL SEGREGATION BANNED

Turnpike Bonds Authorized So Suit Can Start

Supreme Court Will Clear Legal Air in Friendly Action

The Kansas Turnpike authority Monday formally approved issuance of 160 million dollars in revenue bonds for the 234-mile proposed Kansas turnpike.

In so doing, the KTA deliberately stuck its neck out in a legal way to become a target of a friendly-type suit warranto suit by the state to determine the legality of the KTA's actions and the law under which it operates.

A quo warranto action in substance inquires of the defendant "by what right do you act in this matter?"

The state agency also incorporated in resolutions other actions and a set of bylaws thought necessary to offer Atty. Gen. Harold R. Fatzer a legal...

Laying Track at the Fairgrounds for 'Cyrus Holliday'

This special crew from the Santa Fe railroad was hard at work Monday morning putting down a 300-foot strip of track on which the 1880 Cyrus K. Holliday locomotive and one car will chug into the Centennial pageant. The operation was almost identical to the type of work done in early days to move the tracks.

Supreme Court Refutes Doctrine of Separate but Equal Education

High Tribunal Fails to Specify When Practice of Dual Schools Must Be Dropped by States

Washington, May 17 (AP)—The Supreme court ruled unanimously Monday that segregation of Negro and white students in public schools is unconstitutional. But it said it will hear further arguments this fall on how and when to end the practice.

Thus many months—perhaps more time will elapse—before the historic ruling actually wipes out the separate schools now in existence in many states.

Chief Justice Warren read the court's opinion which declared: "We conclude that in the field of public education the doctrine of separate but equal has no place. Separate educational facilities are inherently unequal."

"THEREFORE," he said that...

Court Ruling Hailed

Segregation Already Ending Here, Say School Officials

Jacob A. Dickinson, president of the Topeka Board of Education, hailed the Supreme court's segregation ruling Monday as "in the finest spirit of the law and true de-

Civil Disobedience: The Dockum's Drugstore Sit-In

Brown v. Board of Education of Topeka did not change America overnight. The struggle for civil rights continued. The NAACP and other organizations continued to fight for the rights of African Americans through legal means. In Wichita, the NAACP youth group decided to do something different. They decided to challenge discrimination through *civil disobedience*. Civil disobedience means to take action against laws and customs without the use of violence.

In the 1950s, drugstores had lunch counters where shoppers could eat food and soft drinks. In Wichita, the white-owned drug stores would not serve African Americans at their lunch counters. There was usually a place near the kitchen where black customers could order food for take-out. But if an African American sat down at the counter, he or she would be refused service. This was not the law, it was store policy.

There had been attempts to fight discrimination in Wichita before. White and black students had tried to eat together in

How Do We Know This?

A Building as Evidence

When the U.S. Supreme Court announced its decision on *Brown v. Board of Education of Topeka* it wrote,

Does segregation of children in public schools solely on the basis of race, even though the physical facilities and other "tangible" factors may be equal, deprive the children of the minority group of equal educational opportunities? We believe that it does... Separate educational facilities are inherently unequal. Therefore, we hold that the plaintiffs...are...deprived of the equal protection of the laws guaranteed by the Fourteenth Amendment.

The lawsuit was about testing the idea of "separate but equal." To do so, the NAACP needed a case where the white and black schools looked equal. Topeka offered them that chance. In Topeka, African American teachers were highly qualified and generally paid the same as the white teachers. The textbooks were nearly the same. The buildings were in good repair and offered many of the same opportunities. How do we know this?

The Monroe Elementary School stands today as a National Park Service site. By studying the brick school we can tell that it is typical of many schools in Kansas built during the 1920s. The school we see today is actually the third Monroe School. It was the newest of the African American schools.

The same architect who built many of Topeka's other schools designed Monroe School. If we compare the school with schools that served the white students we would see similarities. This was important to *Brown v. Board of Education of Topeka*. If the white and black schools were obviously unequal they could not test the "separate but equal" idea. By making the Topeka case the lead in the legal appeal, the case could truly be made that "separate but equal is inherently unequal."

The Monroe School helps tell the story of the landmark civil rights case Brown v. Topeka Board of Education.

area restaurants and been refused service. Black students had tried to sit in the "white-only" section of movie theaters. But none of these actions had changed policies.

Against the advice of the national NAACP, the Wichita youths began planning their sit-in at Dockum's Drugstore. They wanted to peacefully disrupt the business and hopefully shame the owners into changing their policy. The sit-in began on July 19, 1958 when a group of well-dressed African American youths entered Dockum's and sat down at the lunch counter. The youngest protester was 15 and the oldest one was 22. The youth sat quietly at the counter looking straight ahead, waiting to be served.

The students would peacefully sit at the counter every Thursday and Saturday from lunchtime through dinnertime. The staff continued to refuse to serve them. As long as the youth were sitting at the counter, no business was being conducted and the store was losing money. Several weeks into the sit-in, the youth decided to add more days to their protest. On Monday, August 11, the store changed its policy and decided to serve the African American youths. The owner said he was losing too much money. The black students at the lunch counter ordered soft drinks and drank them in silent victory.

This was the first successful lunch counter sit-in during the struggle for civil rights, and it had a big impact. Dockum's was part of a chain of drugstores in Kansas. After the sit-in, they changed their policy in all of their stores. Word spread to other youth groups in the region. Similar acts of civil disobedience took place in Oklahoma City, Winfield, Coffeyville, and eventually in the Deep South.

What do you think?

There are many ways to change a policy or law you do not like. Sometimes you can negotiate a change. At other times you might use your vote to make a difference. During the struggle for civil rights some groups practiced civil disobedience. What do you think is the best way to cause things to change?

Kansas PORTRAIT

Gordon Parks
1912 - 2006

Gordon Parks began life in Fort Scott, Kansas. After his mother died, Parks lived with his older sister and her husband in Minnesota. After a disagreement with his sister's husband, Parks found himself homeless at 16. He found work as a piano player, a busboy, and a basketball player.

Parks became one of the most influential photographers in the world. He said, "I chose my camera as a weapon against all the things I dislike about America." As a photojournalist, he told stories in pictures. They were often stories of poverty and discrimination. He was the first African American photographer to work for *Life*. Parks also photographed many famous people as a fashion photographer for *Vogue*.

Parks captured his memories of growing up in Kansas in a novel *The Learning Tree*. Parks made the novel into a film, which he directed. It was one of the first Hollywood movies directed by an African American. *The Learning Tree* was among the first 25 films put into the Library of Congress collection.

Gordon Parks also composed music and has written a ballet about the life of civil rights leader Martin Luther King, Jr. Gordon Parks is one of the most respected artists of the 20th century.

Gordon Parks is shown directing a film made from his novel, The Learning Tree.

The Cold War

At the end of World War II the United States and the Soviet Union became the only two superpowers in the world. The Soviet Union was a *communist* country made up of several Eastern European nations, the largest being Russia. The United States did not trust the Soviet Union, and felt it was a threat to the security of the free world. The United States was also concerned that the spread of communism would threaten our way of life. The Soviet Union was equally fearful that the spread of American *capitalism* would have a similar effect on its way of life.

The tensions between the two superpowers resulted in what became known as the Cold War. In the beginning, the Cold War focused on Eastern Europe where the Soviet Union was supporting communist governments. In response, the United States wanted to stop communism in other parts of the world. The United States practiced a policy of containment. The goal was to prevent the Soviet Union from expanding its influence.

Both the United States and the Soviet Union built up a supply of weapons and missiles to defend themselves and their allies. The two countries never directly went to war with each other but entered into conflicts by backing opposing sides throughout the world.

The Korean War

After World War II, Korea was split in half along the 38th parallel. North Korea became a communist country backed by the Soviet Union and China. South Korea formed ties with the United States and formed a democratic government. In June 1950, North Korea invaded South Korea. American troops were sent to defend South Korea.

In Kansas, Fort Riley and Fort Leavenworth became training centers for soldiers going overseas. Several Kansas airbases were expanded to accommodate the jets that were used during the war. Many Kansans served in the Korean War.

As a presidential candidate, Dwight Eisenhower said he would go to Korea to stop the war. When he became president, Eisenhower threatened to use atomic weapons to bring about an end. Three years after the Korean War began, all sides agreed

Of the 33,000 American soldiers killed in the Korean War, 415 were from Kansas. This memorial in Wichita honors their service to their country.

Students at the University of Kansas disrupted the chancellor's review of the ROTC as a protest to the Vietnam War.

to stop fighting. Still, no official end to the war has taken place, and tensions between North Korea and South Korea have never ended.

The Vietnam War

Vietnam in Southeast Asia had gained its independence after a long period of French rule. The United States did not support this independence because the Communist Party of Vietnam had too much power. America's Cold War policy was to contain communism and prevent it from spreading to other parts of the world. The U.S. government was afraid that if Vietnam became a communist country then most of Southeast Asia would follow.

Vietnam became a divided country. The United States backed South Vietnam and the Soviet Union and other communist countries supported North Vietnam. The American involvement in Vietnam started slowly but increased over time. Eventually, 58,000 Americans lost their lives fighting in Vietnam—753 of them were from Kansas.

Many Americans supported the United States involvement in Vietnam, but many others did not. Many young people began protesting against America's involvement in the war. The growth of the anti-war movement was unlike any other in American history. Protests on college campuses spread across the country.

By the end of the 1960s, campus anti-war demonstrations were common. At the University of Kansas, protesters disrupted the chancellor's annual review of ROTC (Reserve Officer Training Corps) cadets in 1969. The protesters, carrying signs that read "ROTC off Campus" and "Stop the War," forced cancellation of the event. By the end of the Vietnam War, some soldiers were protesting the U.S. involvement by wearing peace signs on their combat uniforms.

Over time, more and more Americans disliked our involvement in the Vietnam War. But many of those who did not believe in the war still supported the American men and women who served in the military in Vietnam.

A highpoint in the Space Race happened when Buzz Aldrin and Neil Armstrong landed on the moon.

The Nuclear Age

In the 1950s and 1960s, Americans lived in fear of a *nuclear* attack. In 1945, the United States used an atomic bomb in Japan. Many people felt that the use of atomic weapons ended World War II. The Soviet Union tested its first atomic bomb four years later. Both countries developed hydrogen bombs that were even more powerful. All of these weapons were capable of widespread destruction.

The Space Race

The Soviet Union successfully launched the first satellite into space. It was called "Sputnik" and it made Americans uneasy. Did the Soviet Union have the ability to launch weapons through space? The United States made the development of satellites and rockets a priority. Soon the two countries were in a space race.

The launch of Sputnik changed the lives of schoolchildren in America. In order to win the space race, schools put a greater emphasis on math and science. The federal government put more money into education so the nation could train a generation of scientists. Putting a man on the moon became an important goal. The United States succeeded when astronauts Neil Armstrong and Buzz Aldrin stepped onto the surface of the moon in 1969.

Missiles in Kansas

During the Cold War many important military bases were located in the Midwest.

Students at Jackson Heights High School in Holton go to school in an old missile silo.

Kansas was home to Forbes Air Force Base (Topeka), McConnell Air Force Base (Wichita), and others. These military bases controlled a network of missiles buried throughout the state. Missile silos housed rockets with nuclear weapons that could travel about 6,000 miles. Fortunately, they were never launched.

When the federal government abandoned the missile silos in Kansas some of them were filled with dirt and sealed. Others were sold. Jackson Heights school district in Holton bought one of the old silos for $1. They used it to build Jackson Heights High School. What is now the bus garage once housed a deadly missile. The command center was turned into a classroom. Students today walk through tunnels built for military personnel.

President Eisenhower Warning About the Military-Industrial Complex

All presidents, upon completing their term in office, give a final speech to the nation. In his farewell address, President Eisenhower spoke of America's role in establishing a peaceful world. He also spoke of the importance of the military in keeping the peace. The military needed to be ready for "instant action," in case someone wanted to do this country harm.

But Eisenhower also warned Americans about the influence of what he called the military industrial complex. He pointed out that we had established a large defense industry for the first time in our country's peacetime history. He warned that America needed to guard against the influence of these defense industries. Eisenhower feared that those that made money creating weapons would influence American foreign policy. He believed that the defense industries should respond to America's needs, not create them. Eisenhower was concerned that the country would be convinced to build weapons that were not needed.

Duck and Cover: Civil Defense at Home

During the Cold War the government launched a series of educational programs designed to inform the public what to do in case of a nuclear attack. The programs were developed with the idea that it was possible to survive a nuclear bomb.

"Duck and Cover" was a strategy to survive the initial atomic blast. Students across the country were taught what to do by a cartoon character named Bert the Turtle:

- "Duck to avoid things flying through the air."
- "Cover to keep from getting cut or even badly burned."

If you saw the bright flash of light of a nuclear explosion, you were to drop to the floor and cover your head with your hands. In schools, students were taught to dive beneath their desks and then cover their heads. If you survived the initial blast then you were to look for shelter from the *radioactive* fallout. Public buildings with shelters carried Civil Defense signs.

The building of family fallout shelters was encouraged. These were small underground rooms that were strong enough to survive a nuclear attack. Families would stock their "bomb" or "fallout" shelters with canned food, water, clothing, and first aid supplies.

The school of engineering at Kansas State University designed and built a sample fallout shelter. It was used to show the public how to construct one at home. Designed to hold a family of four, the shelter was 13 feet in diameter and about six and a half feet tall. The structure had bunk beds for sleeping. It was estimated that a family would need $1,000 in materials, and it would take two to three months to build.

The Cold War Ends

The Cold War came to an end gradually. The Soviet Union began to experience difficulties. The Soviet economy suffered greatly. Countries in Eastern Europe wanted their independence. In 1991, the Soviet Union itself broke apart into separate countries. This left the United States as the only remaining superpower.

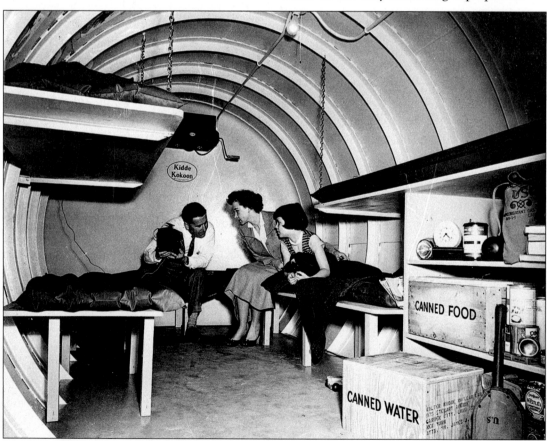

Some families built their own fallout shelters.

Chapter 11 Review

What Do You Remember?

1. How did the attack on Pearl Harbor change the isolationist views of some Americans?
2. What made Dwight D. Eisenhower a strong military leader?
3. How did World War II transform the Kansas economy?
4. Why was Planeview built?
5. Name two ways Americans were asked to do with less during the war.
6. What was the "Temperance Tornado?"
7. Define suburbia.
8. How did growing up in Kansas influence the plays of William Inge?
9. How did Topeka save its drinking water during the 1951 flood?
10. What is the meaning of "separate but equal is inherently unequal?"
11. In what ways did Kansas segregate its schools?
12. In your words, tell the story of the fight to integrate Argentine High School.
13. Who was Gordon Parks and what has he accomplished?
14. What was the Cold War?
15. Why were students taught to "Duck and Cover?"

Think About It!

1. The idea of a military draft is often controversial. Some people feel it is the patriotic duty of all Americans to be willing to fight for their country. Others are concerned that it is too difficult to administer a draft fairly. What do you think? How do you defend your position?

2. President Eisenhower was one of the first politicians to use television in his campaign. Think about how television might have changed political campaigns. Do you think the Internet is having the same effect?

Activities

1. Using newspapers, research The Gulf War, the attack on the United States on September 11, 2001, and the War on Terrorism and compare the public response and experiences to the attack on Pearl Harbor and the United States' entry into World War II. In what way were the experiences the same and in what way were they different?

2. Research the GI Bill of Rights. Interview someone in your community who used the GI Bill. Develop an exhibit board on how the bill changed his or her life.

3. Research a reservoir or lake near your hometown. Was it man-made? Was it built as a flood control project? How did people in the surrounding community feel about the project?

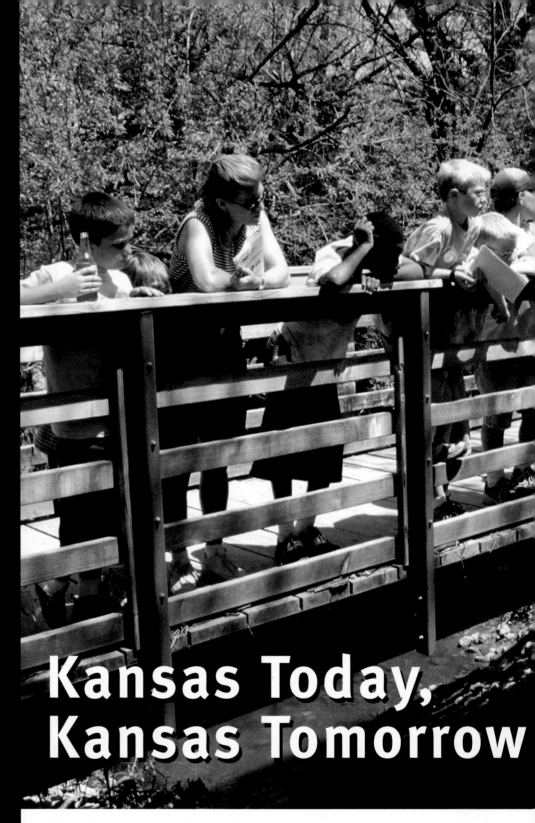

Kansas Today, Kansas Tomorrow

Timeline of Events

1972
Kansas Legislature ratifies the Equal Rights Amendment.
Ron Evans pilots Apollo 17 around the moon.

1985
Ernest Garcia becomes the
first Hispanic to serve
as the U.S. Senate's
sergeant at arms.

1970   1975   1980

1978
Nancy Landon
Kassebaum is elected U.S.
Senator from Kansas.

WORDS TO UNDERSTAND
ancestor
conserve
consolidating
curriculum
ethanol
ethnicity
export
habitat
import
naturalized citizen
preserve
rural depopulation
standardization
tourist

Kansas kids will be making decisions about the future of Kansas. These students are learning why it is important to protect our environment.

1991
Joan Finney becomes the first woman governor of Kansas. Barry Sanders named Pro Football Player of the Year.

1995
Kay McFarland becomes the first woman Chief Justice of the Kansas Supreme Court.

2004
Lynette Woodard is inducted into the Basketball Hall of Fame.

985   1990   1995   2000   2005

1987
The idea of the "Buffalo Commons" is presented.

1996
Senator Bob Dole is nominated as the Republican candidate for president.

273

Kansas: Past, Present, and Future

Many of the issues facing Kansans today have their roots in the past. Those same issues are shaping the future of the state. Addressing the needs of a changing population, keeping the Kansas economy strong, and living in harmony with the environment are just a few of the issues that have been with Kansas throughout its history.

Kansans today enjoy new technologies and opportunities not available to our *ancestors*. But in many ways we are no different than the people who lived before us. We struggle today with many of the same challenges faced by our ancestors. Like the people of the past, our solutions are shaped by the tools and ideas available to us. People, whether past, present, or future, continue to work for a better tomorrow.

Activity

Population of Kansas

The Kansas population increased every decade but one. Can you speculate on why the population may have decreased between 1930 and 1940?

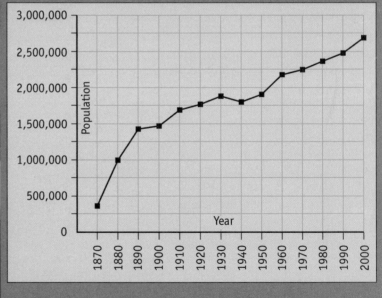

Rows of new homes now fill what had recently been a farmer's field in Overland Park, a city in the fastest growing county in the state.

The Kansas Journey

Kansas' Changing Population

Every 10 years the United States government conducts a census. In the year 2000, Kansas was home to more than 2,500,000 people. Johnson was the fastest growing county in the state. Between 1990 and 2000, Johnson County's population increased by 27 percent. Other urban areas also continued to grow. The communities around Kansas City, Topeka, Lawrence, and Wichita account for most of the state's recent growth.

Although the Kansas population continues to increase, its rate of growth is less than the United States as a whole. This means that other parts of the country are growing faster than Kansas. Today, less than one percent of the United States population lives in Kansas. One hundred years ago more than two percent of the people in the United States resided in Kansas. So even though Kansas is growing, today Kansans are a smaller percentage of the overall U.S. population.

Population Numbers Have Consequences

In terms of land size, Kansas is the 14th largest state in the country. In terms of population our state ranks 32nd. A state's population determines how that state is represented in the U.S. Congress. Congress has two governing bodies and each citizen is represented in two ways. All states have two Senators who represent the entire population of the state. There are 100 U.S. Senators. The smallest state and the largest state have the same number of Senators.

The United States House of Representatives is different. There are a total of 435 representatives, divided among the 50 states. Each state is divided into congressional districts. The districts are based on population, not geographic size. Kansas sends four representatives to Washington D.C., each representing about 670,000 people.

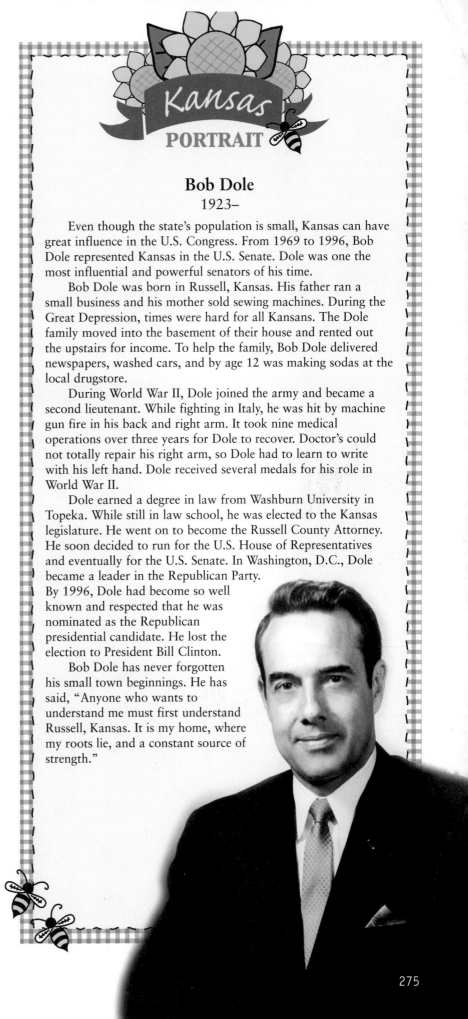

Kansas PORTRAIT

Bob Dole
1923–

Even though the state's population is small, Kansas can have great influence in the U.S. Congress. From 1969 to 1996, Bob Dole represented Kansas in the U.S. Senate. Dole was one the most influential and powerful senators of his time.

Bob Dole was born in Russell, Kansas. His father ran a small business and his mother sold sewing machines. During the Great Depression, times were hard for all Kansans. The Dole family moved into the basement of their house and rented out the upstairs for income. To help the family, Bob Dole delivered newspapers, washed cars, and by age 12 was making sodas at the local drugstore.

During World War II, Dole joined the army and became a second lieutenant. While fighting in Italy, he was hit by machine gun fire in his back and right arm. It took nine medical operations over three years for Dole to recover. Doctor's could not totally repair his right arm, so Dole had to learn to write with his left hand. Dole received several medals for his role in World War II.

Dole earned a degree in law from Washburn University in Topeka. While still in law school, he was elected to the Kansas legislature. He went on to become the Russell County Attorney. He soon decided to run for the U.S. House of Representatives and eventually for the U.S. Senate. In Washington, D.C., Dole became a leader in the Republican Party. By 1996, Dole had become so well known and respected that he was nominated as the Republican presidential candidate. He lost the election to President Bill Clinton.

Bob Dole has never forgotten his small town beginnings. He has said, "Anyone who wants to understand me must first understand Russell, Kansas. It is my home, where my roots lie, and a constant source of strength."

Rural Depopulation

Over time, more and more people have moved from rural to urban areas of Kansas. This is referred to as *rural depopulation*. It means the rural parts of the state are losing people.

The rural economy has traditionally been based in agriculture. Farms have become bigger and bigger as farm equipment has become more mechanized. Technology has allowed fewer people to do the work. Bigger farms create smaller populations in rural Kansas.

Rural depopulation does not happen all at once. It is a slow process. After World War II, many people looked for work in the cities. Low farm prices pushed some farmers off their land. Other farmers bought vacant farms and worked more land to compensate for low prices.

Most small towns depend on farmers to survive. If there are fewer farm families then there are less people to support local stores, services, and schools. If a business loses its customers it is forced to shut down. The people who worked for those businesses then must find work elsewhere. This cycle also leads to rural depopulation.

As families move from rural areas, businesses close and many small towns are left with vacant buildings. This is Margaret's Café in Elgin, Chautauqua County. Elgin is sometimes known as "the town too tough to die."

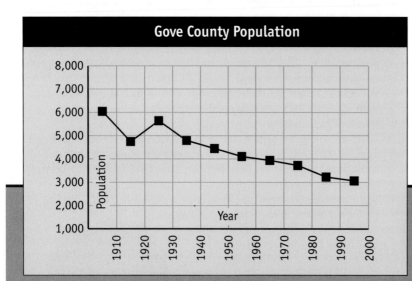

Gove, Kansas

Gove is the county seat of Gove County. The county seat is like the capital of the county. It is home to the county government. When counties were established, towns would often compete to become the county seat. When Gove County was organized, Gove beat out Buffalo Park, Grainfield, and Jerome to be the center of county government.

Gove County has felt the effects of rural depopulation. The county reached its highest population in 1910. Since 1930 the population has been in decline.

Historically Gove was not only the center of county government but also a thriving business community. The city was home to hotels, banks, attorneys, barbers, retail stores, and wagon and car shops. In the 1950s, the town had a hardware store, a grocery store, two gas stations, a construction company, and a newspaper. As the population declined, many of these businesses went away.

By the 1990s, the county government was having trouble functioning in a town without businesses. The people of Gove had an innovative idea. They formed the Gove County Improvement Association and opened a grocery store to serve their community. The citizens of Gove went farther and raised funds to open the County Seat Café. The success of these businesses shows that communities can find solutions to counter some of the affects of rural depopulation.

Possible Solutions to Rural Depopulation

In the 1980s, two professors published an article that suggested that part of the Great Plains be restored to what they called the "Buffalo Commons." They argued that the area was facing depopulation and suggested that the federal government buy the land to turn the region back to the way it was before it was settled. Buffalo Commons was used as a metaphor for the project, suggesting that the land be returned to the buffalo and other wildlife that once roamed the plains.

The idea of the Buffalo Commons was controversial among those that lived on the Great Plains. Many people felt it undervalued their traditional way of life and all that was good about rural America. The idea, however, did get people talking. It initiated serious discussions about the affects of rural depopulation in our state.

Many people have come up with ways to work against depopulation. Some have suggested that the economy of rural Kansas must be diversified. This means offering businesses and industries incentives to locate in rural areas of the state. It also means finding other sources of income from farms. One idea is called "agri-tourism." This allows *tourists* to experience what rural life is like. Families can spend their vacation participating in life on a farm. Another option for farmers is to rent their land to hunters. During hunting seasons, rural motels provide special equipment and accommodations to attract hunters.

Most farmers in Kansas grow products that are sold to someone else to manufacture into products that are sold to consumers. Some Kansas farmers are experimenting with growing products that they can sell directly to the public. By marketing directly to the consumer, the farmer can make more money. Many people believe that if farmers can increase their incomes, then they will stimulate other local businesses which in turn will reverse the trend of rural depopulation.

The Rebirth of Homesteading

Some communities in Kansas are hoping an old idea will bring more people to their communities. To attract new residents, some cities are offering their own version of the Homestead Act of 1862. Marquette, Kansas, is one such community.

Marquette is a small town, of about 600 people, in McPherson County. In order to attract new families to their town, the city bought 50 acres of farmland and divided it into 80 housing lots. If a person qualifies, the city will give him or her a free lot on which to build a house. Just like the Homestead Act, the new resident receives free land and the free land also comes with some conditions. The homesteader must begin construction of their house within 120 days, and the structure must meet certain minimum requirements. The homeowner is required to live in the house for at least one year.

People from all over the country have responded to the offer of free land. If this plan works, the city will have more residents who pay taxes. More taxes give the city and the state increased revenue. Marquette hopes to have more children enrolled in the local school. This will increase school funding. The added residents will support the local businesses by purchasing goods and services.

The Marquette Community Library holds approximately 7,800 books in its collections. It is housed in an historic building that once was a bank. The library uses the old bank vault to store copies of the Marquette Tribune.

Changing Demographics

Demographics is a way of defining the characteristics of a population. Age, gender, and *ethnicity* are all part of population demographics. As Kansas has moved into the 21st century, the state faces changing demographics.

The population of Kansas today is evenly split between men and women. Kids age 10 to 14 years old make up about seven percent of the state's population. More than twice as many Kansans live in urban areas than in rural ones. Each decade, the census reveals that the population of Kansas is getting a little older. Although those over 65 years of age still make up only about 13 percent of the population.

The ethnic and racial makeup of Kansas is also changing. The Hispanic population is the fastest growing group in the state. The state is also seeing a significant increase in its Asian population.

What do you think?

As the characteristics of the population change, so do the issues facing that population. Can you think of some issues that might become more important to Kansans as the population ages? Do you think changing demographics change the priorities for state and local governments?

Continued Immigration

Immigration is not something that exists only in the past. Immigrants come to Kansas every year seeking a better life with new opportunities. Just like in the past, immigrants continue to come to Kansas for many reasons.

Southwest Kansas is home to some of the largest meat-packing plants in the world. Jobs at these plants have attracted many Mexican and Southeast Asian immigrants to Garden City and Dodge City. These cities have a long history with Mexican immigrants, but the Vietnamese, Laotian, and Cambodian immigrants did not arrive in Kansas until the 1980s.

America has long served as a place for immigrants to build a new life, as this 1919 poster shows.

If new immigrants arrive in a city in large numbers, they may have special needs. Cities must be prepared with adequate housing, health care, and educational facilities to accommodate the new immigrants. This is true today, just as it was in the past.

New immigrants bring with them their culture from their homeland. Their traditions soon become part of the Kansas landscape. For example, the entire population of Garden City has learned to enjoy the Vietnamese New Years celebration and Mexican Fiesta.

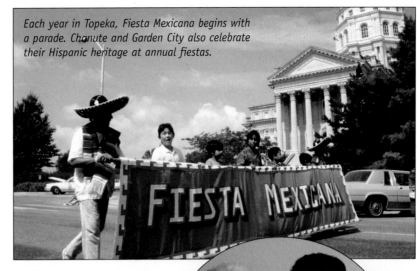

Each year in Topeka, Fiesta Mexicana begins with a parade. Chanute and Garden City also celebrate their Hispanic heritage at annual fiestas.

Activity

Naturalization Ceremony for 150 New Citizens

Not all new immigrants to Kansas become citizens, but many do. Do you know the requirements to become a *naturalized* citizen? Some of the requirements are:

- Residence in the United States
- Ability to read, write, and speak English
- Understanding of U.S. history and government
- Good moral character
- Support of the principles of the U.S. Constitution

Sybil Colin participated in the ceremony to become a new citizen. She now lives in Lawrence and continues to raise money to help children with AIDS in her native South Africa.

An immigrant must apply to become a citizen. When immigrants have met the requirements of citizenship, they usually participate in a ceremony welcoming them as new citizens of this country. On September 8, 2004, the University of Kansas issued the following announcement to the media about a naturalization ceremony to be held at the University of Kansas Dole Institute.

The announcement tells us from what countries these new citizens immigrated. Locate these countries on a map. What activities were involved in the ceremony and what symbolic meaning do they have?

LAWRENCE — Approximately 150 people from 49 nations will take an oath to become American citizens in a ceremony Friday at the Dole Institute of Politics on the University of Kansas campus.

The 2 p.m. ceremony will feature speeches by KU Chancellor Robert Hemenway and Kansas City, Kan., U.S. District Judge Carlos Murguia, a 1982 KU graduate.

The citizens to be naturalized come from Australia, Azerbaijan, Bolivia, Bosnia-Herzegovina, Brazil, Canada, China, Colombia, Cuba, the Dominican Republic, Ecuador, Egypt, El Salvador, Ethiopia, Gambia, Germany, Grenada, Guatemala, Honduras, India, Iran, Italy, Jamaica, Kampuchea, Laos, Lebanon, Malaysia, Mexico, Nepal, Netherlands, Nigeria, North Korea, Pakistan, Paraguay, Peru, Philippines, Russia, South Africa, South Korea, Sri Lanka, Syria, Tanzania, Thailand, Trinidad and Tobago, Ukraine, United Kingdom, Venezuela, Vietnam and Yugoslavia.

U.S. District Court Judge John W. Lungstrum, a 1970 KU graduate, will preside over the ceremony, which will include the singing of the national anthem by Sarah L. Young, a lecturer in the KU English department; the pledge of allegiance and presentation of colors by the Kansas Wing of the Civil Air Force Patrol; and the singing of "America the Beautiful" by Tami Anthony.

Fighting for the Rights of Women

Kansas has a long history of fighting for the rights of women. This did not end when women achieved the right to vote. In 1923, the first equal rights amendment to the U.S. Constitution was introduced. It gave men and women equal rights under the law. At first the amendment did not pass the U.S. Congress. It continued to be introduced in Congress each year until it finally passed in 1972.

The 1972 amendment read, "Equality of rights under the law shall not be denied or abridged by the United States or by any state on account of sex." In order to become part of the U.S. Constitution, 38 states needed to ratify the amendment. Kansas was one of 22 states to do so in the first year. Eventually, 12 more states ratified the amendment. To the disappointment of the many supporters of the Equal Rights Amendment, it was never ratified by the required 38 states.

Although the time ran out on the 1972 amendment, it has been reintroduced in Congress every year since 1982. This bill has never again been resubmitted to the states.

Women in Kansas Politics

Throughout the state's history, Kansas women have been involved in politics. In recent years, women have been increasingly successful in being elected to political offices.

In 1991, Joan Finney became the first woman to serve as governor of Kansas. A native of Topeka, Finney earned a degree in economic history from Washburn University. After being active in local politics, she was elected state treasurer. It was after serving five terms in that office that Joan Finney became the first women governor of Kansas.

In 2002, another Kansas woman was elected governor. Kathleen Sebelius became the first daughter of a U.S. governor to be elected to that same position. Her father, John Gilligan, served as governor of Ohio. Before becoming governor, Sebelius was a member of the Kansas House of Representatives and served two terms as the state's Insurance Commissioner.

Other Kansas women have distinguished themselves in public office.

Kansas PORTRAIT

Nancy Landon Kassebaum Baker
1932–

Nancy Landon grew up in Topeka hearing her father Alf Landon talk politics. But some of her fondest childhood memories are of spending time "hiking the woods or on the sandbars on the Kaw River." She once reminisced, "my dad...loved to ride horseback through the woods. He was the one who in many ways encouraged us to learn about the trees, and we'd gather gooseberries in the woods. I came to appreciate...at that time just how much I loved living in the country."

Nancy Landon Kassebaum grew up, married, and had children. She obtained degrees from the University of Kansas and the University of Michigan. She first entered public life by serving on the school board in Maize, Kansas. In 1978, she was elected to the U.S. Senate. She served Kansas in that capacity for 18 years.

Kassebaum became the first woman to ever chair a major senate committee. She remembers her time as chair of the Committee on Labor and Human Services saying, "I cared a lot about education issues. That's why going on the Labor and Human Resources committee, which had education and health care, labor issues, was such an interesting committee." After she retired from the U.S. Senate, she married former Tennessee Senator Howard Baker.

The Honorable Kay McFarland is the first woman Chief Justice of the Kansas Supreme Court. Sheila Frahm became the first woman lieutenant governor and was appointed to the U.S Senate. Today, women make up about one-third of the Kansas legislature and hold many local political offices.

Issues Facing State Government in the 21st Century

Governor Kathleen Sebelius took office in 2003. In her inaugural address she said, "The role of government is to empower citizens to come together and provide services we can't provide by ourselves—to build roads, organize schools, secure our borders and our neighborhoods, and promote commerce. Government must compliment and enhance the work of private citizens, not impede the progress of individuals."

The issues facing Kansas state government in the 21st century are similar to those faced by earlier generations. The struggle is always about prioritizing the needs of the people. The state government, like Kansas families, has a limited amount of money to spend each year. Determining how to spend that money is often hard— especially when the needs of the people continue to grow.

Working for a Strong Economy

A strong economy is a priority for state government. If the economy is strong, there are more jobs for Kansans. If the economy stays strong, there is more revenue coming into the state. As we move through the 21st century, Kansas needs to maintain and grow a diversified economy.

The Kansas economy is connected to worldwide markets. As a state, we trade with other states and nations. Kansas *imports* goods from all over the world. Take a look at the labels in your clothing. Where were they made? Where was your television set manufactured? There is a good chance that these goods were made outside of Kansas.

The state also *exports* goods to other nations. Kansas beef, wheat, and airplanes are sold all over the world. Processed foods and computer and electronic products are some of the manufactured goods that the state exports. The countries that buy the largest number of Kansas exports are our neighboring countries of Canada and Mexico.

Today, our state's economy depends as much on manufacturing as it does on agriculture. In fact, four times more Kansans work in manufacturing than in farming-though not all Kansas manufacturing companies are big. Small and medium sized manufacturing companies in Kansas produce more than one-quarter of all our state's exports.

Farming is still an important part of the Kansas economy. Kansas grows the most wheat of any state in the country. Our state is also a leading producer of sorghum, corn, hay, soybeans, and sunflowers. Raising cattle and the meat-packing industry are also important aspects of our state's economy. Kansas also produces oil, natural gas, and helium.

More and more Kansans work in service industries. These include workers who provide support or a service to the public. Service industries include transportation, finance, professional and technical support, health care, food service, and recreation.

Cessna exports aircraft to customers around the world. At this Wichita plant, employees build business jets.

Living with the Environment

Keeping our air and water clean presents a challenge. There are over 1,100 public water sources in Kansas. Most of these sources serve less than 1,000 water customers each. Citizens and our government must work together to insure safe air and water for future generations.

The Clean Air Act of 1970 allows state government to fight pollution in two ways. State government can regulate industries and businesses that add pollutants to the air and water. State government also provides money to local communities to control pollution coming into streams and rivers from runoff.

Air quality measurements show that Kansas air is relatively clean. By continuing to monitor and regulate air quality, especially in urban areas, we can be sure the air in Kansas will be clean into the next century.

Providing adequate energy for Kansans is another concern. There must be a balance between the energy produced and the energy consumed. Energy is used to produce electricity, to power transportation, and to run industry. Energy can come through burning coal, oil, or natural gas or it can be from nuclear energy, wind power, or *ethanol*, a type of alcohol. Ethanol is made primarily from corn, but can also be made from plant parts that farmers discard when they harvest corn, milo, oats, barley, and wheat. Processing plants ferment these materials into ethanol. It has been used as an additive to gasoline, but researchers are looking for other ways to use ethanol to meet energy needs.

Reliable energy is important not just for Kansas families, but also for businesses and industries. New businesses will come to our state only if there is enough energy for their needs. Kansas must find a way to provide enough energy without harming the environment.

What do you think?

Creating energy by burning coal uses a limited resource. Where will we get energy when the coal is gone? How does using wind energy impact the environment and the Kansas landscape? How would using more ethanol impact Kansas farmers and the Kansas economy?

Wolf Creek Nuclear Power Plant near Burlington produces enough electricity to power 800,000 homes.

The Kansas Journey

Education has always been a priority in Kansas. At the Kansas Museum of History students can learn first hand what it was like to go to a one-room school.

The Priority of Education

Kansans have always placed a high priority on education. The Wyandotte Constitution, under which Kansas became a state, called for a "uniform system" of schools. By 1908, the state had 8,689 organized school districts. Most of these were rural one-room schools. By the beginning of the 20th century, most school districts offered instruction through the 8th grade. A high school education was only available in the cities and towns of the state.

Today, the state constitution reads, "Local public schools under the general supervision of the state board of education shall be maintained, developed and operated by locally elected boards." This statement encompasses issues that have been a part of education in Kansas for at least 100 years. The State Board of Education oversees all public schools in the state and provides for some level of *standardization*. At the same time, local school boards control many aspects of Kansas schools. This is referred to as "local control."

In the early 20th century, the state began *consolidating* school districts. Smaller school districts joined together to become one. At the same time there was a movement to standardize schools. At first, the state focused its attention on requirements for teachers, and the standardization of school facilities. Today, the State Board of Education adopts *curriculum* standards. These standards insure all Kansas students will learn the same basic information. As long as there are schools, there will always be discussions about what is appropriate for the state to require and what should be left up to the local community to decide.

The funding of schools has been an issue throughout the state's history. From the beginning, the state legislature placed a tax on all property to fund the state's educational system. Over time, both local property taxes and a state sales tax have been used to pay for schools. The state allocates funding to school districts based on the number of students. Additional funds are also provided to equalize the school districts, so that all students in Kansas receive an equal opportunity to learn. Kansas schools today receive the largest part of the state's budget. Debates about school finance are likely to continue into the future.

Kansans in the News

Kansans don't always live in Kansas. Many people consider themselves to be Kansans even if they live in New York, California, or the other side of the world. They are Kansans, because they have lived or studied in Kansas. They believe Kansas is an important part of who they are. Kansans can be found in almost every facet of business and industry and in every corner of the globe. Some of these Kansans are well known and they often speak of the values they learned growing up in their home state.

Kansans in Sports

Kansas has produced many famous athletes. Among them is Lynette Woodard, who made her mark in basketball. Woodard's first basketball was a stuffed sock but by the time she was ten, she was in demand as a basketball player in her hometown of Wichita. She played at Wichita North High School and the University of Kansas. She was co-captain of the American women's basketball team in 1984 that brought home an Olympic gold medal. Woodard went on to play professional basketball. She became the first female player on the Harlem Globetrotters, a professional African American basketball team. Woodard eventually returned to

Mike Torrez recreates his wind-up for a pitch from his career in baseball.

Kansas to coach basketball at the University of Kansas.

Kansans have made their mark in professional football as well. Gale Sayers was born in Wichita in 1943 and attended the University of Kansas where he played football. Known as "the Kansas Comet" Sayers played for the Chicago Bears. Barry Sanders was also born in Wichita and played football in school so he could earn a scholarship to college. Sanders was originally thought to be too short to play football. But he won the prestigious Heisman Trophy in 1988, making him the most valuable college player that year. Sanders played professionally for the Detroit Lions.

Mike Torrez grew up in Topeka where he polished his baseball pitching and hitting skills. His father pushed Mike toward his dream of professional baseball. Torrez put his education first and after graduating from college he signed with the St. Louis Cardinals. Ten years later, he pitched two games in the World Series to help the New York Yankees win the 1977 World Series. During his professional career, Torrez played for seven major league teams. His pitching beat every team in both the National and American leagues. Torrez was the first major league pitcher to accomplish this feat.

Kansans in the Arts

Kansas artists have drawn, painted, photographed, written, and sung about their Kansas roots. One group of artists, a rock band, even named their musical group for their home state. The band *Kansas* would open their act by saying, "good evening ladies and gentlemen, and welcome to KANSAS."

Some Kansas artists think big. Stan Herd is one of them. Herd has become famous for his environmental art, what he calls "earthworks." He creates his images on farm fields. Herd first drove a tractor as a teenager on his family's farm. Herd used his farm experience to create unique art. He plants and plows images into the Kansas landscape.

Francis Blackbear Bosin was born in Oklahoma of Kiowa-Comanche heritage. Bosin is named for his grandfather, Tsate-

Lynette Woodard played professional basketball for the Detroit Shocks in the 1990s.

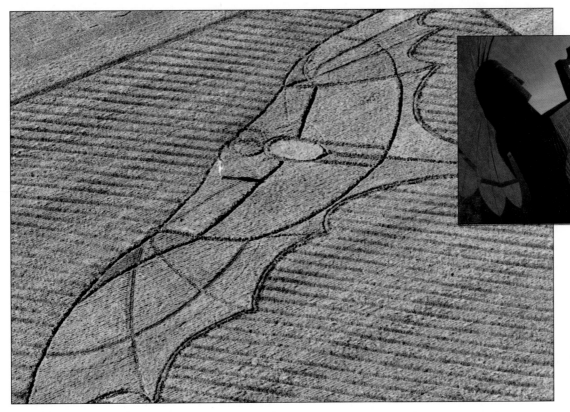

Keeper Of The Plains
*has become a symbol
of Wichita and of
Kansas' American
Indian heritage.*

*Stan Herd uses the land
for his canvas. This
artwork is in a field
near Salina. It is based
on a sketch by Italian
Renaissance artist
Leonardo da Vinci.*

Kongia, which means "Blackbear." He came to Wichita to work as an illustrator for Boeing Aircraft. Blackbear became internationally known for his paintings. His only sculpture, *Keeper Of The Plains*, is a 44-foot steel Indian warrior with hands raised to the sky. Placed at the junction of two rivers in Wichita, the statue is a symbol of the city.

Kansans in Space

Kansas kids have always looked to the stars and some have dreamed of being astronauts. Some have realized that dream. Three Kansan astronauts have flown in space. Born in St. Francis in western Kansas, Ron Evans grew up in Topeka. He flew as a fighter pilot in the Vietnam War before becoming an astronaut. Evans lived his fantasy—to fly to the moon and walk in space. He said, "You can't discover the source of the Missouri [River] any more. So, where are you going to go but space? I'm in this to explore what's out there and what's inside myself."

Joe Engle was born in Dickinson County. He knew as a child that he wanted to fly airplanes and worked to make his dream come true. Engle was a member of the support team for Apollo 10 and as a backup lunar module pilot for Apollo 14. He flew the space shuttle *Columbia* as the first pilot of a "used" spacecraft. Engle flew the shuttle *Discovery*, as well.

Another Kansas astronaut, Steve Hawley, was born in Ottawa and raised in Salina. Hawley studied physics and astronomy at the University of Kansas. Hawley also flew as a crewmember on the shuttle *Discovery*. His job on *Discovery* was to operate the robot arm so the crew could work on the Hubbell space telescope.

*Kansas astronauts
must learn to work
in weightlessness.
Joe Engle trained
underwater to
prepare.*

Bill Kurtis
1940–

Bill Kurtis grew up in Independence, Kansas. After graduating from the University of Kansas and receiving a law degree from Washburn University, Kurtis began a career in television broadcasting. In 1966, he was working for WIBW-TV in Topeka. When a major tornado hit the city, Kurtis received national recognition for his 24-hour coverage of the disaster.

Bill Kurtis moved on to television news in Chicago. He eventually was hired by CBS television to anchor the *CBS Morning News*. Kurtis went on to become a well-known documentary producer. He has produced such televisions shows as *New Explorers*, *Investigative Reports* and *Cold Case Files*. These shows and others have taken Bill Kurtis around the world, but he still considers Kansas his home.

Kurtis has a dream to revitalize small town America. He is doing his part. He has purchased the Red Buffalo Ranch, a working cattle ranch on the tallgrass prairie near Sedan. He is proud to say, "It's as attractive and unique of an area as mountains are to the west, beaches to the south. This is prairie—the heartland of America. There's no place like it in the world."

Kurtis has a great interest in the conservation of the prairie and the preservation of historical resources. He has worked with the people of Sedan to restore the town's downtown. In doing so he sees an economic future, in preserving the past. His interest in conserving the prairie is evident when he says, "I've thought about this ranch and had to get back here. It is a kind of connection with the land. . . . It is like you can stand barefoot on the soil and feel the pulse of the earth beneath your feet."

Preserving Kansas for the Future

What is Kansas? It is a state, but it is so much more than that. Those of us who live here develop what is called a "sense of place." We do this by understanding the history and geography of this place. The stories we hear from the past connect us to the people who have lived here before. The climate, the land, and the plants connect us to a land before our birth. By developing a sense of place, we are connected to all other Kansans, past, present, and future.

Kansans today are working to *conserve* and *preserve* the state for future generations. Conservation is the careful management of natural resources. Agencies like the Kansas Department of Wildlife and Parks actively work to conserve Kansas wildlife and their *habitats*. By protecting and managing our Kansas environment, we

Kansas Wildlife and Parks works to preserve the natural environment of Kansas.

The Kansas Journey

are ensuring the future health of the state.

Preservation is the act of protecting something from being destroyed. Organizations like the Kansas State Historical Society preserve historic documents, artifacts, and buildings. By preserving our past, we are creating a sense of place for future generations.

What do you think?

Conservation and preservation of Kansas takes work. Concerned citizens across the state work hard to conserve environmental regions such as the tallgrass prairie. Others put their energies into preserving the historic buildings in their hometowns. What do you think? What impact do conservation and preservation efforts have on the state? Why might it be important to protect what we have inherited?

In 2004, Governor Sebelius spoke at a Kansas Farm Bureau conference. Why do you think the conference theme was "Responsible Stewardship, Preserving Our Future"?

The Kansas Experience

Many people have written about Kansas. They define it as more than a place. They write about the special nature of Kansas people and what defines their character. They write in wonder about the beauty of the Kansas land. What does Kansas mean to you? As you read the following quotes, think about how you would define this place we call home.

If you want to understand the character of our people, you must understand the fierce sense of independence that sweeps across the plains from Bird City to Kansas City. It's the kind of spirit that resists definition. Like the proud people of my state, there are no easy labels you can pin on that spirit.

—Kansas statesman Bob Dole, 1984

One thing for sure, I never appreciated the prairie as a kid the way I do now... You see vast blue sky and maybe one cloud puff—sort of icing on the cake... People here have a certain character that ties in with that. As a whole, it gives you a certain sense of magnificence.

—Kansas writer, photographer,
and filmmaker Gordon Parks, 1986

...there is something powerful, something significant, something noteworthy about Kansas. This something may be part of the past: a combination of historical events and the mixture of people who struggled against great odds to settle and maintain decent, democratic lives and who succeeded. This something may be part of the present; the shape and beauty of the land and sky, the Kansan's intimacy with the natural world..."

—Kansas writer Thomas Fox Averill, 1991

Chapter 12 Review

What Do You Remember?

1. What is the fastest growing county in Kansas?
2. How does the Kansas population growth compare to that of other states?
3. What are the two ways each Kansan is represented in the U.S. Congress?
4. Define rural depopulation.
5. What is the idea behind the Buffalo Commons?
6. How is Marquette, Kansas working to attract new residents?
7. Name two ways Kansas demographics are changing.
8. What are the requirements to become a naturalized citizen of the United States?
9. What was the Equal Rights Amendment?
10. Name at least three Kansas exports.
11. What is ethanol? Why might it be an important product for the state?
12. Why does the state want to provide for some level of standardization in schools? How is this done?
13. What is the difference between conservation and preservation? How are they alike?

Think About It!

1. In Gove, Kansas the residents have come up with creative ways to solve some of their problems. Every community has challenges, whether it is growing or declining in population. Think about challenges in your community. Can you think of creative solutions to these challenges?

2. How might Kansas diversify its economy, especially in the rural areas? Can you think of ways the state might attract new businesses? What incentives may be needed?

Activities

1. Research what U.S. congressional district you live in. Determine who is your representative. Research who your state senator and state representative are. Using newspaper articles research what issues your representatives are working on at either the federal or state level. Do you agree with your representatives' point of view?

2. Pretend your class is the Kansas legislature. Research bills that are being introduced during the current legislative session. Using the steps a bill must go through to become law, try to pass one of the bills in your classroom legislature. If you succeed, try to write your own legislation on a topic of your choice.

3. Research the accomplishments of a well-known Kansan living today. Write a nomination for that person to be named Kansan of the Year.

4. Read the work of a contemporary Kansas writer. How do you think Kansas has influenced his or her writing?

Glossary

The definitions for words are as they are used in the chapters of this textbook.

A

abolitionist: a person who wanted to bring about the immediate end of slavery

absolute dating: the determination of the age of an object based on measurable physical or chemical qualities or associations with written records

absolute location: location description using longitude and latitude

adaptation: change in behavior in response to new or modified surroundings

amend: to alter, change, or add to

ancestor: a person from whom one is descended

antislavery: opposed to practice of slavery

aquifer: a layer of rock that holds water underground

arbitrate: provide judgment

arid: lacking moisture, dry

armory: a storehouse for arms

artifact: something made or used by people from the past

assimilate: to absorb (immigrants or a culturally distinct group) into the prevailing culture

B

bankrupt: financially ruined

barbed wire: twisted strands of fence wire with barbs at regular intervals

barter: to trade one thing for another without the exchange of money

basin: land drained by a river system

bigotry: the attitude, state of mind, or behavior characteristic of intolerance

boarding: a type of school where students live at the school and are provided food and lodging

border ruffian: Missouri settlers who crossed into Kansas to influence the outcome of the slavery issue in Kansas

botanical: relating to plants or plant life

broadside: something, such as an advertisement or public notice, that is printed on a large piece of paper

bushwhacker: Missouri settlers who raided antislavery settlements in Kansas

C

capital: wealth used in the production of more wealth

capitalism: an economic system in which the means of production and distribution are privately or corporately owned

catalyst: something that causes change

celestial: heavenly

censor: a person authorized to examine books, or films to remove what is considered morally objectionable

chain mail: flexible armor made of joined metal links

chain migration: migration that is caused by the feedback from people who have already immigrated

charter: a document issued by the government, creating a public or private corporation

civil disobedience: refusal to obey civil laws in an effort to induce change

civil rights: the rights belonging to an individual by virtue of citizenship

civilian: one who is not part of the military

class action: a lawsuit brought by a group of people who have a common interest

class system: social structure where people share certain economic, social, or cultural characteristics

collective bargaining: negotiation between organized workers and their employer cooperative: groups created by farmers to help share costs and have greater buying power

commerce: the buying and selling of goods

communal: of, belonging to, or shared by the people of a community

communist: supporting communism

confluence: a flowing together of two or more streams

conformity: similarity in form or character

conscientious: guided by the dictates of conscience

conscription: required enrollment in the armed forces

conserve: to protect from loss or harm

consolidating: to unite into one system or whole

consumer: one who acquires goods or services for direct use or ownership

contaminated: impure

conterminous: contained in the same boundaries

cooperative: organization made of farmers who shared expenses

credit: an arrangement for deferred payment of a loan or purchase

cultivate: to prepare the land for planting crops

currency: money in any form when in actual use as a medium of exchange

curriculum: an integrated course of school studies

D

demographic: relating to the study of the characteristics of human populations

depot: a railroad station

depression: a period of low economic activity marked by rising levels of unemployment

discrimination: treatment based on class or category, such as race, rather than individual merit

disincentive: something that prevents or discourages action

dispatch: a written message

diversified: producing more than product

domesticate: to train or adapt (an animal or plant) to be of use to humans

draft: required enrollment in the armed forces

drought: a prolonged period of below average precipitation

dug out: a pit dug into the ground or on a hillside and used as a shelter

E

ecosystem: a community of living things that depend on each other in order to function as a unit

electioneering: to work actively for a candidate or political party

emancipation: the act of being made free

eminent domain: the right of a government to use private property for public use

entrepreneur: someone who turns an idea into a new business

epidemic: an outbreak of a contagious disease that spreads rapidly and widely

erosion: the process of breaking down, as in the break down of rock by wind and water

ethanol: a renewable clean-burning additive to gasoline

ethnicity: people sharing a common and distinctive racial, national, religious, linguistic, or cultural heritage

expansionist: the practice or policy of territorial or economic expansion

export: to send to a foreign country for trade or sale

extraction: taking from Earth

F

famine: a drastic, wide-reaching food shortage

folklore: traditional beliefs, myths, tales, and practices of a people

foreclosure: the ending of the rights of a debtor to personal property

franchise: a business operated under authorization of a parent company

free-stater: a settler who believed Kansas should not allow slavery

fuselage: the central body of an aircraft which accommodates the crew, passengers, and cargo

G-H

grassroots: of or involving the common people for political change

guerrilla: a member of an irregular military unit operating in small bands in occupied territory to harass and undermine the enemy, as by surprise raids

habitat: a natural place where plants and animals live together

horticultural: the science or art of cultivating fruits, vegetables, or flowers

I

import: to bring in from a foreign country for trade or sale

improvisation: something composed or performed with little or no preparation

inalienable: incapable of being alienated, surrendered, or transferred

inaugural address: a speech given by a person being formally inducted into office

incentive: serving to induce or motivate

incorporated: part of a business corporation

indentured servant: a person who is bonded or contracted to work for another for a specified time

industrialization: to become industrial

infer: imply

inheritance: something received (property or a title, for example) from an ancestor by legal succession or will

installment: payments

integrated: to bring different ethnic groups or people together

irrigation: to supply dry land with water by means of ditches, pipes, or streams

isolationist: abstaining from political or economic relations with other countries

J-L

jayhawker: a free-soil or Unionist guerrilla in Kansas and Missouri during the border disputes

liberate: to set free

lobby: a group of persons trying to influence public officials in favor of a specific cause

lobbyist: a person engaged in trying to influence public officials in favor of a specific cause

M-N

manifest destiny: the idea that America was meant to expand from coast to coast and was blessed by a higher power

martyr: one who chooses to suffer death rather than renounce his or her beliefs

materialism: the attitude that physical well-being and worldly possessions create the greatest good

middle class: The social class between the working class and the upper class

migration: the act of moving from one land or country to settle in another place

monarchy: government by one ruler, such as a king or queen

monopoly: when only one company provides or produces a certain product or service activity

moral: conforming to standards of what is right or just in behavior

naturalized citizen: an immigrant who becomes a citizen

neutrality: the state or policy of being neutral

New World: the term Europeans used for North America in the early days of their exploration

nomadic: having no fixed home and moving according to the seasons from place to place in search of food, water, and grazing land

nuclear: a type of energy used to create nuclear bombs

O-P

obsolete: no longer in use

oral tradition: the spoken preservation, from one generation to the next, of a people's cultural history and ancestry, often by a storyteller in narrative form

ordinance: a local law

organic: material derived from living organisms

pacifist: opposition to war or violence as a means of resolving disputes

parfleche: an article, like a bag, made from an untanned animal hide

per capita: per unit of population

physical feature: the natural landforms and characteristics of a place

physiographic region: land regions that were formed by similar geologic processes

plaintiff: the party that institutes a suit in a court.

plat: a map showing actual or planned features, such as streets and building lots

popular sovereignty: the concept that political and legislative power resides with the citizens

Populism: A U.S. political movement that sought to represent the interests of farmers and laborers in the 1890s

precipitation: the amount of water in the air that falls to the earth as rain or snow

preserve: to keep or maintain intact

primary source: something made or written by someone who was there at the time; an original record

progressive: promoting or favoring progress toward better conditions or new policies, ideas, or methods

prohibition: the period (1920-1933) during which the 18th Amendment forbidding the manufacture and sale of alcoholic beverages was in force

propaganda: material distributed by the advocates or opponents of a doctrine or cause

proslavery: supportive of the practice of slavery

Q-R

quarantine: enforced isolation

quota: a set amount

racism: discrimination or prejudice based on race

radioactive: something that emits radiation

ratify: to approve

ration: a little bit of something divided among many people

refinery: an industrial plant for purifying a crude substance

regulation: controlling or enforcing set standards or rules

relative dating: in archaeology, the arrangement of artifacts or events in a sequence relative to one another

relative location: location description using a place's location in relation to other places

reminiscence: a narration of past experiences

repeal: to revoke

representative government: a form of government in which the citizens delegate authority to elected representatives

reservation: a piece of land set aside by the U.S. government for Native Americans to live on

reservoir: an artificial lake used for the storage and regulation of water

residential: used or designed for the place where people live

retail: the sale of goods in small quantities directly to consumers

revenue: income of a government for the payment of the public expenses

rural: of or relating to people who live in the country

rural depopulation: the decline of population in rural areas

Rural Free Delivery: a program that provided free mail service to rural areas

S

sanitation: relating to health, cleanliness, disposal of garbage or waste

secede: to withdraw from an organization

sections: a parcel or piece of land

sediment: material such as stones and sand deposited by water, wind, or glacier

segregate: to separate by race; to keep apart

servitude: a state of subjection to an owner or master

shelter belt: a barrier of trees and shrubs that protects against the wind and reduces erosion

siege: the surrounding and blockading of a city or town by an army attempting to capture it

Socialism: theories or systems of social organization in which the means of producing and distributing goods is owned collectively or by a centralized government that often plans and controls the economy

sod house: a home made from sod, or grass

sovereign right: authority based on the power of government

specialization: producing one or a small number of products or services

speculation: a conclusion, opinion, or theory reached by supposition

speculator: someone who invests financially in something, with the possibility of great gains or losses

squatter: to settle on unoccupied land without legal claim

standardization: to cause to conform to a standard

stock: the capital or fund that a corporation raises through the sale of shares

subsidy: financial assistance given by a government to a person or group in support of an enterprise that should help the public

subsistence: having enough food or resource to live

suburban: relating to a residential area outlying a city

suffrage: the right or privilege of voting

surplus: an amount or a quantity in excess of what is needed

synonymous: having the same or a similar meaning

T

temperance: restraint in the use of or abstinence from alcoholic liquors

tenant: one who pays rent to use or occupy land, a building, or other property

tourist: people who tour or visit places for pleasure

trade: exchange goods or services for other goods or services or for money

transcontinental: spanning or crossing a continent

transcribe: to translate or make a written copy of something

travois: a frame hung between trailing poles and pulled by a dog or horse

treason: violation of allegiance toward one's country

tuberculosis: a disease that affects the lungs but may spread to other areas and is characterized by fever, cough, and difficulty in breathing

U-Z

unconstitutional: not in accord with the principles set forth in the constitution of a nation or state

underdog: one that is at a disadvantage

union: a group of workers who get together to solve problems or cause change

urban: of or relating to people who live in the city

utopian: characterized by or aspiring to impracticable perfection

veto: to reject a bill from becoming a law

vocation: an occupation

yield: an amount produced

Index

The Kansas Journey

Index

——————————————————————

Alton, Thad 106
Anderson, Neil 49
AP/Wide World Press 102, 222 (bottom), 223 (right), 232 (top), 265, 270, 274, 281, 284 (bottom left), 285 (top middle), 287 (top)
Wichita Convention and Visitors Center 285 (top right)
NASA 285 (bottom)
Berryman, Gene vi-v, vi-vii, 2-3, 8, 17, 288
Davis, Jon/Jim Reed Photography 15
Franklin D. Roosevelt Library 232-233 (bottom)
Good, Karol D. 14 (top)
Granger Collection 116-117 (top), 132 (bottom), 166 (top), 247, 250
Haynes, Michael 50-51
Johnson County Museum 256-257 (top)
Kansas Geological Survey 9 (both), 11 (bottom), 12 (both), 13, 20, 21 (right), 22 (both), 27 (top), 276
Kansas Secretary of State Office 103
Ponting, Liz 277
Kansas State Historical Society 4-5, 11 (top), 14 (bottom), 19 (bottom), 24-25, 26 (left), 28 (bottom left), 29, 30, 32, 34 (top), 35 (top middle and right, bottom middle and right), 36 (both), 37 (both), 38, 39, 40, 41 (both), 42, 44-45 (painting by David H Overmyer), 46 (top, painting by Albert Reid), 46 (bottom), 47 (both), 48, 52 (bottom), 53 (both), 54, 56, 57 (left), 58 (both), 59 (bottom right), 61 (all), 62-63 (painting by Charles Goslin), 66-67 (painting by John Steuart Curry), 70 (top), 71, 72, 74 (both), 75, 76 (both), 77 (top), 78 (all), 79 (both), 80 (top), 82 (both), 83 (all), 84, 86, 87 (both), 88, 89 (both), 90 (all),

92 (both), 93 (both), 94, 96-97 (painting by Henry Worrall), 98 (both), 100, 101, 104, 107 (all), 109, 110 (both on top), 111 (drawing by Sherman Enderton), 112, 113 (both), 114 (both), 118 (top), 120-121, 123, 124 (both), 126 (both), 128-129 (all), 130 (both), 131 (both), 132 (top), 133, 134, 135 (both), 136, 137 (top), 138 (top, painting by Marijana Grisnik), 138 (bottom), 140-141, 142 (both), 144-145 (all), 146, 147, 149, 150, 151, 152 (left), 153, 154, 155, 156, 157 (both), 158 (top), 162 (bottom left), 163, 165, 166 (bottom left), 167, 168, 171 (top), 172-173, 174 (both), 175 (all), 176-177, 178, 179, 180-181 (all), 182 (both), 186, 188-189 (both), 190, 192 (both), 194 (both), 195, 196, 197, 198, 199, 200, 201, 202, 203, 206-207 (both), 208 (bottom), 210-211, 212, 213 (both), 214, 215, 216, 217, 219 (top), 221, 222 (top), 223 (left), 225, 228, 230-231 (paintings by John Steuart Curry), 233 (right), 234-235 (both), 236 (right and bottom), 238 (both), 243, 244, 248, 252, 253, 254 (both), 256 (bottom), 257 (right)), 258 (both), 263, 264, 272-273, 275, 279 (top), 280, 282, 283, 286, 286-287 (bottom)
The Kansas Adjutant General's Department Korean War Commemoration Partner Program Committee 266
Lewis and Clark College 245
Library of Congress 52 (top), 64 (painting by John Gast), 85, 122, 152 (middle), 158 (bottom), 160-161, 162 (bottom right), 164, 169, 187, 204, 208 (top), 220 (top), 227, 240-241, 242, 246, 255, 278

Maryland Historical Society 171 (bottom)
Montana State Historical Society 118 (bottom)
National Archives 70 (bottom), 224, 251, 268
National Museum of American Indian 73
National Museum of Health and Medicine, Armed Forces Institute of Pathology 205
New York Public Library 91
North Wind Picture Archives 69
NRCS 229 (photo by Jeff Vanuga)
Photos.com 18 (both), 19 (top), 34 (bottom), 35 (top left), 80 (bottom), 81
Rare Book Collection, Columbia University 77 (bottom)
Rasmussen, Gary 26 (top), 27 (bottom), 28 (bottom right)
Richter, Cheryl 137 (bottom)
St. Louis Public Library 184-185
Sween, Nancy 262
The Boeing Company 249
The Martin and Osa Johnson Safari Museum 237 (top)
Topeka Capitol-Journal 269, 284 (top left)
Lawrence Journal-World 279 (middle right)
University of Kansas Special Collections 260, 267
Varner, Dan 10
Wichita State University Department of Special Collections, 218, 219 (bottom)
Wichita-Sedgwick County Historical Museum 220 (bottom)
Worley, Barry 21 (top)